Becker Professional Education, a global leader in professional educatic  is
for ACCA for more than 20 years, and thousands of candidates studyii
succeeded in their professional examinations through its Platinum and ɪnd
Eastern Europe and Central Asia.*

Becker Professional Education has also been awarded ACCA Approvᵥ als
for the Diploma in International Financial Reporting (DipIFR).

Nearly half a million professionals have advanced their careers through Becker Professional Education's courses. Throughout its more than 50-year history, Becker has earned a strong track record of student success through world-class teaching, curriculum and learning tools.

We provide a single destination for individuals and companies in need of global accounting certifications and continuing professional education.

*Platinum – Moscow, Russia and Kiev, Ukraine. Gold – Almaty, Kazakhstan

Becker Professional Education's ACCA Study Materials

All of Becker's materials are authored by experienced ACCA lecturers and are used in the delivery of classroom courses.

Study System: Gives complete coverage of the syllabus with a focus on learning outcomes. It is designed to be used both as a reference text and as part of integrated study. It also includes the ACCA Syllabus and Study Guide, exam advice and commentaries and a Study Question Bank containing practice questions relating to each topic covered.

Revision Question Bank: Exam style and standard questions together with comprehensive answers to support and prepare students for their exams. The Revision Question Bank also includes past examination questions (updated where relevant), model answers and alternative solutions and tutorial notes.

Revision Essentials*: A condensed, easy-to-use aid to revision containing essential technical content and exam guidance.

*Revision Essentials are substantially derived from content reviewed by ACCA's examining team.

Becker Professional Education
is an ACCA approved content provider

BECKER
PROFESSIONAL EDUCATION®

ACCA

PAPER P1

GOVERNANCE, RISK AND ETHICS

REVISION QUESTION BANK

For Examinations to June 2016

This training material has been prepared and published by Becker Professional Development International Limited:

16 Elmtree Road
Teddington
TW11 8ST
United Kingdom

ISBN: 978-1-78566-123-5

Acknowledgement

Past ACCA examination questions are the copyright of the Association of Chartered Certified Accountants and have been reproduced by kind permission.

CONTENTS

The current exam format is a 50 mark case study question and a choice of two from three 25 mark questions. Questions of different mark allocations are provided for additional syllabus coverage.

Tutorial notes: *Answers to past exam questions are indicative of the style and quality of the answer expected by the examiner. However, they may not be indicative of the length of answer expected as such "suggested solutions" usually contain far more points and detail than is needed to obtain a good pass. In particular, specific references to academic and literature sources are for illustrative purposes.*

Question 1 PRIVATE, LISTED AND PUBLIC SECTOR GOVERNANCE

(a)   Although the concept of corporate governance has been a feature of corporate entities ever since the first company was formed, it has only been in the last 20 to 30 years that the principles of corporate governance have been codified and recognised as being fundamental to the continued growth of the wealth generated by corporations for the benefit of corporate stakeholders.

Required:

Describe the main principles of corporate governance in the private sector   (8 marks)

(b)   "The principles of corporate governance do not apply to the public sector because the objectives of state owned enterprises and public services are different from those of the private sector."

Required:

Construct an argument against this assertion.   (12 marks)

(c)   Agency and stakeholder relationships apply throughout the private and public sectors as well as throughout society as a whole.

Required:

Explain the principal differences between the private and public sector application of agency and stakeholder approaches.   (5 marks)

(25 marks)

Question 2 PUBLIC SECTOR GOVERNANCE ARRANGEMENTS

At a recent conference on public sector governance, two keynote speakers, Jack Russell (CEO of the Kayland stock exchange) and Sunny Xhengj (government health minister of the emerging nation, Emland), were involved in a debate entitled "Corporate Governance: Improvement and Trust in Public Services".

Jack argued that the introduction of corporate governance codes from the mid-1990s and their continued refinement and improvement (e.g. on matters such as diversity and integrated reporting) had led to a significant improvement in the investment climate, in investors' confidence in the market and in the core underlying growth of corporate value and the wealth of shareholders. In addition to shareholders, many other stakeholders (for example employees, customers, suppliers, communities and the environment) had also benefited from sound corporate governance. Although corporate scandals would never go away, they had become fewer and far between.

In his view, the principles of sound corporate governance, such as transparency, integrity, responsibility, accountability, honesty and probity, could be applied to any entity – public, private, governmental, not-for-profit, NGO – it did not matter. He gave examples from Kayland where corporate governance principles had been introduced into government processes. He admitted that it was taking a long time for the ideas to take root, but with strong governmental support, progress was beginning to be seen.

From her perspective as a senior governmental minister, Sunny considered that trying to implement corporate governance principles and arrangements, which from its very name and nature was aimed at listed corporations, was not practical in a non-corporate environment.

As a government minister she said that there were so many variations of public sector organisations that a typical corporate governance "one size fits all" approach could never work in the public sector in Emland. As just one example, she explained the complexities in her ministry of having national level, subnational level and supranational levels of health organisations; all of which, in her view, needed to be controlled by the senior minister.

Sunny also pointed out that the ethos of public service was totally different to that of, for example, listed companies. There were no shareholders, no products produced and sold, no profit-driven motives, no immoral tax avoidance or evasion schemes and no scandals.

Required:

(a) **Describe and contrast the national, subnational and supranational level of public services.** (6 marks)

(b) **Briefly describe appropriate principles for good governance in the public sector.** (9 marks)

(c) **Critically assess Sunny's view that trying to implement corporate governance principles and arrangements is not practical in a non-corporate environment.** (10 marks)

(25 marks)

Question 3 HORACE HOI

In the country of Laland, aid organisations registered as charities are not subject to the same financial reporting requirements as limited companies (this is not the case in many other countries where they are treated equally in law). One person to take advantage of this is Horace Hoi who has led his vigorous campaign in favour of animal protection for the past 25 years. As a highly competent self-publicist for his charity and an engaging media performer, he has raised the public profile of his charity substantially. He can and does raise large amounts of money for his charity through his personal charm and passionate appeals on television and in large meetings of supporters. His charity is called the "Horace Hoi Organisation" (HHO) and its stated aim is to "stop animals suffering".

Mr Hoi has recently become the subject of criticism by the media because of allegations that he lived a lavish lifestyle and personally owned a large mansion and a number of classic cars. The HHO recently bought a private jet to support Mr Hoi in his travels around the world for speaking engagements and for his work for the HHO charity. One journalist reported that most of the donors to HHO are well-meaning individuals, mainly of modest means, that care greatly about animal suffering and who would be "horrified" if they knew of the luxury in which Mr Hoi lived.

Despite the fact that Mr Hoi had claimed that he personally takes only a modest salary from the organisation for his work, a journalist recently estimated Mr Hoi's personal wealth, thought to be gained from the HHO, to be around $10 million. When challenged to disclose the financial details of the HHO and Mr Hoi's own personal earnings, a HHO spokesman simply replied that this was not required under the law in Laland and that the HHO was therefore fully compliant with the law. The HHO has refused to join a group of other charities that have undertaken to make full financial disclosures despite it not being mandatory in law. The HHO says that although it does produce financial information for the charity and tax authorities, it has no intention of making this information public. The HHO also makes no disclosures about its governance structures and was once criticised as being "intentionally opaque in order to hide bad practice".

In yielding to the media pressure to provide some information on its financial affairs, HHO eventually published a pie chart on its website saying that its expenditure was divided between animal shelters (57%), field work helping animals (32%), administration (6%) and other causes (5%). This was the totality of its public financial disclosure.

Required:

(a)   Discuss the ways in which charities differ from public listed companies and explain how these differences affect their respective governance structures.   (9 marks)

(b)   Define "transparency" and construct the case for greater transparency in the governance of the Horace Hoi Organisation.   (8 marks)

(c)   Audit committees can have a role in reviewing internal controls and addressing areas of deficiency.

Required:

Explain how an audit committee might assist in addressing the apparent internal control deficiencies at HHO.   (8 marks)

(25 marks)

Question 4 STAKEHOLDERS, DIRECTORS AND FIDUCIARY DUTIES

Private sector companies have multiple stakeholders who are likely to have divergent interests. The directors of a company are also stakeholders of that company, but bound by their fiduciary duties.

Required:

(a)   Identify five stakeholder groups and briefly discuss their financial and other objectives.   (10 marks)

(b)   Explain the concept of fiduciary duty and describe the fiduciary responsibilities of directors.   (7 marks)

(c)   Examine the extent to which good corporate governance procedures can help manage the problems arising from the divergent interests of multiple stakeholder groups.   (8 marks)

(25 marks)

Question 5 ROSH & CO

Mary Hobbes joined the board of Rosh and Company, a large retailer, as finance director earlier this year. Whilst she was glad to have finally been given the chance to become finance director after several years as a financial accountant, she also quickly realised that the new appointment would offer her a lot of challenges. In the first board meeting, she realised that not only was she the only woman but she was also the youngest by many years.

Rosh was established almost 100 years ago. Members of the Rosh family have occupied senior board positions since the outset and even after the company's flotation 20 years ago a member of the Rosh family has either been executive chairman or chief executive. The current longstanding chairman, Timothy Rosh, has already prepared his slightly younger brother, Geoffrey (also a longstanding member of the board) to succeed him in two years' time when he plans to retire. The Rosh family, who still own 40% of the shares, consider it their right to occupy the most senior positions in the company so have never been very active in external recruitment. They only appointed Mary because they felt they needed a qualified accountant on the board to deal with changes in international financial reporting standards.

Several former executive members have been recruited as non-executives immediately after they retired from full-time service. A recent death, however, has reduced the number of non-executive directors to two. These sit alongside an executive board of seven that, apart from Mary, have all been in post for over ten years.

Mary noted that board meetings very rarely contain any significant discussion of strategy and never involve any debate or disagreement. When she asked why this was, she was told that the directors had all known each other for so long that they knew how each other thought. All of the other directors came from similar backgrounds, she was told, and had worked for the company for so long that they all knew what was "best" for the company in any given situation. Mary observed that notes on strategy were not presented at board meetings and she asked Timothy Rosh whether the existing board was fully equipped to formulate strategy in the changing world of retailing. She did not receive a reply.

Required:

(a) **Explain "agency" in the context of corporate governance and criticise the governance arrangements of Rosh and Company.** (12 marks)

(b) **Explain the roles of a nominations committee and assess the potential usefulness of a nominations committee to the board of Rosh and Company.** (8 marks)

(c) **Define "retirement by rotation" and explain its importance in the context of Rosh and Company.** (5 marks)

(25 marks)

Question 6 DING COMPANY

Sam Mesentery was appointed a director of Ding Company in October this year taking on the role of financial controller. He had moved himself and his family to a new country to take up the post and was looking forward to the new challenges. When he arrived he learned that he was on the "operating board" of Ding Company and that there was a "corporate board" above the operating board that was senior to it. This surprised him as in the companies he had worked for in his own country, all directors in the company were equal. The corporate board at Ding was small, with five directors in total, while the operating board was larger, with ten members.

After a few days in the job he received an e-mail requiring him to report to Annette Hora, the managing director. She said that she had regretfully received two complaints from another senior colleague about Sam's behaviour. First, Sam had apparently made a highly inappropriate remark to a young female colleague and second, his office was laid out in the wrong way. Not only was his desk positioned in breach of fire regulations but also, he was told that it was normal to have the desk facing towards the door so that colleagues felt more welcomed when they went in. "It's company policy" she said abruptly. Sam remembered the conversation with the young female colleague but was unaware of anything inappropriate in what he had said to her. He said that he positioned his desk so he could get the best view out of the window when he was working.

The following day he arrived at work to find that the corporate board was in an emergency meeting. There had been a sudden and dramatic change in the circumstances of one of Ding's major suppliers and the corporate board later said that they needed to meet to agree a way forward and a strategy to cope with the change. Annette said that because of the competitive nature of its resource markets, Ding had to act fast and preferably before its competitors. Hence the necessity of a two-tier board structure. She said there was no time for lengthy discussions which was why the operating board was excluded. Sam was told that Ding operated in a "complex and turbulent" environment and when strategic factors in the environment changed, the company often had to respond quickly and decisively.

It was a month later that Sam first met with Arif Zaman, Ding's non-executive chairman. After Arif asked Sam how he was settling in, Sam asked Arif why he preferred a two-tier board structure and Arif replied that actually it was Annette's idea. He said that she prefers it that way and because he is a non-executive member doesn't feel able to challenge her opinion on it. Because "it seems to work" he had no plans to discuss it with her. He went on to say that he was an old friend of Annette's and was only in post to satisfy the corporate governance requirements to have a non-executive chairman. He said that he saw his role as mainly ceremonial and saw no need to take any direct interest in the company's activities. He said that he chaired some board meetings when he was available and he sometimes wrote the chairman's statement in the annual report.

Required:

(a) **Explain the content of a director's induction programme and assess the advantages of such a programme for Sam.** (8 marks)

(b) **Using information from the case, critically evaluate Annette's belief that two-tier boards are preferable in complex and turbulent environments such as at Ding Company.** (8 marks)

(c) **Assess Arif Zaman's understanding of his role as non-executive chairman.** (9 marks)

(25 marks)

Question 7 KK

KK is a large listed company. When a non-executive directorship of KK became available, John Soria was nominated to fill the vacancy. John is the brother-in-law of KK's chief executive Ken Kava. John is also the CEO of Soria Supplies, KK's largest single supplier and is, therefore, very familiar with KK and its industry. He has sold goods to KK for over 20 years and is on friendly terms with all of the senior officers in the company. In fact last year, Soria Supplies appointed KK's finance director, Susan Schwab, to a non-executive directorship on its board. The executive directors of KK all know and like John and so plan to ask the nominations committee to appoint him before the next AGM.

KK has recently undergone a period of rapid growth and has recently entered several new overseas markets, some of which, according to the finance director, are riskier than the domestic market. Ken Kava, being the dominant person on the KK board, has increased the risk exposure of the company according to some investors. They say that because most of the executive directors are less experienced, they rarely question his overseas expansion strategy. This expansion has also created a growth in employee numbers and an increase in the number of executive directors, mainly to manage the increasingly complex operations of the company. It was thought by some that the company lacked experience and knowledge of international markets as it expanded and that this increased the risk of the strategy's failure. Some shareholders believed that the aggressive strategy, led by Ken Kava, has been careless as it has exposed KK to some losses on overseas direct investments made before all necessary information on the investment was obtained.

As a large listed company, the governance of KK is important to its shareholders. Fin Brun is one of KK's largest shareholders and holds a large portfolio of shares including 8% of the shares in KK. At the last AGM he complained to KK's chief executive, Ken Kava, that he needed more information on directors' performance. Fin said that he didn't know how to vote on board reappointments because he had no information on how they had performed in their jobs. Mr Kava said that the board intended to include a corporate governance section in future annual reports to address this and to provide other information that shareholders had asked for. He added, however, that he would not be able to publish information on the performance of individual executive directors as this was too complicated and actually not the concern of shareholders. It was, he said, the performance of the board as a whole that was important and he (Mr Kava) would manage the performance targets of individual directors.

Required:

(a) **Explain the term "conflict of interest" in the context of non-executive directors and discuss the potential conflicts of interest relating to KK and Soria Supplies if John Soria were to become a non-executive director of KK.** (8 marks)

(b) **Assess the advantages of appointing experienced and effective non-executive directors to the KK board during the period in which the company was growing rapidly.** (7 marks)

(c) **Explain the typical contents of a "best practice" corporate governance report within an annual report and how its contents could help meet the information needs of Fin Brun.**

(10 marks)

(25 marks)

Question 8 LUM CO

Lum Co is a family business that has been wholly-owned and controlled by the Lum family since 1925. The current chief executive, Mr Gustav Lum, is the great grandson of the company's founder and has himself been in post as CEO since 2001. Because the Lum family wanted to maintain a high degree of control, they operated a two-tier board structure: four members of the Lum family comprised the supervisory board and the other eight non-family directors comprised the operating board.

Despite being quite a large company with 5,000 employees, Lum Co never had any non-executive directors because they were not required in privately-owned companies in the country in which Lum Co was situated.

The four members of the Lum family valued the control of the supervisory board to ensure that the full Lum family's wishes (being the only shareholders) were carried out. This also enabled decisions to be made quickly, without the need to take everything before a meeting of the full board.

Starting in 2011, the two tiers of the board met in joint sessions to discuss a flotation (issuing public shares on the stock market) of 80% of the company. The issue of the family losing control was raised by the CEO's brother, Mr Crispin Lum. He said that if the company became listed, the Lum family would lose the freedom to manage the company as they wished, including supporting their own long-held values and beliefs. These values, he said, were managing for the long term and adopting a paternalistic management style. Other directors said that the new listing rules that would apply to the board, including compliance with the stock market's corporate governance codes of practice, would be expensive and difficult to introduce.

The flotation went ahead in 2014. In order to comply with the new listing rules, Lum Co took on a number of non-executive directors (NEDs) and formed a unitary board. A number of problems arose around this time with NEDs feeling frustrated at the culture and management style in Lum Co, whilst the Lum family members found it difficult to make the transition to managing a public company with a unitary board. Gustav Lum said that it was very different from managing the company when it was privately owned by the Lum family. The human resources manager said that an effective induction programme for NEDs and some relevant continuing professional development (CPD) for existing executives might help to address the problems.

Required:

(a) **Compare the typical governance arrangements between a family business and a listed company, and assess Crispin's view that the Lum family will "lose the freedom to manage the company as they wish" after the flotation.** (10 marks)

(b)   Assess the benefits of introducing an induction programme for the new NEDs, and requiring continual professional development (CPD) for the existing executives at Lum Co after its flotation.   (8 marks)

(c)   Distinguish between unitary and two-tier boards, and discuss the difficulties that the Lum family might encounter when introducing a unitary board.   (7 marks)

(25 marks)

Question 9 SONIA TAN

Sonia Tan, a fund manager at institutional investor Sentosa House, was reviewing the annual report of one of the major companies in her portfolio. The company, Eastern Products, had recently undergone a number of board changes as a result of a lack of confidence in its management from its major institutional investors of which Sentosa House was one. The problems started two years ago when a new chairman at Eastern Products (Thomas Hoo) started to pursue what the institutional investors regarded as very risky strategies whilst at the same time failing to comply with a stock market requirement on the number of non-executive directors on the board.

Sonia rang Eastern's investor relations department to ask why it still was not in compliance with the requirements relating to non-executive directors. She was told that because Eastern was listed in a principles-based jurisdiction, the requirement was not compulsory. It was simply that Eastern chose not to comply with that particular requirement. When Sonia asked how its board committees could be made up with an insufficient number of non-executive directors, the investor relations manager said he didn't know and that Sonia should contact the chairman directly. She was also told that there was no longer a risk committee because the chairman saw no need for one.

Sonia telephoned Thomas Hoo, the chairman of Eastern Products. She began by reminding him that Sentosa House was one of Eastern's main shareholders and currently owned 13% of the company. She went on to explain that she had concerns over the governance of Eastern Products and that she would like Thomas to explain his non-compliance with some of the stock market's requirements and also why he was pursuing strategies viewed by many investors as very risky. Thomas reminded Sonia that Eastern had outperformed its sector in terms of earnings per share in both years since he had become chairman and that rather than question him, she should trust him to run the company as he saw fit. He thanked Sentosa House for its support and hung up the phone.

Required:

(a)   Explain what an "agency cost" is and discuss the problems that might increase agency costs for Sentosa House in the case of Eastern Products.   (7 marks)

(b)   Describe, with reference to the case, the conditions under which it might be appropriate for an institutional investor to intervene in a company whose shares it holds. (10 marks)

(c)   Evaluate the contribution that a risk committee made up of non-executive directors could make to Sonia's confidence in the management of Eastern Products.   (4 marks)

(d)   Assess the opinion given to Sonia that because Eastern Products was listed in a principles-based jurisdiction, compliance with the stock market's rules was "not compulsory".   (4 marks)

(25 marks)

Question 10 HAITCHLAND

After the government of Haitchland decided to privatise its monopoly gas supplier (transferring it from government control to private ownership by issuing and selling shares), there was a period of transition as the new board took shape. A great deal of internal reorganisation and culture change was deemed necessary as the company moved to the private sector. The new company, called Dale Gas, set up a committee structure in readiness to comply with stock exchange listing rules. During this transitional period, some directors left and new ones, more familiar with operating in listed companies but unfamiliar with the gas industry, joined the board.

It was unanimously agreed by the new board that the previous chief executive, Helen Evans, should continue in her role after the privatisation. Tom Nwede, a fund manager at XY Investments, one of the company's major new institutional shareholders, said that the company would be exposed to higher market risk if she were to leave the company, so it was very important that she stayed on. She was seen as a highly competent CEO with excellent strategic and communication skills. She commanded the confidence and trust of the employees and also the new institutional investors.

One of the first actions of the new remuneration committee was to propose a doubling of Mrs Evans's salary. The committee said that she had been underpaid when the company was state-controlled because of government constraints on the salaries of public servants. The committee said that she now needed to receive a salary commensurate with the importance of the job and in line with other public listed companies of similar size. This proposal was widely publicised. Some criticised it on the basis that if her previous salary was considered sufficient then, why was it now felt necessary to double her rewards after privatisation?

Her new salary was put to the vote at the company's first annual general meeting after privatisation. Although many small shareholders (some protesting at the AGM itself) voted against her salary increase, it was easily passed by the proxy votes of the large institutional shareholders who did not attend the meeting in person. Tom Nwede, the XY Investments fund manager, said that the votes of the institutional shareholders were crucial in ensuring that Mrs Evans was retained, thereby mitigating market risk.

Required:

(a)   **Explain the purposes of a chief executive's reward package and review the factors that might influence the level of reward for Mrs Evans after the privatisation.**   (10 marks)

(b)   **Define "market risk" and justify, giving reasons, Tom Nwede's belief that retaining Mrs Evans was crucial in mitigating market risk.**   (10 marks)

(c)   **Define, and explain the advantages of, "proxy voting" in the context of the case.**
     (5 marks)

     (25 marks)

Question 11 GEELAND

There has been a debate in the country of Geeland for some years about the most appropriate way to regulate corporate governance. Several years ago, there were a number of major corporate failures and "scandals" caused in part by a number of single powerful individuals dominating their boards. Business leaders and policy-makers were sceptical about a rules-based approach, and this led the Geeland stock exchange to issue guidance in the "Geeland Code" as follows:

"Good corporate governance is not just a matter of prescribing particular corporate structures and complying with a number of rules. There is a need for broad principles. All stakeholders should then apply these flexibly to the varying circumstances of individual companies."

Given the causes of the Geeland corporate governance failures, there was a debate about whether the separation of the roles of chairman and chief executive should be made a legal requirement. This resulted in the stock exchange issuing guidance that whilst a rules-based or "box ticking" approach would specify that "the roles of chairman and chief executive officer should never be combined... We do not think that there are universally valid answers on such points."

One company to take advantage of the flexibility in Geeland's principles-based approach was Anson Company. In July 2014, Anson Company announced that it had combined its roles of chairman and chief executive in a single role carried out by one individual. In accordance with the Geeland listing rules, it made the following "comply or explain" statement in its 2015 annual report:

"Throughout the year the company complied with all Geeland Code provisions with the exception that from 1 July 2014 the roles of chairman and chief executive have been exercised by the same individual, William Klunker. We recognise that this has been out of line with best practice. We understand the concerns of shareholders but believe that we have maintained robust governance while at the same time benefiting from having Mr Klunker in control. On 31 July 2016 Mr Klunker will step down as executive chairman, remaining as chairman until we conclude our search for a non-executive chairman to succeed him, no later than March 2017."

Required:

(a)   **Briefly distinguish between rules and principles-based approaches to corporate governance. Critically evaluate the Geeland stock exchange's guidance that "all stakeholders should then apply these flexibly to the varying circumstances of individual companies".**   (12 marks)

(b)   **Explain why a separation of the roles of chairman and chief executive is considered best practice in most jurisdictions.**   (8 marks)

(c)   **Assess the "comply or explain" statement made by Anson Company in its 2015 annual report.**   (5 marks)

(25 marks)

Question 12 ZOGS COMPANY

John Louse, the recently retired chief executive of Zogs Company, a major listed company, was giving a speech reflecting on his career and some of the aspects of governance he supported and others of which he was critical. In particular, he believed that board committees were mainly ineffective. A lot of the ineffectiveness, he said, was due to the lack of independence of many non-executive directors (NEDs). He believed that it was not enough just to have the required number of non-executive directors; they must also be "truly independent" of the executive board. It was his opinion that it was not enough to have no material financial connection with a company for independence: he believed that in order to be truly independent, NEDs should come from outside the industry and have no previous contact with any of the current executive directors.

In relation to risk committees, he said that in his experience, the company's risk committee had never stopped any risk affecting the company and because of this, he questioned its value. He said that the risk committee was "always asking for more information, which was inconvenient" and had such a "gloomy and pessimistic" approach to its task. He asked, "why can't risk committees just get on with stopping risk, and also stop making inconvenient demands on company management? Do they think middle managers have nothing else to do?" He viewed all material risks as external risks and so the risk committee should be looking outwards and not inwards.

Since retiring from Zogs, Mr Louse had taken up a non-executive directorship of SmallCo, a smaller private company in his town. In a meeting with Alan Ng, the new chief executive of Zogs, Mr Ng said that whilst risk management systems were vital in large companies like Zogs, fewer risk controls were needed in smaller companies like SmallCo.

Required:

(a)   **Define "independence" in the context of corporate governance and critically evaluate Mr Louse's comment that greater independence of non-executive directors is important in increasing the effectiveness of board committees.** (8 marks)

(b)   **Describe the roles of a risk committee and criticise Mr Louse's understanding of the risk committee in Zogs Company.** (9 marks)

(c)   **Assess whether risk committees and risk mitigation systems are more important in larger companies, like Zogs, than in smaller companies like SmallCo.** (8 marks)

(25 marks)

Question 13 OLAND

After a recent financial crisis in the country of Oland, there had been a number of high profile company failures and a general loss of confidence in business. As a result, an updated corporate governance code was proposed, with changes to address these concerns.

Before the new code was published, there was a debate in Oland society about whether corporate governance provisions should be made rules-based, or remain principles-based as had been the case in the past. One elected legislator, Martin Mung, whose constituency contained a number of the companies that had failed with resulting rises in unemployment, argued strongly that many of the corporate governance failures would not have happened if directors were legally accountable for compliance with corporate governance provisions. He said that "you can't trust the markets to punish bad practice", saying that this was what had caused the problems in the first place. He said that Oland should become a rules-based jurisdiction because the current "comply or explain" was ineffective as a means of controlling corporate governance.

Mr Mung was angered by the company failures in his constituency and believed that a lack of sound corporate governance contributed to the failure of important companies and the jobs they supported. He said that he wanted the new code to make it more difficult for companies to fail.

The new code was then issued, under a principles-based approach. One added provision in the new Oland code was to recommend a reduction in the re-election period of all directors from three years to one year. The code also required that when seeking re-election, there should be "sufficient biographical details on each director to enable shareholders to take an informed decision". The code explained that these measures were "in the interests of greater accountability".

Required:

(a)   **Examine how sound corporate governance can make it more difficult for companies to fail, clearly explaining what "corporate governance" means in your answer. (10 marks)**

(b)   Martin Mung believes that Oland should become a rules-based jurisdiction because the current "comply or explain" approach is ineffective as a means of controlling corporate governance.

Required:

Explain the difference between rules-based and principles-based approaches to corporate governance regulation, and argue against Martin Mung's belief that "comply or explain" is ineffective.   (8 marks)

(c)   Explain what "accountability" means, and discuss how the proposed new provisions for shorter re-election periods and biographical details might result in "greater accountability" as the code suggests.   (7 marks)

(25 marks)

Question 14 CORPORATE SOCIAL RESPONSIBILITY

"Clearly the power of corporations is the predominant power in the society. The problem is how to limit it.   The concern of public policy, which can be summed up in the expression "social responsibility", is derived from the perception of a commercial society and controls which a government may have to impose on economic ventures that generate unforeseen consequences far beyond intentions, or power of control, of the initiating parties".

Required:

(a)   Explain the term "corporate social responsibility".   (6 marks)

(b)   Give FOUR examples of activities by a company that could be described as showing an awareness of corporate social responsibility.   (4 marks)

(c)   Construct a case to support the assertion that awareness of corporate social responsibility is crucial for good corporate governance.   (10 marks)

(d)   Describe the relationship between integrated reporting and corporate social responsibility.   (5 marks)

(25 marks)

Question 15 SHAREHOLDERS AND ANNUAL GENERAL MEETINGS

Shareholders occupy a position of central importance in a company because they are its legal owners and they expect high levels of economic performance. But the company is not always run solely for their benefit, so they contend with management and the board of directors for control of company policies.   This is where the Annual General Meeting plays an important role in ensuring proper communication with shareholders.

Required:

(a)   Explain the difference between private and institutional shareholders, including the role of private equity and venture capital.   (6 marks)

(b)   Explain the term "minority shareholders" and the ways in which they may be unfairly treated by the majority shareholders.   (6 marks)

(c)   Explain the typical provisions included within corporate governance codes covering the rights and equitable treatment of shareholders.   (8 marks)

(d)   Explain how corporate governance codes aim to improve the quality of AGMs. (5 marks)

(25 marks)

Question 16 GLUCK AND GOODMAN

Susan Paullaos was recently appointed as a non-executive member of the internal audit committee of Gluck and Goodman, a public listed company producing complex engineering products. Barney Chester, the executive finance director who chairs the committee, has always viewed the purpose of internal audit as primarily financial in nature and as long as financial controls are seen to be fully in place, he is less concerned with other aspects of internal control. When Susan asked about operational controls in the production facility Barney said that these were not the concern of the internal audit committee. This, he said, was because as long as the accounting systems and financial controls were fully functional, all other systems may be assumed to be working correctly.

Susan, however, was concerned with the operational and quality controls in the production facility. She spoke to production director Aaron Hardanger, and asked if he would be prepared to produce regular reports for the internal audit committee on levels of specification compliance and other control issues. Mr Hardanger said that the internal audit committee had always trusted him because his reputation as a manager was very good. He said that he had never been asked to provide compliance evidence to the internal audit committee and saw no reason as to why he should start doing so now.

At board level, the non-executive chairman, George Allejandra, said that he only instituted the internal audit committee in the first place in order to be seen to be in compliance with the stock market's requirement that Gluck and Goodman should have one. He believed that internal audit committees didn't add materially to the company. They were, he believed, one of those "outrageous demands" that regulatory authorities made without considering the consequences in smaller companies nor the individual needs of different companies. He also complained about the need to have an internal auditor. He said that Gluck and Goodman used to have a full time internal auditor but when he left a year ago, he wasn't replaced. The audit committee didn't feel it needed an internal auditor because Barney Chester believed that only financial control information was important and he could get that information from his management accountant.

Susan asked Mr Allejandra if he recognised that the company was exposing itself to increased market risks by failing to have an effective audit committee. Mr Allejandra said he didn't know what a market risk was.

Required:

(a)   Internal control and audit are considered to be important parts of sound corporate governance.

      (i)   **Describe FIVE general objectives of internal control.**   (5 marks)

      (ii)   **Explain the organisational factors that determine the need for internal audit in public listed companies.**   (5 marks)

(b)   **Criticise the internal control and internal audit arrangements at Gluck and Goodman as described in the case scenario.**   (10 marks)

(c)   **Define "market risk" for Mr Allejandra and explain why Gluck and Goodman's market risk exposure is increased by failing to have an effective audit committee.**   (5 marks)

(25 marks)

Question 17 TREADWAY COMMISSION

The Committee of Sponsoring Organisations (COSO) of the Treadway Commission is an American voluntary, private sector organisation and is unconnected to government or any other regulatory authority. It was established in 1985 to help companies identify the causes of fraudulent reporting and to create internal control environments able to support full and accurate reporting. It is named after its first chairman, James Treadway, and has issued several guidance reports over the years including important reports in 1987, 1992 and 2006.

In 2009, COSO issued new "Guidance on monitoring internal control systems" to help companies tighten internal controls and thereby enjoy greater internal productivity and produce higher quality reporting. The report, written principally by a leading global professional services firm but adopted by all of the COSO members, noted that "unmonitored controls tend to deteriorate over time" and encouraged organisations to adopt wide ranging internal controls. It went on to say that, the "assessment of internal controls [can] ... involve a significant amount of ... internal audit testing".

After its publication, the business journalist, Mark Rogalski, said that the latest report contained "yet more guidance from COSO on how to make your company less productive by burdening it even more with non-productive things to do" referring to the internal control guidance the 2009 report contains. He said that there was no industry sector-specific advice and that a "one-size-fits-all" approach to internal control was "ridiculous". He further argued that there was no link between internal controls and external reporting, and that internal controls are unnecessary for effective external reporting.

Another commentator, Claire Mahmood, wrote a reply to Rogalski's column pointing to the views expressed in the 2009 COSO report that, "over time effective monitoring can lead to organisational efficiencies and reduced costs associated with public reporting on internal control because problems are identified and addressed in a proactive, rather than reactive, manner". She said that these benefits were not industry sector specific and that Rogalski was incorrect in his dismissal of the report's value. She also said that although primarily concerned with governance in the USA, the best practice guidance from COSO could be applied by companies anywhere in the world. She said that although the USA, where COSO is based, is concerned with the "rigid rules" of compliance, the advice ought to be followed by companies in countries with principles-based approaches to corporate governance because it was best practice.

Required:

(a)   **Distinguish between rules-based and principles-based approaches to internal control system compliance as described by Claire Mahmood and discuss the benefits to an organisation of a principles-based approach.** (7 marks)

(b)   Mr Rogalski is sceptical over the value of internal control and believes that controls must be industry-specific to be effective.

Required:

Describe the advantages of internal control that apply regardless of industry sector and briefly explain the meaning of the statement "unmonitored controls tend to deteriorate over time". Your answer should refer to the case scenario as appropriate. (10 marks)

(c)   The COSO report explains that "assessment of internal controls [can] ... involve a significant amount of ... internal audit testing".

Required:

Define "internal audit testing" and explain the roles of internal audit in helping ensure the effectiveness of internal control systems. (8 marks)

(25 marks)

Question 18 YAYA COMPANY

In Yaya Company, operations director Ben Janoon recently realised there had been an increase in products failing the final quality checks. These checks were carried out in the QC (quality control) laboratory, which tested finished goods products before being released for sale. The product failure rate had risen from 1% of items two years ago to 4% now, and this meant an increase of hundreds of items of output a month which were not sold on to Yaya's customers. The failed products had no value to the company once they had failed QC as the rework costs were not economic. Because the increase was gradual, it took a while for Mr Janoon to realise that the failure rate had risen.

A thorough review of the main production operation revealed nothing that might explain the increased failure and so attention was focused instead on the QC laboratory. For some years, the QC laboratory at Yaya, managed by Jane Goo, had been marginalised in the company, with its two staff working in a remote laboratory well away from other employees. Operations director Ben Janoon, who designed the internal control systems in Yaya, rarely visited the QC lab because of its remote location. He never asked for information on product failure rates to be reported to him and did not understand the science involved in the QC process. He relied on the two QC staff, Jane Goo and her assistant John Zong, both of whom did have relevant scientific qualifications.

The two QC staff considered themselves low paid. Whilst in theory they reported to Mr Janoon, in practice, they conducted their work with little contact with colleagues. The work was routine and involved testing products against a set of compliance standards. A single signature on a product compliance report was required to pass or fail in QC and these reports were then filed away with no-one else seeing them.

It was eventually established that Jane Goo had found a local buyer to pay her directly for any of Yaya's products which had failed the QC tests. The increased failure rate had resulted from her signing products as having "failed QC" when, in fact, they had passed. She kept the proceeds from the sales for herself, and also paid her assistant, John Zong, a proportion of the proceeds from the sale of the failed products.

Required:

(a)   **Explain typical reasons why an internal control system might be ineffective.**   (5 marks)

(b)   **Explain the internal control deficiencies that led to the increased product failures at Yaya.**   (10 marks)

(c)   **Discuss the general qualities of useful information, stating clearly how they would be of benefit to Mr Janoon, and recommend specific measures which would improve information flow from the QC lab to Mr Janoon.**   (10 marks)

(25 marks)

Question 19 BELIK

Belik is a listed company on a recognised stock exchange. One of the company's internal auditors uncovered an accounting malpractice, whereby the company had recorded nearly $4 million in revenue expenditure as capital expenditure, thereby falsely increasing the company's profits. She informed the head of internal audit of her findings, but was alarmed to discover at a later date that he had not included this in any of his reports to the audit committee or the board. When asked why he had not included her findings within his reports, he said that he considered the amounts not to be material.

Required:

(a)   **Explain the concept of "whistleblowing" in the context of this case and its importance to ensuring good corporate governance practice.**   (7 marks)

(b)   Identify what may be considered as best practice on "whistleblowing".   (7 marks)

(c)   Describe the role of an audit committee in respect of the financial statements, internal audit and whistleblowing.   (6 marks)

(20 marks)

Question 20 FRANKS & FISHER

The board of Franks & Fisher, a large manufacturing company, decided to set up an internal control and audit function. The proposal was to appoint an internal auditor at mid-management level and also to establish a board level internal audit committee made up mainly of non-executive directors.

The initiative to do so was driven by a recent period of rapid growth. The company had taken on many more activities as a result of growth in its product range. The board decided that the increased size and complexity of its operations created the need for greater control over internal activities and that an internal audit function was a good way forward. The need was highlighted by a recent event where internal quality standards were not enforced, resulting in the stoppage of a production line for several hours. The production director angrily described the stoppage as "entirely avoidable" and the finance director, Jason Kumas, said that the stoppage had been very costly.

Mr Kumas said that there were problems with internal control in a number of areas of the company's operations and that there was a great need for internal audit. He said that as the head of the company's accounting and finance function, the new internal auditor should report to him. The reasons for this, he said, were because as an accountant, he was already familiar with auditing procedure and the fact that he already had information on budgets and other "control" information that the internal auditor would need.

It was decided that the new internal auditor needed to be a person of some experience and with enough personality not to be intimidated nor diverted by other department heads who might find the internal audits an inconvenience. One debate the board had was whether it would be better to recruit to the position from inside or outside the company. A second argument was over the limits of authority that the internal auditor might be given. It was pointed out that while the board considered the role of internal audit to be very important, it didn't want it to interfere with the activities of other departments to the point where their operational effectiveness was reduced.

Required:

(a)   Explain, with reference to the case, the factors that are typically considered when deciding to establish internal audit in an organisation.   (10 marks)

(b)   Construct the argument in favour of appointing the new internal auditor from outside the company rather than promoting internally.   (6 marks)

(c)   Critically evaluate Mr Kumas's belief that the internal auditor should report to him as finance director.   (4 marks)

(d)   Define "objectivity" and describe characteristics that might demonstrate an internal auditor's professional objectivity.   (5 marks)

(25 marks)

Question 21 AGREX

You have been appointed Chairman of Agrex in order to assist the CEO and the board in their preparations to take Agrex to a listing. One of your first tasks will be to obtain a preliminary understanding of the company's internal control systems as the basis for drafting a report to shareholders on internal controls.

Required:

Prepare a checklist to assist you in understanding the effectiveness of the company's internal control systems.

(20 marks)

Question 22 ULTRA-UBER

During the global economic recession that began in mid-2008, many companies found it difficult to gain enough credit in the form of short-term loans from their banks and other lenders. In some cases, this caused working capital problems as short-term cash flow deficits could not be funded.

Ultra-Uber (UU), a large manufacturer based in an economically depressed region, had traditionally operated a voluntary supplier payment policy in which it was announced that all trade payables would be paid at or before 20 days and there would be no late payment. This was operated despite the normal payment terms being 30 days. The company gave the reason for this as "a desire to publicly demonstrate our social responsibility and support our valued suppliers, most of whom, like UU, also provide employment in this region". In the 20 years the policy had been in place, the UU website proudly boasted that it had never been broken. Brian Mills, the chief executive often mentioned this as the basis of the company's social responsibility. "Rather than trying to delay our payments to suppliers", he often said, "we support them and their cash flow. It's the right thing to do". Most of the other directors, however, especially the finance director, think that the voluntary supplier payment policy is a mistake. Some say that it is a means of Brian Mills exercising his own ethical beliefs in a way that is not supported by others at UU.

When UU itself came under severe cash flow pressure in the summer of 2009 as a result of its bank's failure to extend credit, the finance director told Brian Mills that UU's liquidity problems would be greatly relieved if they took an average of 30 rather than the 20 days to pay suppliers.

In addition, the manufacturing director said that he could offer another reason why the short-term liquidity at UU was a problem. He said that the credit control department was poor, taking approximately 50 days to receive payment from each customer. He also said that his own inventory control could be improved and he said he would look into that. It was pointed out to the manufacturing director that cost of goods sold was 65% of turnover and this proportion was continuously rising, driving down gross and profit margins. Due to poor inventory controls, excessively high levels of inventory were held in store at all stages of production. The long-serving sales manager wanted to keep high levels of finished goods so that customers could buy from existing inventory and the manufacturing director wanted to keep high levels of raw materials and work-in-progress to give him minimum response times when a new order came in.

One of the non-executive directors (NEDs) of UU, Bob Ndumo, said that he could not work out why UU was in such a situation as no other company in which he was a NED was having liquidity problems. Bob Ndumo held a number of other NED positions but these were mainly in service-based companies.

Required:

(a)   **Define "liquidity risk" and explain why it might be a significant risk to UU.**   (5 marks)

(b)   **Define "risk embeddedness" and explain the methods by which risk awareness and management can be embedded in organisations.**   (7 marks)

(c)   **Examine the obstacles to embedding liquidity risk management at UU.**   (8 marks)

(d)   **Criticise the voluntary supplier payment policy as a means of demonstrating UU's social responsibility.**   (5 marks)

(25 marks)

Question 23 YGT

The board of YGT discussed its need for timely risk information. The consensus of the meeting was that risk consultants should be engaged to review the risks facing the company. One director, Raz Dutta, said that she felt that this would be a waste of money as the company needed to concentrate its resources on improving organisational efficiency rather than on gathering risk information. She said that many risks "didn't change much" and "hardly ever materialised" and so can mostly be ignored. The rest of the board, however, believed that a number of risks had recently emerged whilst others had become less important and so the board wanted a current assessment as it believed previous assessments might now be outdated.

The team of risk consultants completed the risk audit. They identified and assessed six potential risks (A, B, C, D, E and F) and the following information was discussed when the findings were presented to the YGT board:

Risk A was assessed as unlikely and low impact whilst Risk B was assessed as highly likely to occur and with a high impact. The activities giving rise to both A and B, however, are seen as marginal in that whilst the activities do have value and are capable of making good returns, neither is strategically vital.

Risk C was assessed as low probability but with a high potential impact and also arises from an activity that must not be discontinued although alternative arrangements for bearing the risks are possible. The activity giving rise to Risk C was recently introduced by YGT as a result of a new product launch.

Risk D was assessed as highly likely but with a low potential impact, and arose as a result of a recent change in legislation. It cannot be insured against nor can it be outsourced. It is strategically important that the company continues to engage in the activity that gives rise to Risk D although not necessarily at the same level as is currently the case.

In addition, Risks E and F were identified. Risk E was an environmental risk and Risk F was classed as a reputation risk. The risk consultants said that risks E and F could be related risks. In the formal feedback to the board of YGT, the consultants said that the company had to develop a culture of risk awareness and that this should permeate all levels of the company.

Required:

(a)   **Criticise Raz Dutta's beliefs about the need for risk assessment. Explain why risks are dynamic and therefore need to be assessed regularly.**   (8 marks)

(b)   **Using the TARA framework, select and explain the appropriate strategy for managing each risk (A, B, C and D). Justify your selection in each case.**   (6 marks)

(c)   **Explain what "related risks" are and describe how Risks E and F might be positively correlated.**   (5 marks)

(d)   The risk consultants reported that YGT needed to cultivate a culture of risk awareness and that this should permeate all levels of the company.

       Required:

       Explain and assess this advice.   (6 marks)

                                                                            (25 marks)

Question 24 JH GRAPHICS

The board of JH Graphics, a design and artwork company, was debating an agenda item on the possible adoption of a corporate code of ethics. Jenny Harris, the chief executive and majority shareholder, was a leading supporter of the idea. She said that many of the large companies in the industry had adopted codes of ethics and that she thought it would signal the importance that JH Graphics placed on ethics. She also said that she was personally driven by high ethical values and that she wanted to express these through her work and through the company's activities and policies.

Alan Leroy, the creative director, explained that he would support the adoption of the code of ethics as long as it helped to support the company's long-term strategic objectives. He said that he could see no other reason as the company was "not a charity" and had to maximise shareholder value above all other objectives. In particular, he was keen, as a shareholder himself, to know what the code would cost to draw up and how much it would cost to comply with it over and above existing costs.

Jenny argued that having a code would help to resolve some ethical issues, one of which, she suggested, was a problem the company was having over a particular image it had recently produced for a newspaper advertisement. The image was produced for an advertising client and although the client was pleased, it had offended a particular religious group because of its content and design.

When it was discovered who had produced the "offending" image, some religious leaders criticised JH Graphics for being insensitive and offensive to their religion. For a brief time, the events were a major news story. As politicians, journalists and others debated the issues in the media, the board of JH Graphics was involved in intense discussions and faced with a dilemma as to whether or not to issue a public apology for the offence caused by the image and to ask the client to withdraw it.

Alan argued that having a code of ethics would not have helped in that situation, as the issue was so complicated. His view was that the company should not apologise for the image and that he didn't care very much that the image offended people. He said it was bringing the company free publicity and that was good for the business. Jenny said that she had sympathy for the viewpoint of the offended religious leaders. Although she disagreed with them, she understood the importance to some people of firmly-held beliefs. The board agreed that as there seemed to be arguments both ways, the decision on how the company should deal with the image should be Jenny's as chief executive.

Required:

(a)   Analyse Jenny's and Alan's motivations for adopting the code of ethics using the normative-instrumental forms of stakeholder theory.   (8 marks)

(b)   Assess Jenny's decision on the possible apology for the "offending" image from conventional and pre-conventional moral development perspectives.   (4 marks)

(c)   Explain and assess the factors that the board of JH Graphics might consider in deciding how to respond to the controversy over the offending image.   (10 marks)

(d)   Comment on the legitimacy of the religious group's claims on JH Graphics' activities.
                                                                                 (3 marks)

                                                                         (25 marks)

Question 25 RAILWAY DEVELOPMENT COMPANY

Railway Development Company (RDC) was considering two options for a new railway line connecting two towns. Route A involved cutting a channel through an area designated as being of special scientific importance because it was one of a very few suitable feeding grounds for a colony of endangered birds. The birds were considered to be an important part of the local environment with some potential influences on local ecosystems.

The alternative was Route B which would involve the compulsory purchase and destruction of Eddie Krul's farm. Mr Krul was a vocal opponent of the Route B plan. He said that he had a right to stay on the land which had been owned by his family for four generations and which he had developed into a profitable farm. The farm employed a number of local people whose jobs would be lost if Route B went through the house and land. Mr Krul threatened legal action against RDC if Route B was chosen.

An independent legal authority has determined that the compulsory purchase price of Mr Krul's farm would be $1 million if Route B was chosen. RDC considered this a material cost, over and above other land costs, because the projected net present value (NPV) of cash flows over a ten-year period would be $5 million without buying the farm. This would reduce the NPV by $1 million if Route B was chosen.

The local government authority had given both routes provisional planning permission and offered no opinion of which it preferred. It supported infrastructure projects such as the new railway line, believing that either route would attract new income and prosperity to the region. It took the view that as an experienced railway builder, RDC would know best which to choose and how to evaluate the two options. Because it was very keen to attract the investment, it left the decision entirely to RDC. RDC selected Route A as the route to build the new line.

A local environmental pressure group, "Save the Birds", was outraged at the decision to choose Route A. It criticised RDC and also the local authority for ignoring the sustainability implications of the decision. It accused the company of profiting at the expense of the environment and threatened to use "direct action" to disrupt the building of the line through the birds' feeding ground if Route A went ahead.

Required:

(a) **Use Tucker's "five question" model to assess the decision to choose Route A.** (10 marks)

(b) **Discuss the importance to RDC of recognising all of the stakeholders in a decision such as deciding between Route A and Route B.** (8 marks)

(c) **Explain what a stakeholder "claim" is, and critically assess the stakeholder claims of Mr Krul, the local government authority and the colony of endangered birds.** (7 marks)

(25 marks)

Question 26 ESKADA

Eskada, a bank listed on a recognised Stock Exchange, has enjoyed real annual growth in excess of 30% per annum over the last ten years under the direction of its autocratic chief executive, David Hake. This had been achieved by a strategy of takeover and aggressive selling of the bank's products and services. David is feared by his fellow board executives and senior managers. He has earned the nickname "Hacker" because of his reputation in disciplining executives and managers who do not meet their targets and in cutting staff and costs in the bank and those banks Eskada acquired. A typical example of his attitude to those who did not agree with him was the dismissal of the bank's senior risk manager two years ago who had been warning the audit committee (all independent non-execs) that the bank was taking risks that the board did not fully understand that many of the products it was dealing with were building up systemic risk. The role of the risk manager was given to the bank's top sales manager, who was given a significant increase in remuneration, reporting directly to David.

Just before the bank's last acquisition one year ago, the BCM Banking Group, David confided (in a rare friendly chat) to the bank's Chairman that he wanted to be the "king" of the largest international banking group – he referred to it as his "empire". His rationale in making the acquisition was to prevent the bank in question from joining a rival banking group. With little regard to due diligence (David's attitude was that it was a waste of time and an outdated practice in the modern banking world) Eskada's board recommended the take over which was duly approved by the shareholders following a series of meetings between David and the major shareholders.

Nine months after BCM was taken over, it was becoming clear to David that the acquisition was a total disaster. Eskada's share price was showing signs that it was beginning to free fall and David decided that it was time to get out. In negotiations with the bank's remuneration committee (all independent non-exec directors) it was agreed that David would receive all his due bonuses (amounting to over $5 million), the bank would pay ten years of additional pension fund contribution (at least $20 million) and that he could start to immediately draw his pension ($1 million per year) as if he had retired at the normal retirement age of 60 (David was 51).

After David had left Eskada, the details of his resignation and severance deal became public knowledge. Because of the furore that followed, the Chairman and all of the non-executive directors were forced to resign without any compensation. The business press demanded to know why the bank had poor corporate governance and why a culture of poor moral and ethical behaviour had permeated throughout the bank.

Required:

(a)   **Identify the corporate governance issues created at Eskada and explain how they could have been avoided.**   (10 marks)

(b)   **Explain the importance of personal morality and ethics, relating to the role of David within Eskada.**   (8 marks)

(c)   In the context of Integrated Reporting <IR>, "integrated thinking is the active consideration by an organisation of the relationships between its various operating and functional units and the capitals that the organisation uses or affects". The long-term vision of the International Integrated Reporting Council (IIRC) is that integrated thinking should be embedded within mainstream business practice, facilitated by <IR> as the corporate reporting norm.

Explain how integrated thinking could have helped to manage the issues at Eskada.
(7 marks)

(25 marks)

Question 27 BIGGO

When Biggo Manufacturing (a public listed company) needed to build an extension to its factory, it obtained planning permission to build it on an adjacent field. The local government authority was keen to attract the new jobs that would go with the expansion and so granted the permission despite the objections of a number of residents, who were concerned that the new factory extension would mean the loss of a children's play area.

When the board of Biggo met after the building approval had been given, the chief executive read out a letter from Albert Doo, leader of the local government authority, saying that although permission to build had been given, the company should consider making a sizeable contribution towards creating a new children's play area in a nearby location. Mr Doo said that Biggo "should recognise its social responsibility". He said that the company should consider itself a citizen of society and should, accordingly, "recognise its responsibilities as well as its legal rights".

One of Biggo's directors, Robert Tens, said he thought the request was entirely reasonable given the displacement of the play area. He also said that they could use the donation strategically to help cultivate the company's reputation locally to help in future recruitment. It might also, he said, help to reduce resistance to any future expansion the company might need to make.

Margaret Heggs, in contrast, argued that the company should not make the donation as it was likely that company profits would be low in the current year. She said that the acquisition of the land and the gaining of planning permission were done through the normal legal channels and so the company had no further contractual or ethical duties to the local government, nor to the local community. She said that Biggo provided local employment and produced excellent products and so it was unreasonable for the request for a donation to have been made. "This board is accountable to the shareholders of Biggo and not to the local community or the local government authority", she said.

Required:

(a)   **Explain the meaning of "rights" and "responsibilities" in the context of Biggo and describe how these terms are interpreted at the two ends of the Gray, Owen & Adams "continuum".**   (10 marks)

(b)   **Justify, using evidence from the case, which of Gray, Owen & Adams's positions are best described by the comments made by Robert Tens and also Margaret Heggs.**
                                                                                                                        (6 marks)

(c)   **Define "social responsibility" as used by Albert Doo. Contrast how short and long-term shareholder interest perspectives may affect Biggo's attitude to the requested contribution for the children's play area.**   (9 marks)

                                                                                                                    (25 marks)

Question 28 HAPPY AND HEALTHY

"Happy and healthy" is a traditional independent health food business that has been run as a family company for 40 years by Ken and Steffi Potter. As a couple they have always been passionate campaigners for healthy foods and are more concerned about the quality of the foods they sell than the financial detail of their business. Since the company started in 1970, it has been audited by Watson Shreeves, a local audit firm. Mr Shreeves has overseen the Potters' audit for all of the 40 year history (rotating the engagement partner) and has always taken the opportunity to meet with Ken and Steffi informally at the end of each audit to sign off the financial statements and to offer a briefing and some free financial advice in his role as what he calls, "auditor and friend". In these briefings, Mr Shreeves, who has become a close family friend of the Potters over the years, always points out that the business is profitable (which the Potters already knew without knowing the actual figures) and how they might increase their margins. But the Potters have never been too concerned about financial performance as long as they can provide a good service to their customers, make enough to keep the business going and provide continued employment for themselves and their son, Ivan. Whilst Ken and Steffi still retain a majority shareholding in "Happy and healthy" they have gradually increased Ivan's proportion over the years. They currently own 60% to Ivan's 40%. Ivan was appointed a director, alongside Ken and Steffi, in 2013.

Ivan grew up in the business and has helped his parents out since he was a young boy. As he grew up, Ken and Steffi gave him more and more responsibility in the hope that he would one day take the business over. By the end of 2014, Ken made sure that Ivan drew more salary than Ken and Steffi combined as they sought to ensure that Ivan was happy to continue in the business after they retired.

During the audit for the year ended 31 March 2015, a member of Watson Shreeves was performing the audit as usual when he noticed a dramatic drop in the profitability of the business as a whole. He noticed that whilst food sales continued to be profitable, a large amount of inventory had been sold below cost to Barong Company with no further explanation and it was this that had caused the reduction in the company's operating margin. Each transaction with Barong Company had, the invoices showed, been authorised by Ivan.

Mr Shreeves was certain Ken and Steffi would not know anything about this and he prepared to tell them about it as a part of his annual end of audit meeting. Before the meeting, however, he carried out some checks on Barong Company and found that it was a separate business owned by Ivan and his wife. Mr Shreeves's conclusion was that Ivan was effectively stealing from "Happy and healthy" to provide inventory for Barong Company at a highly discounted cost price. Although Mr Shreeves now had to recommend certain disclosures to the financial statements in this meeting, his main fear was that Ken and Steffi would be devastated if they found out that Ivan was stealing and that it would have long-term implications for their family relationships and the future of "Happy and healthy".

Required:

(a) **Explain how a family (or insider-dominated) business differs from a public listed company and, using evidence from the case, explore the governance issues of a family or insider-dominated business.** (10 marks)

(b) **Mr Shreeves is a professional accountant and auditor. Explain why he is considered a professional by society and describe the fundamental principles (or responsibilities) of professionalism that society expects from him and all other accountants.** (7 marks)

(c) **Discuss the professional and ethical dilemma facing Mr Shreeves in deciding whether or not to tell Ken and Steffi about Ivan's activity. Advise Mr Shreeves of the most appropriate course of action.** (8 marks)

(25 marks)

Question 29 HOGG PRODUCTS

Hogg Products Company (HPC), based in a developing country, was recently wholly acquired by American Overseas Investments (AOI), a North American holding company. The new owners took the opportunity to completely review HPC's management, culture and systems. One of the first things that AOI questioned was HPC's longstanding corporate code of ethics.

The board of AOI said that it had a general code of ethics that HPC, as an AOI subsidiary, should adopt. Simon Hogg, the chief executive of HPC, disagreed however, and explained why HPC should retain its existing code. He said that HPC had adopted its code of ethics in its home country which was often criticised for its unethical business behaviour.

Some other companies in the country were criticised for their "sweat shop" conditions. HPC's adoption of its code of ethics, however, meant that it could always obtain orders from European customers on the guarantee that products were made ethically and in compliance with its own highly regarded code of ethics. Mr Hogg explained that HPC had an outstanding ethical reputation both locally and internationally and that reputation could be threatened if it was forced to replace its existing code of ethics with AOI's more general code.

When Ed Tanner, a senior director from AOI's head office, visited Mr Hogg after the acquisition, he was shown HPC's operation in action. Mr Hogg pointed out that unlike some other employers in the industry, HPC didn't employ child labour. Mr Hogg explained that although it was allowed by law in the country, it was forbidden by HPC's code of ethics. Mr Hogg also explained that in his view, employing child labour was always ethically wrong. Mr Tanner asked whether the money that children earned by working in the relatively safe conditions at HPC was an important source of income for their families. Mr Hogg said that the money was important to them but even so, it was still wrong to employ children, as it was exploitative and interfered with their education. He also said that it would alienate the European customers who bought from HPC partly on the basis of the terms of its code of ethics.

Required:

(a) Describe the purposes and typical contents of a corporate code of ethics. (9 marks)

(b) "Strategic positioning" is about the way that a company as a whole is placed in its environment and concerns its "fit" with the factors in its environment.

With reference to the case as appropriate, explain how a code of ethics can be used as part of a company's overall strategic positioning. (7 marks)

(c) Assess Mr Hogg's belief that employing child labour is "always ethically wrong" from deontological and teleological (consequentialist) ethical perspectives. (9 marks)

(25 marks)

Question 30 MRS YTTRIA & MR MORDUE

In a major policy speech, Government finance minister Mrs Wei Yttria said that the audit and assurance industry's work should always be judged by the effect it has on public confidence in business. She said that it was crucial that professional services such as audit and assurance should always be performed in the public interest and that there should be no material threats to the assurer's independence. Enron and other corporate failures happened, she said, because some accountants didn't understand what it was to act in the public interest. She stressed that it was important that firms should not provide more than one service to individual clients. If a firm audited a client then, she said, it shouldn't provide any other services to that client.

Mr Oggon Mordue, a financial journalist who had worked in audit and assurance for many years, was in the audience. He suggested that the normal advice on threats to independence was wrong. On the contrary in fact, the more services that a professional services firm can provide to a client the better, as it enables the firm to better understand the client and its commercial and accounting needs. Mrs Yttria disagreed, saying that his views were a good example of professional services firms not acting in the public interest.

Mr Mordue said that when he was a partner at a major professional services firm, he got to know his clients very well through the multiple links that his firm had with them. He said that he knew all about their finances from providing audit and assurance services, all about their tax affairs through tax consulting and was always in a good position to provide any other advice as he had acted as a consultant on other matters for many years including advising on mergers, acquisitions, compliance and legal issues. He became very good friends with the directors of client companies, he said. The clients, he explained, also found the relationship very helpful and the accounting firms did well financially out of it.

Another reporter in the audience argued with Mr Mordue. Ivor Nahum said that Mr Mordue represented the "very worst" of the accounting profession. He said that accounting was a "biased and value laden" profession that served minority interests, was complicit in environmental degradation and could not serve the public interest as long as it primarily served the interests of unfettered capitalism. He said that the public interest was badly served by accounting, as it did not address poverty, animal rights or other social injustices.

Required:

(a) Explain, using accounting as an example, what "the public interest" means as used by Mrs Yttria in her speech. (5 marks)

(b) This requirement concerns ethical threats. It is very important for professional accountants to be aware of ethical threats and to avoid these where possible.

Required:

(i)   With reference to the case as appropriate, describe five types of ethical threat.

(5 marks)

(ii) Assess the ethical threats implied by Mr Mordue's beliefs.   (8 marks)

(c)   Assess Ivor Nahum's remarks about the accounting profession in the light of Gray, Owen & Adams' deep green (or deep ecologist) position on social responsibility.

(7 marks)

(25 marks)

Question 31 MBABO COMPANY

John Wang is a junior partner and training manager at Miller Dundas, a medium sized firm of auditors. He oversees the progress of the firm's student accountants. One of those under John's supervision, Lisa Xu, recently wrote in her progress and achievement log about a situation in an audit that had disturbed her.

On the recent audit of Mbabo Company, a medium sized, family-run business and longstanding client of Miller Dundas, Lisa was checking non-current asset purchases when she noticed what she thought might be an irregularity. There was an entry of $100,000 for a security system for an address in a well-known holiday resort with no obvious link to the company. On questioning this with Ellen Tan, the financial controller, Lisa was told that the system was for Mr Martin Mbabo's holiday cottage (Martin Mbabo is managing director and a minority shareholder in the Mbabo Company). She was told that Martin Mbabo often took confidential company documents with him to his holiday home and so needed the security system on the property to protect them. It was because of this, Ellen said, that it was reasonable to charge the security system to the company.

Ellen Tan expressed surprise at Lisa's concerns and said that auditors had not previously been concerned about the company being charged for non-current assets and operational expenses for Mr Mbabo's personal properties.

Lisa told the engagement partner, Potto Sinter, what she had found and Potto simply said that the charge could probably be ignored. He did agree, however, to ask for a formal explanation from Martin Mbabo before he signed off the audit. Lisa wasn't at the final clearance meeting but later read the following in the notes from the clearance meeting: "discussed other matter with client, happy with explanation". When Lisa discussed the matter with Potto afterwards she was told that the matter was now closed and that she should concentrate on her next audit and her important accounting studies.

When John Wang read about Lisa's concerns and spoke to her directly, he realised he was in an ethical dilemma. Not only should there be a disclosure requirement of Mr Mbabo's transaction, but the situation was made more complicated by the fact that Potto Sinter was senior to John Wang in Miller Dundas and also by the fact that the two men were good friends.

Required:

(a)   Explain the meaning of "integrity" and its importance in professional relationships such as those described in the case.   (5 marks)

(b)   Criticise Potto Sinter's ethical and professional behaviour in the case.   (10 marks)

(c)   Critically evaluate the alternatives that John Wang has in his ethical dilemma. (10 marks)

(25 marks)

Question 32 JOJO AUDITORS

Jojo Auditors is an audit practice with five partners. The five partners have worked together for several years and, as well as being work colleagues, are personal friends with each other. At Jojo it is customary for the performance of all student accountants to be appraised after their first year of a training contract using a range of criteria including examination success, technical ability and professionalism. Three levels of outcome are possible:

(1)   "Good", allowing students to continue with no issues;
(2)   "Some concerns", meaning students are counselled and then allowed to continue; and
(3)   "Poor", where students are dismissed from the audit practice.

The appraisal committee is comprised of three people: managing partner Jack Hu, the training manager (both of whom are professional accountants) and the person responsible for human resources. The committee receives confidential reports on each student and makes decisions based on the views of relevant engagement partners and also exam results. It is normally the training manager who makes the recommendation and in most cases his appraisal is agreed and then acted upon accordingly. Because the appraisals are confidential between the student and the firm, the list of students and their appraisal categories are not publicised within the firm.

When the 2014 intake was being appraised last year, one student was appraised by the training manager as "poor" but was not dismissed. Polly Shah was unpopular among other students because she was considered lazy and technically weak. She also failed a number of her exams. Other students who were appraised as "poor" were dismissed, but Polly received a brief counselling session from Jack Hu and then returned to her duties. Polly stayed for another year and then, having failed more exams, left Jojo to pursue other career interests outside accounting.

Polly's departure triggered some discussion amongst Jojo's partners as to why she had been retained when other poor performers had not. It later emerged that Jack Hu was a close friend of Polly's parents and had enjoyed free holidays in the Shah family's villa for several years. Because he was the managing partner, Mr Hu was able to insist on retaining Polly, despite the objections of the training manager and the human resources representative, although the training manager was reported to be furious at the decision to retain Polly.

Required:

(a)   **Define "conflict of interest" and assess the consequences of Jack Hu's behaviour after Polly Shah's appraisal.**   (10 marks)

(b)   **Describe four ethical safeguards that could be used in Jojo to prevent a recurrence of the events like those described in the case.**   (8 marks)

(c)   The case raises issues of the importance of senior management performance measurement. In a public company, this refers to directors, and in a privately-owned partnership like Jojo, it refers to partners. The managing partner (Mr Hu's position) is equivalent to the role of chief executive.

         Required:

         Explain the typical criteria used in the performance measurement of individual directors and discuss the reasons why individual performance measurement of partners may be difficult to implement at Jojo.   (7 marks)

                                                                                      (25 marks)

Question 33 INTEGRATED REPORTING

The International Integrated Reporting Council (IIRC) developed the International <IR> Framework that, based on the concept of integrated thinking, combines financial, environmental, social and governance information in a clear, concise, consistent and comparable format – the integrated report.

The aim of the Framework is to help to develop more comprehensive and comprehensible information (historic, current and future) about organisations (both private and public), to meet the needs of a more sustainable, global economy. The Framework provides guiding principles and content elements that help to shape the information provided and to explain why the inclusion of the information provided is important.

Integrated reporting combines financial and non-financial information in one report with the aim of maximising the value of information provided to stakeholders with a variety of interests in an organisation.

The goals of integrated reporting are:

■   to improve the quality of information available to providers of financial capital;

■   to promote a more cohesive and efficient approach to corporate reporting that better reflects all of the factors that materially affect the ability of an organisation to create value over time;

■   to enhance accountability and stewardship for all forms of capital;

■   to promote the understanding of the interdependencies among the various capitals; and

■   to support integrated thinking in decision-making and actions which create value over the short, medium and long term.

Required:

(a)   **Explain the concept of integrated thinking and how it is related to integrated reporting.**

(3 marks)

(b)   **Describe each of the Guiding Principles that underpin the preparation of an integrated report.**   (7 marks)

(c)   **Explain how the Content Elements help to ensure a suitable level of comparability between organisations.**   (8 marks)

(d)   Integrated thinking and reporting results in a more expansive coverage of information than traditional financial reporting. Integrated reporting more clearly demonstrates an organisation's use of and dependence on different resources and relationships or "capitals" and the organisation's access to and effect on them.

       Explain the concept of capitals in integrated reporting.   (7 marks)

(25 marks)

Question 34 HYDRASPORTS

Hydrasports Co, a national leisure group, has 16 centres around the country and a head office. The group was originally started by five individuals who each contributed $10,000 to start the organization. Each of these individuals have worked in fitness instruction and training for over 10 years. Facilities at each centre are of a standard design which incorporates a heated swimming pool, sauna, air-conditioned gym, fitness studios, state-of-the-art entertainment system throughout the centre and supervised childcare. The fitness instructors and childcare supervisors at each centre must hold recognised qualifications and be appropriately certified. Each centre is managed on a day-to-day basis, by a centre manager, in accordance with company policies.

Members pay a $100 joining fee, plus either $100 per month for "platinum" membership (opening times including the pool), $70 per month for "standard" membership (same as platinum but no pool) and $40 "off-peak" membership (daytime until 17.00, no use of pool). Standard and off-peak members can use the pool for a $30 supplement per month). Pensioners are entitled to a 50% discount on off-peak membership. Fees are not usually refundable.

The centre at Verne was closed from July to September 2015 after a chemical spill in the sauna caused a serious accident. Although the centre was re-opened, Hydrasports has recommended to all centre managers that sauna facilities be suspended until further notice.

In response to complaints to the local authorities about its childcare facilities, Hydrasports has issued centre managers with revised guidelines for minimum levels of supervision.

Staff lateness is a recurring problem and a major cause of "early bird" customer dissatisfaction with sessions which are scheduled to start at 07.00. New employees are generally attracted to the industry in the short-term for its non-cash benefits, including free use of the facilities – but leave when they require increased financial rewards. Turnover of centre managers is also high, due to the constraints imposed on them by company policy.

Three of the centres are expected to have run at a loss for the year to 31 December 2015 due to falling membership.

Hydrasports has invested heavily in a hydrotherapy pool at one of these centres, with the aim of attracting retired members with more leisure time. Financing for the new hydrotherapy pool is through a bank loan. The pool has several new features that have never been used before in hydrotherapy. The features were designed by one of the founders of Hydrasports and the company has applied for a patent on the design. Water from a recently discovered hot thermal spring under the centre will be used in the pool. The pool is expected to open in February 2016.

Cash flow difficulties in the current year have put back the planned replacement of gym equipment for most of the centres.

Insurance premiums for liability to employees and the public have increased by nearly 45%. Rather than passing on this increased cost through an increase in membership fees, Hydrasports has met the additional expense by reducing its insurance coverage on its plant and equipment from a replacement cost basis to a net realisable value basis.

The company is planning to issue its first integrated report that will incorporate a social and environmental statement.

Required:

(a)   **Suggest performance indicators that could be set to increase the centre managers' awareness of Hydrasports' social and environmental responsibilities and the evidence which should be available to provide assurance on their accuracy.** (13 marks)

(b) Identify examples of the types of capital, according to the International <IR> Framework, relevant to Hydrasports and explain where the company needs to work to improve or increase these capitals. (12 marks)

(25 marks)

Question 35 JGP CHEMICALS

At a board meeting of JGP Chemicals, the directors were discussing some recent negative publicity arising from the accidental emission of a chemical pollutant into the local river. As well as it resulting in a large fine from the courts, the leak had created a great deal of controversy in the local community that relied on the polluted river for its normal use (including drinking). A prominent community leader spoke for those affected when she said that a leak of this type must never happen again or JGP would suffer the loss of support from the community. She also reminded JGP that it attracts 65% of its labour from the local community.

As a response to the problems that arose after the leak, the JGP board decided to consult an expert on whether the publication of a full annual environmental report might help to mitigate future environmental risks. The expert, Professor Appo (a prominent academic), said that the company would need to establish an annual environmental audit before they could issue a report. He said that the environmental audit should include, in addition to a review and evaluation of JGP's safety controls, a full audit of the environmental impact of JGP's supply chain. He said that these components would be very important in addressing the concerns of a growing group of investors who are worried about such things. Professor Appo said that all chemical companies had a structural environmental risk and JGP was no exception to this. As major consumers of natural chemical resources and producers of potentially hazardous outputs, Professor Appo said that chemical companies should be aware of the wide range of ways in which they can affect the environment. CEO Keith Miasma agreed with Professor Appo and added that because JGP was in chemicals, any environmental issue had the potential to affect JGP's overall reputation among a wide range of stakeholders.

When the board was discussing the issue of sustainability in connection with the environmental audit, the finance director said that sustainability reporting would not be necessary as the company was already sustainable because it had no "going concern" issues. He said that JGP had been in business for over 50 years, should be able to continue for many years to come and was therefore sustainable. As far as he was concerned, this was all that was meant by sustainability.

In the discussion that followed, the board noted that in order to signal its seriousness to the local community and to investors, the environmental audit should be as thorough as possible and that as much information should be made available to the public "in the interests of transparency". It was agreed that contents of the audit (the agreed metrics) should be robust and with little room left for interpretation – they wanted to be able to demonstrate that they had complied with their agreed metrics for the environmental audit.

Required:

(a) Explain "sustainability" in the context of environmental auditing and criticise the finance director's understanding of sustainability. (6 marks)

(b) Explain the three stages in an environmental audit and explore, using information from the case, the issues that JGP will have in developing these stages. (9 marks)

(c) Define "environmental risk". Distinguish between strategic and operational risks and explain why the environmental risks at JGP are strategic. (10 marks)

(25 marks)

Question 36 R & M

Rowlands & Medeleev (R&M), a major listed European civil engineering company, was successful in its bid to become principal (lead) contractor to build the Giant Dam Project in an East Asian country. The board of R&M prided itself in observing the highest standards of corporate governance. R&M's client, the government of the East Asian country, had taken into account several factors in appointing the principal contractor including each bidder's track record in large civil engineering projects, the value of the bid and a statement, required from each bidder, on how it would deal with the "sensitive issues" and publicity that might arise as a result of the project.

The Giant Dam Project was seen as vital to the East Asian country's economic development as it would provide a large amount of hydroelectric power. This was seen as a "clean energy" driver of future economic growth. The government was keen to point out that because hydroelectric power did not involve the burning of fossil fuels, the power would be environmentally clean and would contribute to the East Asian country's ability to meet its internationally agreed carbon emission targets. This, in turn, would contribute to the reduction of greenhouse gases in the environment. Critics, such as the environmental pressure group "Stop-the-dam", however, argued that the project was far too large and the cost to the local environment would be unacceptable. Stop-the-dam was highly organised and, according to press reports in Europe, was capable of disrupting progress on the dam by measures such as creating "human barriers" to the site and hiding people in tunnels who would have to be physically removed before proceeding. A spokesman for Stop-the-dam said it would definitely be attempting to resist the Giant Dam Project when construction started.

The project was intended to dam one of the region's largest rivers, thus creating a massive lake behind it. The lake would, the critics claimed, not only displace an estimated 100,000 people from their homes, but would also flood productive farmland and destroy several rare plant and animal habitats. A number of important archaeological sites would also be lost. The largest community to be relocated was the indigenous First Nation people who had lived on and farmed the land for an estimated thousand years. A spokesman for the First Nation community said that the "true price" of hydroelectric power was "misery and cruelty". A press report said that whilst the First Nation would be unlikely to disrupt the building of the dam, it was highly likely that they would protest and also attempt to mobilise opinion in other parts of the world against the Giant Dam Project.

The board of R&M was fully aware of the controversy when it submitted its tender to build the dam. The finance director, Sally Grignard, had insisted on putting an amount into the tender for the management of "local risks". Sally was also responsible for the financing of the project for R&M. Although the client was expected to release money in several "interim payments" as the various parts of the project were completed to strict time deadlines, she anticipated a number of working capital challenges for R&M, especially near the beginning where a number of early stage costs would need to be incurred. There would, she explained, also be financing issues in managing the cash flows to R&M's many subcontractors. Although the major banks financed the client through a lending syndicate, R&M's usual bank said it was wary of lending directly to R&M for the Giant Dam Project because of the potential negative publicity that might result. Another bank said it would provide R&M with its early stage working capital needs on the understanding that its involvement in financing R&M to undertake the Giant Dam Project was not disclosed. A press statement from Stop-the-dam said that it would do all it could to discover R&M's financial lenders and publicly expose them. Sally told the R&M board that some debt financing would be essential until the first interim payments from the client became available.

When it was announced that R&M had won the contract to build the Giant Dam Project, some of its institutional shareholders contacted Richard Markovnikoff, the chairman. They wanted reassurance that the company had fully taken the environmental issues and other risks into account. One fund manager asked if Mr Markovnikoff could explain the sustainability implications of the project to assess whether R&M shares were still suitable for his environmentally sensitive clients. Mr Markovnikoff said, through the company's investor relations department, that he intended to give a statement at the next annual general meeting (AGM) that he hoped would address these environmental concerns. He would also, he said, make a statement on the importance of confidentiality in the financing of the early stage working capital needs.

(a) Any large project such as the Giant Dam Project has a number of stakeholders.

Required:

(i) **Define the terms "stakeholder" and "stakeholder claim", and identify from the case FOUR of R&M's external stakeholders as it carries out the Giant Dam Project;** (6 marks)

(ii) **Describe the claim of each of the four identified stakeholders.** (4 marks)

(b) **Describe a framework to assess the risks to the progress of the Giant Dam Project. Your answer should include a diagram to represent the framework.** (6 marks)

(c) **Using information from the case, assess THREE risks to the Giant Dam Project.** (9 marks)

(d) **Prepare the statement for Mr Markovnikoff to read out at the AGM. The statement you construct should contain the following.**

(i) **A definition and brief explanation of "sustainable development";** (3 marks)

(ii) **An evaluation of the environmental and sustainability implications of the Giant Dam Project;** (8 marks)

(iii) **A statement on the importance of confidentiality in the financing of the early stage working capital needs and an explanation of how this conflicts with the duty of transparency in matters of corporate governance.** (6 marks)

Professional marks for layout, logical flow and persuasiveness of the statement. (4 marks)

(e) Internal controls are very important in a complex civil engineering project such as the Giant Dam Project.

Required:

Describe the difficulties of maintaining sound internal controls in the Giant Dam Project created by working through sub-contractors. (4 marks)

(50 marks)

Question 37 SWAN HILL

The scientists in the research laboratories of Swan Hill Company (SHC), a public listed company, recently made a very important discovery about the process that manufactured its major product. The scientific director, Dr Sonja Rainbow, informed the board that the breakthrough was called the "sink method". She explained that the sink method would enable SHC to produce its major product at a lower unit cost and in much higher volumes than the current process.

It would also produce lower unit environmental emissions and would substantially improve product quality compared to its current process and indeed compared to all of the other competitors in the industry.

SHC currently has 30% of the global market with its nearest competitor having 25% and the other twelve producers sharing the remainder. The company, based in the town of Swan Hill, has a paternalistic management approach and has always valued its relationship with the local community. Its website says that SHC has always sought to maximise the benefit to the workforce and community in all of its business decisions and feels a great sense of loyalty to the Swan Hill locality which is where it started in 1900 and has been based ever since.

As the board considered the implications of the discovery of the sink method, chief executive Nelson Cobar asked whether Sonja Rainbow was certain that SHC was the only company in the industry that had made the discovery and she said that she was. She also said that she was certain that the competitors were "some years" behind SHC in their research.

It quickly became clear that the discovery of the sink method was so important and far reaching that it had the potential to give SHC an unassailable competitive advantage in its industry. Chief executive Nelson Cobar told board colleagues that they should clearly understand that the discovery had the potential to put all of SHC's competitors out of business and make SHC the single global supplier. He said that as the board considered the options, members should bear in mind the seriousness of the implications upon the rest of the industry.

Mr Cobar said there were two strategic options. Option one was to press ahead with the huge investment of new plant necessary to introduce the sink method into the factory whilst, as far as possible, keeping the nature of the sink technology secret from competitors (the "secrecy option"). A patent disclosing the nature of the technology would not be filed so as to keep the technology secret within SHC. Option two was to file a patent and then offer the use of the discovery to competitors under a licensing arrangement where SHC would receive substantial royalties for the twenty-year legal lifetime of the patent (the "licensing option"). This would also involve new investment but at a slower pace in line with competitors. The licence contract would, Mr Cobar explained, include an "improvement sharing" requirement where licensees would be required to inform SHC of any improvements discovered that made the sink method more efficient or effective.

The sales director, Edwin Kiama, argued strongly in favour of the secrecy option. He said that the board owed it to SHC's shareholders to take the option that would maximise shareholder value. He argued that business strategy was all about gaining competitive advantage and this was a chance to do exactly that. Accordingly, he argued, the sink method should not be licensed to competitors and should be pursued as fast as possible. The operations director said that to gain the full benefits of the sink method with either option would require a complete refitting of the factory and the largest capital investment that SHC had ever undertaken.

The financial director, Sean Nyngan, advised the board that pressing ahead with investment under the secrecy option was not without risks. First, he said, he would have to finance the investment, probably initially through debt, and second, there were risks associated with any large investment. He also informed the board that the licensing option would, over many years, involve the inflow of "massive" funds in royalty payments from competitors using the SHC's patented sink method. By pursuing the licensing option, Sean Nyngan said that they could retain their market leadership in the short term without incurring risk, whilst increasing their industry dominance in the future through careful investment of the royalty payments.

The non-executive chairman, Alison Manilla, said that she was looking at the issue from an ethical perspective. She asked whether SHC had the right, even if it had the ability, to put competitors out of business.

Required:

(a) **Assess the secrecy option using Tucker's model for decision-making.** (10 marks)

(b) **Distinguish between strategic and operational risks, and explain why the secrecy option would be a source of strategic risk.** (10 marks)

(c) Mr Cobar, the chief executive of SHC, has decided to draft two alternative statements to explain both possible outcomes of the secrecy/licensing decision to shareholders. Once the board has decided which one to pursue, the relevant draft will be included in a voluntary section of the next corporate annual report.

Required:

(i) **Draft a statement in the event that the board chooses the secrecy option. It should make a convincing business case and put forward ethical arguments for the secrecy option. The ethical arguments should be made from the stockholder (or pristine capitalist) perspective.** (8 marks)

(ii) **Draft a statement in the event that the board chooses the licensing option. It should make a convincing business case and put forward ethical arguments for the licensing option. The ethical arguments should be made from the wider stakeholder perspective.** (8 marks)

(iii) **Professional marks for the persuasiveness and logical flow of arguments: two marks per statement.** (4 marks)

(d) Corporate annual reports contain both mandatory and voluntary disclosures.

Required:

(i) **Distinguish, using examples, between mandatory and voluntary disclosures in the annual reports of public listed companies.** (6 marks)

(ii) **Explain why the disclosure of voluntary information in annual reports can enhance the company's accountability to equity investors.** (4 marks)

(50 marks)

Question 38 GLOBAL-BANK

Global-bank is a prominent European bank with branches throughout Europe and investment arms in many locations throughout the world. It is regarded as one of the world's major international banks. Through its network of investment offices throughout the world, fund managers trade in local investment markets and equities. Futures and derivative traders also operate. Its primary listing is in London although it is also listed in most of the other global stock markets including New York, Hong Kong, Frankfurt and Singapore. As with similar banks in its position, Global-bank's structure is complicated and the complexity of its operations makes the strategic management of the company a demanding and highly technical process. Up until the autumn of 2008, investors had a high degree of confidence in the Global-bank board as it had delivered healthy profits for many years.

In the autumn of 2008, it came to light that Jack Mineta, a Global-bank derivatives trader in the large city office in Philos, had made a very large loss dealing in derivatives over a three-month period. It emerged that the losses arose from Mr Mineta's practice of ignoring the company trading rules which placed limits on, and also restricted, the type of financial instruments and derivatives that could be traded.

The loss, estimated to be approximately $7 billion, was described by one analyst as "a huge amount of money and enough to threaten the survival of the whole company". As soon as the loss was uncovered, Mr Mineta was suspended from his job and the police were called in to check for evidence of fraud. The newspapers quickly reported the story, referring to Mr Mineta as a "rogue trader" and asking how so much money could be lost without the bank's senior management being aware of it. It turned out that Mr Mineta's line manager at the Philos office had ignored the trading rules in the past in pursuit of higher profits through more risky transactions. Mr Mineta had considerably exceeded his trading limit and this had resulted in the huge loss. It later emerged that Mr Mineta had been dealing in unauthorised products which were one of the riskiest forms of derivatives.

At a press conference after Mr Mineta's arrest, Global-bank's chief executive, Mrs Barbara Keefer, said that her first priority would be to ask the Philos office why the normal internal controls had not been effective in monitoring Mr Mineta's activities. It emerged that Mr Mineta had in the past been one of Global-bank's most profitable derivatives traders. Some journalists suggested to Mrs Keefer that the company was happy to ignore normal trading rules when Mr Mineta was making profits because it suited them to do so.

Another derivatives trader in the Philos office, Emma Hubu, spoke to the media informally. She said that Mr Mineta was brilliant and highly motivated but that he often said that he didn't care about the trading rules. Miss Hubu explained that Mr Mineta didn't believe in right and wrong and once told her that "I'm in this job for what I can get for myself – big risks bring big returns and big bonuses for me." She also explained that the culture of the Philos office was driven by Mr Mineta's line manager, Juan Evora. She said that Mr Evora knew that Mr Mineta was breaking trading rules but was also very profits driven and kept compliance information from head office so that the nature of Mr Mineta's trading was not uncovered. The compliance information was required by head office but several failures to return the information had not been acted upon by head office. Mr Evora's bonus was directly linked to the size of the Philos office's profits and all of the derivatives traders, including Mr Mineta, were regularly reminded about the importance of taking risks to make big returns. Miss Hubu said that trading rules were not enforced and that head office never got involved in what went on in Philos as long as the annual profits from the Philos derivative traders were at or above expectations.

It emerged that the lack of correct information from Philos and elsewhere meant that Global-bank's annual report statement of internal control effectiveness was not accurate and gave an unduly favourable impression of the company's internal controls. In addition, the company's audit committee had been recently criticised by the external auditors for a lack of thoroughness. Also, the audit committee had recently lost two non-executive members that had not been replaced.

The amount lost by Mr Mineta made it necessary to refinance the Global-bank business and when the board recommended a $5 billion rights issue, some of the institutional investors demanded an extraordinary general meeting (EGM). Global-bank's largest single shareholder, the Shalala Pension Fund, that held 12% of the shares, was furious about the losses and wanted an explanation from Mrs Keefer on why internal controls were so ineffective. When the Shalala trustees met after the losses had been reported, it was decided to write an urgent letter to Mrs Keefer expressing the trustees' disappointment at her role in the internal control failures at Global-bank. The letter would be signed by Millau Haber, the chairman of the Shalala trustees.

At the EGM, Mrs Keefer made a statement on behalf of the Global-bank board. In it she said that Mineta had been a rogue trader who had wilfully disregarded the company's internal controls and was, in breaking the company's trading rules, criminally responsible for the theft of company assets. She denied that the main Global-bank board had any responsibility for the loss and said that it was a "genuinely unforeseeable" situation.

(a) Kohlberg's theory of the development of moral reasoning contains three levels, with each level containing two stages or "planes". It is a useful framework for understanding the ways in which people think about ethical issues.

Required:

(i) **Explain the three levels of Kohlberg's theory.** (6 marks)

(ii) **Identify the level that Mr Mineta operated at and justify your choice using evidence from the case.** (4 marks)

(iii) **Identify, with reasons, the stage (or "plane") of Kohlberg's moral development most appropriate for a professional bank employee such as Mr Mineta as he undertakes his trading duties.** (2 marks)

(b) **Explain FIVE typical causes of internal control failure and assess the internal control performance of Global-bank in the case scenario.** (10 marks)

(c) **Analyse the agency relationship that exists between the board of Global-bank and the trustees of the Shalala Pension Fund.** (4 marks)

(d) **Distinguish between narrow and wide stakeholders and identify three narrow stakeholders in Global-bank (based on Evan & Freeman's definition) from information in the case. Assess the potential impact of the events described on each narrow stakeholder identified.** (10 marks)

(e) **You have been asked to draft a letter from Millau Haber, chairman of the Shalala trustees, to Mrs Keefer as a result of concerns over the events described in the case. The letter should explain the roles and responsibilities of the chief executive in internal control, and criticise Mrs Keefer's performance in that role.** (10 marks)

Professional marks are available in part (e) for the structure, content, style and layout of the letter. (4 marks)

(50 marks)

Question 39 SEA SHIPS COMPANY

The Mary Jane was a large passenger and vehicle ferry operating between the two major ports of Eastport and Northport across a busy section of ocean known as the "Northport route". Prior to this, the Mary Jane had operated for many years in the much calmer waters of the "Southsea route" but she had been transferred to the Northport route because her large size meant that more profit could be made by carrying more passengers and vehicles per journey. She was capable of carrying up to 1,000 passengers, 300 cars and 100 lorries per trip. The Mary Jane belonged to Sea Ships Company, a long established international company with a fleet of five ships operating on routes in other parts of the world. The Mary Jane had large doors at both the front and rear. Vehicles would drive in through the rear doors in Eastport and when she arrived in Northport, the Mary Jane would dock the other way round so that the vehicles could drive straight out using the forward doors. There were two doors at each end, upper and lower, and it was important that all four doors were securely closed before setting out to sea.

As with all marine operations, the safety procedures aboard the Mary Jane were subject to regulation, but her design left one weakness which was eventually to prove a disaster. From the main control bridge of the ship, it was not possible to see the front or rear doors, which meant that it wasn't possible to check from the main control bridge that they were closed upon departure from a port. On the night of 7 November, the Mary Jane was leaving Eastport in a storm for a crossing to Northport, a journey which should have taken five hours. It was dark and the weather was very poor. When she was only a few kilometres out from the Eastport harbour, water entered the car decks through the upper rear doors that had been left open after the Mary Jane had left port. The stormy conditions meant that the waves were very high and on this occasion, high enough so that when a large wave hit, the water entered through the open rear doors. Once enough water had entered her car decks, the Mary Jane began to lean to 30 degrees before completely falling over onto her side. The speed of the event, less than two minutes, meant that escape via lifeboats wasn't possible and the Mary Jane sank with the loss of many lives.

Among the survivors was first officer Ned Prop. Mr Prop later told how a recent change to staff reporting procedures had produced a situation in which the responsibility for checking that the rear doors were closed before sailing had changed. He said that, under the new system, two people were responsible for safety on the car deck but each person assumed that the other had checked that the upper rear doors had been closed. A reporting system in which each department head (car deck, navigation, etc.) on the ship separately reported readiness for sea to the captain at the beginning of each journey had been abandoned because it was too inconvenient to operate. Mr Prop said that the normal procedure was that if they didn't hear anything to the contrary by the departure time, he and Captain Mullett assumed that all was well throughout the ship and they could put to sea.

Mr Prop told how procedures on board ship often relied on "human teamwork" rather than "following paperwork systems". It also emerged that, on the day of the disaster, a mistake in loading vehicles onto the wrong decks had delayed the ship's departure and created pressure to leave as soon as possible after all the vehicles were loaded. Mr Prop said that this too may have been a contributory factor to the confusion over who should have checked that the rear doors were closed. Mr Prop's superior officer, Captain Mullet, was drowned in the disaster.

Sea Ships Company, the Mary Jane's owner, was one of the longest established and most respected companies listed on the stock exchange. Although best known for its ferry operations, it had diversified into other activities in recent years. It was considered by investment analysts to be a "steady and reliable" investment and the company chief executive, Wim Bock, had often said that Sea Ships Company employed "the highest standards of corporate ethics". It also valued its reputation as a well-run company and believed that the company's value was primarily due to its reputation for "outstanding customer care". The board often claimed that Sea Ships was a socially responsible company.

When Sea Ships' board met to discuss how to proceed after the disaster, Wim Bock said that the company could expect to receive substantial claims from victims' relatives. He also reported that, because of a regrettable oversight in the company's legal department, only a proportion of that liability would be covered by the company's insurance. There would also be punitive fines from the courts, the size of which would, a legal advisor said, reflect the scale of Sea Ship's negligence in contributing to the disaster. The finance director, Jill Wha, reported that if the company met the expected uninsured liabilities in full, even if reduced on appeal, it would severely threaten future cash flows as it would most likely have to sell non-current assets (most of its ships) to settle the claims. If large punitive fines were also imposed after the legal process, Mr Bock said that the company may not survive.

The government ordered an enquiry and a senior official was appointed to investigate the disaster. In her conclusions, enquiry chairman Caroline Chan said that in addition to the human error in not ensuring that the upper rear doors had been closed, it had also emerged that the Mary Jane had been travelling above the local shipping speed limit out of Eastport harbour. The excess speed had caused increased turbulence in the water and this was made much worse by the storm on the night in question. The combination of these factors meant that water gradually entered the open upper rear doors and this eventually caused the ship to lean and then capsize. Mrs Chan said that contrary to the board's perception of itself as a well-run company, she had encountered a "culture of carelessness" at Sea Ships and that the internal control systems were inadequate for safely operating a fleet of ships. She reserved particular criticism for the board of Sea Ships saying that it was unbalanced, lacked independent scrutiny and, because none of the existing directors had ever served on board a ship, lacked representation from technically qualified nautical officers.

After the enquiry was concluded, but before the level of claims and punitive damages had been set by the courts, a document emerged within the company confirming that certain independent advice had been received from an external consultant. The advice was received at the time of the Mary Jane's transfer from the Southsea route to the Northport route. Because the Northport route is a much rougher area of sea, the advice concerned structural changes to the Mary Jane that would make her safer in rougher seas. Had the advice been followed, the Mary Jane would have had additional doors inserted inside the car deck to act as a second internal bulkhead to prevent water flooding the whole deck. Water would still have entered through the open rear doors on the night of 7 November, but would have been kept sealed in that rear section of the car deck and the Mary Jane would not have sunk. The company had received the advice but had not acted upon it as it would have required an expensive refit for the Mary Jane. This advice was then "lost" in the company and only emerged later on.

Required:

(a) The independent consultant's advice was that the Mary Jane should have received structural work to make her safe for operating in the rougher seas of the Northport route. Sea Ships Company did not act on the advice.

Using the seven-step American Accounting Association (AAA) model for ethical decision-making, examine the company's dilemma on whether or not to disclose this information publicly. (14 marks)

(b) **Using information from the case, identify and analyse the internal control failures at Sea Ships Company and on the Mary Jane.** (12 marks)

(c) **Assess the contribution that non-executive directors might have made in improving the corporate governance at Sea Ships Company.** (8 marks)

(d)   **Draft a memo from chief executive Wim Bock to the senior officers on the other ships in the Sea Ships fleet informing them of vital internal control and risk issues following the loss of the Mary Jane. The memo should include the following, all placed in the context of the case.**

      (i)   **An assessment, based on information in the case, of the importance for the board of Sea Ships to have all the information relating to key operational internal controls and risks;**   (6 marks)

      (ii)   **An explanation of the qualitative characteristics of information needed by the Sea Ships' board for the assessment of internal controls and risks.**   (6 marks)

Professional marks will additionally be awarded in part (d) for drafting a memo that is clear, has a logical flow, is persuasive and is appropriately structured.   (4 marks)

(50 marks)

Question 40 COASTAL OIL

Coastal Oil is one of the world's largest petrochemical companies. It is based in Deeland and is responsible alone for 10% of Deeland's total stock market value. It employs 120,000 people in many countries and has an especially strong presence in Effland because of Effland's very large consumption of oil and gas products and its large oil reserves. Coastal Oil is organised, like most petrochemical companies, into three vertically integrated business units: the exploration and extraction division; the processing and refining division; and the distribution and retailing division.

Because of the risks and the capital investment demands, Coastal Oil has joint venture (JV) agreements in place for many of its extraction operations (i.e. its oil and gas rigs), especially those in the deep-water seas. A joint venture is a shared equity arrangement for a particular project where control is shared between the JV partners. In each of its JVs, Coastal Oil is the largest partner, although operations on each rig are divided between the JV member companies and the benefits are distributed according to the share of the JV.

As a highly visible company, Coastal Oil has long prided itself on its safety record and its ethical reputation. It believes both to be essential in supporting shareholder value. Its corporate code of ethics, published some years ago, pledges its commitment to the "highest standards" of ethical performance in the following areas: full compliance with regulation in all jurisdictions; safety and care of employees; transparency and communication with stakeholders; social contribution; and environmental responsibility. In addition, Coastal Oil has usually provided a lot of voluntary disclosure in its annual report and on its website. It says that it has a wide range of stakeholders and so needs to provide a great deal of information.

One of the consequences of dividing up the different responsibilities and operations on an oil or gas rig is that Coastal Oil does not have direct influence over some important operational controls. The contractual arrangements on any given oil rig can be very complex and there have often been disagreements between JV partners on some individual legal agreements and responsibilities for health and safety controls. Given that Coastal Oil has JV interests in hundreds of deep-water oil and gas rigs all over the world, some observers have said that this could be a problem should an accident ever occur.

This issue was tragically highlighted when one of its deep-water rigs, the Effland Coastal Deep Rig, had an explosion earlier this year. It was caused by the failure of a valve at the "well-head" on the sea floor. The valve was the responsibility of Well Services, a minor partner in the JV. Eight workers were killed on the rig from the high pressure released after the valve failure, and oil gushed into the sea from the well-head, a situation that should have been prevented had the valve been fully operational. It was soon established that Well Services' staff failed to inspect the valve before placing it at the well-head at the time of installation, as was required by the company's normal control systems. In addition, the valve was attached to a connecting part that did not meet the required technical specification for the water depth at which it was operating. The sea bed was 1,000 metres deep and the connecting part was intended for use to a depth of up to 300 metres. There was a suggestion that the need to keep costs down was a key reason for the use of the connecting part with the inferior specification.

Reports in the media on the following day said that the accident had happened on a rig "belonging to Coastal Oil" when in fact, Coastal Oil was technically only a major partner in the joint venture. Furthermore, there was no mention that the accident had been caused by a part belonging to Well Services. A journalist did discover, however, that both companies had operated a more lax safety culture on the deep-water rigs than was the case at facilities on land (the "land-side"). He said there was a culture of "out of sight, out of mind" on some offshore facilities and that this meant that several other controls were inoperative in addition to the ones that led to the accident. Information systems reporting back to the "land-side" were in place but it was the responsibility of management on each individual rig to enforce all internal controls and the "land-side" would only be informed of a problem if it was judged to be "an exceptional risk" by the rig's manager.

The accident triggered a large internal argument between Coastal Oil and Well Services about liability and this meant that there was no public statement from Coastal Oil for seven days while the arguments continued. Lawyers on both sides pointed out that liability was contractually ambiguous because the documentation on responsibilities was far too complex and unclear. And in any case, nobody expected anything to go wrong. In the absence of any official statement from Coastal Oil for those seven days, the media had no doubts who was to blame: Coastal Oil was strongly criticised in Effland with the criticism growing stronger as oil from the ruptured valve was shown spilling directly into the sea off the Effland coast. With no contingency plan for a deep-water well-head rupture in place, the ruptured valve took several months to repair, meaning that many thousands of tonnes of crude oil polluted the sea off Effland. Images of seabirds covered in crude oil were frequently broadcast on television and thousands of businesses on the coast reported that the polluted water would disrupt their business over the vital tourist season. Public statements from Coastal Oil that it was not responsible for the ruptured valve were seemingly not believed by the Effland public. Senior legislators in Effland said that the accident happened on "a rig belonging to Coastal Oil" so it must be Coastal Oil's fault.

A review by the Coastal Oil board highlighted several areas where risk management systems might be tightened to reduce the possibility of a similar accident happening again. Finance director, Tanya Tun, suggested that the company should disclose this new information to shareholders as it would be value-relevant to them. In particular, she said that a far more detailed voluntary statement on environmental risk would be material to the shareholders. The annual report would, she believed, be a suitable vehicle for this disclosure.

Because of the high media profile of the event, politicians from Effland involved themselves in the situation. Senator Jones's constituency on the coast nearest the rig was badly affected by the oil spill and many of his constituents suffered economic loss as a result. He angrily retorted in a newspaper interview that Coastal Oil's CEO, Susan Ahmed, "should have known this was going to happen", such was the poor state of some of the internal controls on the Effland Coastal Deep Rig.

As the oil spill continued and the media interest in the events intensified, CEO Mrs Ahmed was summoned to appear before a special committee of the Effland national legislature "to explain herself to the citizens of Effland". The Coastal Oil board agreed that this would be a good opportunity for Mrs Ahmed to address a number of issues in detail and attempt to repair some of the company's damaged reputation. The board agreed that Mrs Ahmed should provide as full a statement as possible on the internal control failures to the special committee.

Required:

(a)   Describe the general purposes of a corporate code of ethics and evaluate Coastal Oil's performance against its own stated ethical aims as set out in its code of ethics.

(10 marks)

(b)   Explain, using examples, the difference between voluntary and mandatory disclosure, and assess Tanya Tun's proposition that additional voluntary disclosure on environmental risk management would be material to the shareholders.   (10 marks)

(c)   In preparing to appear before the special committee of the Effland national legislature, CEO Mrs Ahmed has been informed that she will be asked to explain the causes of the accident and to establish whether she can give assurances that an accident of this type will not re-occur.

Required:

Prepare a statement for Mrs Ahmed to present before the committee that explains the following:

(i)   The internal control failures that gave rise to the accident;   (10 marks)

(ii)   The difference between subjective and objective risk assessment (using examples). Argue against Senator Jones's view that Mrs Ahmed "should have known this was going to happen";   (8 marks)

(iii)   "Health and safety" risk and the factors that can increase this risk in an organisation;   (4 marks)

(iv)   Why Coastal Oil cannot guarantee the prevention of further health and safety failures, using the ALARP (as low as reasonably practicable) principle;   (4 marks)

Professional marks will be awarded in part (c) for logical flow, persuasiveness, format and tone of the answers.   (4 marks)

(50 marks)

Question 41 HAYHO

Hayho is a large international company with direct investments in 65 countries. It is a manufacturer of high technology products, with each Hayho factory typically employing over 3,000 people. Hayho factories also support local supply chains employing many more people so each Hayho plant is considered a vital part of the regional economy in which it is located.

Several years ago, Hayho was widely criticised for its operations in Arrland, a developing country with an oppressive and undemocratic government. Investigative journalists produced material showing the poor conditions of workers, and pollution around the Hayho factories in Arrland. They also showed evidence suggesting that Hayho had paid bribes to the Arrland government so that local opposition to the Hayho operation could be forcefully stopped. After this episode, the company became very sensitive to criticism of its operations in developing countries. A press statement at the time said that Hayho, in future, would always uphold the highest standards of integrity, human rights and environmental protection whilst at the same time "responsibly" supporting developing countries by providing jobs and opportunities to enable greater social and economic development.

The board of Hayho is now deciding between two possible large new investments, both directly employing about 3,000 people. Both options have a number of advantages and disadvantages and Mr Woo, Hayho's finance director, has recently made clear that only one can be chosen at this stage. The two options are of similar investment value and are referred to as the "Jayland option" and the "Pealand option".

The "Jayland option" is to build a new large factory in Jayland and to recruit a completely new local workforce to work in it. Jayland is a developing country with few environmental and labour regulations. It has a poorly developed education and training system, and is generally considered to be undemocratic. Its president, Mr Popo, has been in office since he seized power in a military coup 30 years ago. Human rights organisations say that he maintains order by abusing the rights of the people and cruelly suppressing any dissent against him. In early exploratory talks between Hayho and the Jayland government, Hayho was given assurances that it could pursue its activities with little regulation from the government as long as the Jayland president, Mr Popo, received a personal annual "royalty" (effectively a bribe) for allowing Hayho to operate in his country.

Finance director Mr Woo said that some stakeholders would probably criticise Hayho, perhaps in the international media, for investing in Jayland. Hayho may be accused of supporting the dictatorship of Mr Popo in that country, especially if the "royalty" was ever discovered. Mr Woo calculated that the NPV (net present value) of projected pre-tax returns of the Jayland option over a ten-year period was $2 billion but that there was also a risk of potential political instability in Jayland during the lifetime of the investment.

The "Pealand option" is to buy an existing plant in Pealand which would then be refurbished to facilitate the manufacture of Hayho products. This would involve "inheriting" the workforce of the previous owners. Pealand is a "new democracy", and a transitional economy, having gained its independence ten years ago. In an attempt to purge the corrupt business practices associated with its past, the Pealand government has become very thorough in ensuring that all inward investments, including Hayho's factory purchase, meet exacting and demanding standards of environmental protection and work conditions. Mr Woo, the finance director, said that the NPV of projected pre-tax returns over a ten-year period was $1 billion for the Pealand option but that the risk of political instability in Pealand was negligible. Both of the returns, the forecast $2 billion for Jayland and the $1 billion for Pealand, were considered to be acceptable in principle.

Mr Woo also said that there were issues with the two options relating to the effectiveness of necessary internal controls. Whichever option was chosen (Jayland or Pealand), it would be necessary to establish internal controls to enable accurate and timely reporting of production and cost data back to head office. So a number of systems would need to be put in place to support the production itself. One staff member, Emily Baa, who had previously worked in Jayland for another company, gave her opinion to the board about some of the issues that Hayho might encounter if it chose the Jayland option. She said that Jayland was very under developed until relatively recently and explained how the national culture was unfamiliar with modern business practice and behaviour. She said that property security may be a problem and that there was a potential risk to assets there. She also said that, in her opinion, there was a lack of some key job skills among the potential workforce in Jayland such as quality control and accounting skills. She explained that quality control skills would be necessary to ensure product specifications were met and that accounting skills would be necessary for the provision of internal and external reporting. As a manufacturer of very technologically advanced products, a number of stringent international product standards applied to Hayho products wherever in the world they were produced.

Meanwhile, news that Hayho was considering a large investment in Jayland leaked out to the press. In response, Hayho's chief executive, Helen Duomo received two letters. The first was from a prominent international human rights lobbying organisation called "Watching Business" (WB). In the letter, the lobby group said that because of its "terrible track record" in Arrland and elsewhere, Hayho was being carefully monitored for its "unethical business practices". WB said its interest in Hayho's activities had been rekindled since it had received intelligence about the possible investment in Jayland and warned Mrs Duomo not to make the investment because it would provide credibility for the "brutal dictatorship" of Mr Popo.

Whilst Mrs Duomo, known for her forthright manner, would normally dismiss threats from groups of this type, she knew that WB had a lot of support among senior politicians and legislators in many parts of the world. She believed that WB could achieve some power through mobilising public opinion through effective use of mass media, such as newspapers and television. WB was also respected as a research organisation and its advice was often sought by politicians and trade organisations.

Mrs Duomo said she was frustrated whenever anybody got in the way of her accountability to the Hayho shareholders, but that some interests could not be ignored because of their potential to influence. WB fell into this category.

The second letter she received was from the head of Quark Investments, Hayho's single biggest institutional shareholder. The letter sought to remind Mrs Duomo that the Hayho board was employed by its shareholders and that Mrs Duomo should be determined and resolute in maximising shareholder returns. The letter encouraged the board not to be diverted by "well-meaning but misinformed outsiders concerned with things that were actually none of their business".

Aware that she had to manage two competing demands placed on her, Mrs Duomo sought advice from Emily Baa, who had experience of life in Jayland. So she asked Emily Baa to prepare some notes for the next board meeting to clarify whom the board of Hayho was actually accountable to and how it might respond to the letter from WB.

Required:

(a)   **Explain "risk appetite" and demonstrate how different risk appetites might affect the selection of investments between Jayland and Pealand.** (6 marks)

(b)   **Use the AAA (American Accounting Association) seven-step model to examine the ethical decision whether to select the Jayland option or the Pealand option.** (14 marks)

(c)   **Describe the general purposes of an internal control system and, based on Emily Baa's views, assess the main internal control challenges that Hayho might encounter if it chose the Jayland option.** (12 marks)

(d)   Prepare briefing notes from Emily Baa to prepare chief executive of Hayho, Helen Duomo, for the board meeting as requested in the case. The notes should cover the following:

(i)   A discussion of the meaning of accountability at Hayho and of how the Mendelow framework can be used to predict the influence of the Watching Business pressure group;   (7 marks)

(ii)   A brief explanation of the agency relationship between the board of Hayho and Quark Investments, and advice on why the demands from Watching Business should be carefully considered.   (7 marks)

Professional marks will be awarded in part (d) for the clarity, flow, persuasiveness and structure of the briefing notes.   (4 marks)

(50 marks)

Question 42 P&J

P&J is a long-established listed company based in Emmland, a highly developed and relatively prosperous country. For the past 60 years, P&J has been Emmland's largest importer and processor of a product named X32, a compound used in a wide variety of building materials, protective fabrics and automotive applications. X32 is a material much valued for its heat resistance, strength and adaptability, but perhaps most of all because it is flexible and also totally fireproof. It is this last property that led to the growth of X32 use and made P&J a historically successful company and a major exporter.

X32 is mined in some of the poorest developing countries where large local communities depend heavily on X32 mining for their incomes. The incomes from the mining activities are used to support community development, including education, sanitation and health facilities in those developing countries. The X32 is then processed in dedicated X32 facilities near to the mining communities, supporting many more jobs. It is then exported to Emmland for final manufacture into finished products and distribution.

Each stage of the supply chain for X32 is dedicated only to X32 and cannot be adapted to other materials. In Emmland, P&J is the major employer in several medium-sized towns. In Aytown, for example, P&J employs 45% of the workforce and in Betown, P&J employs 3,000 people and also supports a number of local causes including a children's nursery, an amateur football club and a number of adult education classes. In total, the company employs 15,000 people in Emmland and another 30,000 people in the various parts of the supply chain (mining and processing) in developing countries. Unlike in Emmland, where health and safety regulations are strong, there are no such regulations in most of the developing countries in which P&J operates.

Recently, some independent academic research discovered that X32 was very harmful to human health, particularly in the processing stages, causing a wide range of fatal respiratory diseases, including some that remain inactive in the body for many decades. Doctors had suspected for a while that X32 was the cause of a number of conditions that P&J employees and those working with the material had died from, but it was only when Professor Harry Kroll discovered how X32 actually attacked the body that the link was known for certain. The discovery caused a great deal of distress at P&J, and also in the industries which used X32.

The company was faced with a very difficult situation. Given that 60% of P&J's business was concerned with X32, Professor Kroll's findings could not be ignored. Although demand for X32 remained unaffected by Kroll's findings in the short to medium term, the company had to consider a new legal risk from a stream of potential litigation actions against the company from employees who worked in environments containing high levels of X32 fibre, and workers in industries which used X32 in their own processes.

In order to gain some understanding of the potential value of future compensation losses, P&J took legal advice and produced two sets of figures, both describing the present value of cumulative future compensation payments through litigation against the company. These forecasts were based on financial modelling using another product of which the company was aware, which had also been found to be hazardous to health.

	In 5 years $m	In 15 years $m	In 25 years $m	In 35 years $m
Best case	5	30	150	400
Worst case	20	80	350	1,000

The finance director (FD), Hannah Yin, informed the P&J board that the company could not survive if the worst-case scenario was realised. She said that the actual outcome depended upon the proportion of people affected, the period that the illness lay undetected in the body, the control measures which were put in place to reduce the exposure of employees and users to X32, and society's perception of X32 as a material. She estimated that losses at least the size of the best case scenario were very likely to occur and would cause a manageable but highly damaging level of losses.

The worst case scenario was far less likely but would make it impossible for the company to survive. Although profitable, P&J had been highly geared for several years and it was thought unlikely that its banks would lend it any further funds. Hannah Yin explained that this would limit the company's options when dealing with the risk. She also said that the company had little by way of retained earnings.

Chief executive officer, Laszlo Ho, commissioned a study to see whether the health risk to P&J workers could be managed with extra internal controls relating to safety measures to eliminate or reduce exposure to X32 dust. The confidential report said that it would be very difficult to manage X32 dust in the three stages of the supply chain unless the facilities were redesigned and rebuilt completely, and unless independent breathing apparatus was issued to all people coming into contact with X32 at any stage. FD Hannah Yin calculated that a full refit of all of the company's mines, processing and manufacturing plants (which Mr Ho called "Plan A") was simply not affordable given the current market price of X32 and the current costs of production. Laszlo Ho then proposed the idea of a partial refit of the Aytown and Betown plants because, being in Emmland, they were more visible to investors and most other stakeholders.

Mr Ho reasoned that this partial refit (which he called "Plan B") would enable the company to claim it was making progress on improving internal controls relating to safety measures whilst managing current costs and "waiting to see" how the market for X32 fared in the longer term. Under Plan B, no changes would be made to limit exposure to X32 in the company's operations in developing countries.

Hannah Yin, a qualified accountant, was trusted by shareholders because of her performance in the role of FD over several years. Because she would be believed by shareholders, Mr Ho offered to substantially increase her share options if she would report only the "best case" scenario to shareholders and report "Plan B" as evidence of the company's social responsibility. She accepted Mr Ho's offer and reported to shareholders as he had suggested. She also said that the company was aware of Professor Kroll's research but argued that the findings were not conclusive and also not considered a serious risk to P&J's future success.

Eventually, through speaking to an anonymous company source, a financial journalist discovered the whole story and felt that the public, and P&J's shareholders in particular, would want to know about the events and the decisions that had been taken in P&J. He decided to write an article for his magazine, *Investors in Companies*, on what he had discovered.

Required:

(a)   **Define "social footprint" and describe, from the case, four potential social implications of Professor Kroll's discovery about the health risks of X32.**   (10 marks)

(b)   **Describe what "risk diversification" means and explain why diversifying the risk related to the potential claims against the use of X32 would be very difficult for P&J.**   (10 marks)

(c)   As an accountant, Hannah Yin is bound by the IFAC fundamental principles of professionalism.

   Required:

   Criticise the professional and ethical behaviour of Hannah Yin, clearly identifying the fundamental principles of professionalism she has failed to meet.   (9 marks)

(d)   Writing as the journalist who discovered the story, draft a short article for the magazine *Investors in Companies*. You may assume the magazine has an educated readership. Your article should achieve the following:

   (i)   **Distinguish between strategic and operational risk and explain why Professor Kroll's findings are a strategic risk to P&J;**   (8 marks)

   (ii)   **Discuss the board's responsibilities for internal control in P&J and criticise Mr Ho's decision to choose Plan B.**   (9 marks)

Professional marks will be awarded in part (d) for the structure, logical flow, persuasiveness and tone of the article.   (4 marks)

(50 marks)

JUNE 2013

Question 1 HOPPO COMPANY

A report was recently published by an international accounting organisation on the future of certain rare chemicals used in industrial processes. The report said that some of these chemicals, crucial to many industrial processes, were now so scarce that there was a threat to supply chains for items such as computer circuitry and the rechargeable batteries used in electronic goods. One of these scarce and rare chemicals, the highly toxic trans-Y13 (TY13), has become increasingly rare and, therefore, very expensive. It requires careful processing and, although used in small quantities in each product, its high cost means that even small inefficiencies in its treatment can disproportionately affect final product costs.

The report's conclusions included this statement: "Put simply, we are living beyond the planet's means. Businesses that use these materials will experience new risks. It may even become seen as socially unacceptable to use some of these materials. Finally, if supply stops, then manufacturing stops."

One company which depends on a continuous and reliable supply of TY13 is Hoppo Company. Hoppo is a listed company based in the highly developed country of Essland. It has, for several years, designed and developed its products in Essland and then outsourced manufacturing to another company, Red Co, which is based in the developing country of Teeland. This means that Red Co manufactures Hoppo's products for an agreed price and to Hoppo's designs and technical specifications.

Because Red Co is based in Teeland (a developing country with lower land and labour costs than Essland), working with Red Co has offered Hoppo cost advantages over manufacturing its products in its home country. As a company which outsources many of its functions, Hoppo tries to ensure that in each case of outsourcing, working conditions and environmental responsibility are the same at each outsourcing company as they would be if carried out in its highly-regulated home country of Essland.

Hoppo itself is one of the most valuable companies on the Essland stock exchange and has strategically positioned itself as a company that is seen as a trustworthy and responsible producer that is also responsible in its social and environmental behaviour. In its press statements and annual reports, it has frequently highlighted the high value it places on integrity and transparency as fundamental values in its corporate governance. It has recently considered producing an annual environmental report, as it believes its shareholders would value the information it contains.

Red Co is an experienced producer of electronic circuits and has a long history of working with TY13. It has relationships with the main TY13 suppliers going back many years, and these relationships ensure that it can normally obtain supplies even during periods when world supply is short. Because the supply quality of TY13 varies widely, Red Co has developed finely-tuned methods of ensuring that the TY13 received is of suitable quality. The performance of the finished product is very sensitive to the quality of the TY13 and so this pre-production testing is considered vital. In addition, TY13's toxicity and high cost mean that other systems are put in place at Red Co to ensure that it is safely stored until needed for manufacture.

Earlier this year, however, two issues arose at Red Co which caused Hoppo to reconsider its outsourcing relationship.

The first one was the publication of an international media report showing evidence that, despite Hoppo's claims about having the same working conditions at all of its outsourcing clients, labour conditions were unacceptably poor at Red Co. Because labour regulations were less stringent in Teeland, Red Co had been forcing employees to work excessively long hours without breaks, and other measures that would not have been permitted in Essland. It was reported that workers were being bullied, and threatened with dismissal if they complained about their working conditions.

The second problem was a leakage of unprocessed TY13 from the Red Co factory. Not only was this seen as wasteful and careless, it also poisoned a local river, killing many fish and contaminating local farmland. The community living nearby said that it would be unable to use the contaminated land for many years and that this would affect local food supply.

When a journalist, Bob Hob, discovered information about these two issues, the media interpreted the story as a problem for Hoppo, partly because of its reputation as a responsible company. Hoppo's own research had shown that many of its customers valued its environmental reputation and that some of its key employees were attracted to Hoppo for the same reason.

Some important customers began to associate Hoppo directly with the problems at Red Co, even though it was Red Co which had actually been responsible for the employee issues and also the TY13 leak. Hoppo's share price fell when some investors considered the problems to be important enough to undermine future confidence in Hoppo's management and brand value.

In an effort to protect its reputation in future, Hoppo began to review its outsource arrangement with Red Co. The board considered the options for taking manufacturing under its own direct control by building a new factory in another low-cost country, which would be owned and operated by Hoppo. It quickly realised that stopping the outsourcing relationship with Red Co would mean the loss of about 1,000 jobs there and could also raise the likelihood of legal action by Red Co against Hoppo for loss of contract. As Hoppo's manufacturing contract is so valuable to Red Co, some people thought it likely that Red Co would sue Hoppo for loss of future earnings, despite the terms of the contract being legally ambiguous. This lack of clarity in the contract arose because of differences in Essland and Teeland law and as a consequence of poor legal advice that Hoppo received when drawing up the contract. It was believed that any legal action would be widely reported because of Hoppo's international profile and that this may result in some unfavourable publicity.

When considering its options for a directly-owned factory, Hoppo's plan was to build a modern and efficient plant with "state of the art" environmental controls. Yuland was chosen as a suitable country and Hoppo narrowed the choice down to two possible sites in Yuland for its new factory: Ootown and Aatown. The mayors of both towns wrote to Hoppo's chief executive saying that they would welcome any potential investment from Hoppo. In addition, the mayor of Ootown asked for a "personal gift" (relatively immaterial although not a trivial amount to Hoppo but a large amount of money locally) to facilitate a trouble-free passage of the necessary planning permission for a new Hoppo factory in the town.

When deciding between Ootown and Aatown in Yuland, the general view was that, all other things being equal, Ootown was a better location. But there was some discussion about whether the "personal gift" requested by the mayor of Ootown was ethical. The board thought that the decision was an important one and so took some time to reflect before reaching a decision on whether to continue with Red Co or to build a new factory in either Ootown or Aatown.

Having become aware that investing in Ootown and paying the money to its mayor was being considered by Hoppo, a member of the chief executive's office staff informed the journalist, Bob Hob, and a story appeared in an Essland national newspaper saying, "Hoppo considers paying a bribe to get preferred site in Yuland". Bob Hob made remarks challenging Hoppo's claims about integrity and transparency, and suggested that recent events had shown that it had demonstrated neither. Public discussion then took place on the internet saying that Hoppo, previously considered a highly ethical company, had been corrupt and incompetent, both in allowing Red Co to breach employment and environmental best practice, and then to consider paying a bribe to the mayor of Ootown.

It was decided that, in seeking to restore its reputation, the company needed to publish a detailed press statement responding to the issues raised in the media. Because Hoppo's reputation for integrity and transparency were considered to be strategically important and had been questioned, it was decided that the statement should also contain reassurances about these important themes.

Required:

(a) Briefly explain "related" and "correlated" risks. Explore the correlation between legal risk and reputation risk for Hoppo if it were to cancel its contract with Red Co.

(10 marks)

(b) Describe an environmental report, including its purpose and contents, and discuss the potential advantages of an environmental report for Hoppo and its shareholders.

(10 marks)

(c) Briefly explain how internal controls can be strategic in nature. Explain, using detailed examples from the case, why developing sound internal controls over the supply and processing of TY13 would be important if Hoppo opted to build its own factory in Yuland. (10 marks)

(d) Draft the press release as discussed in the case. It should:

   (i) Define and explain the importance of "integrity" and "transparency" in the context of the case. (6 marks)

   (ii) Construct an argument against paying the bribe to the mayor of Ootown from both business and ethical perspectives. Your ethical arguments should include both deontological and consequentialist perspectives. (10 marks)

   Professional marks will be awarded in part (d) for the format, tone, logical flow and persuasiveness of the press release. (4 marks)

(50 marks)

Question 2 BLUP CO

When Blup Co (a listed company involved in water supply) decided to establish an internal audit function, in line with new listing rules, the board approached Karen Huyer, an external consultant. She explained that internal audit is especially important in highly regulated industries but that it could also offer benefits to companies regardless of the industry context.

Karen was particularly keen to talk to John Xu, the head of the audit committee. John explained that because Blup Co was a water supply company and was thus highly regulated, he considered it important that all of the members of the audit committee were professional water engineers so that they fully understood the industry and its technical challenges. All three members of the audit committee were non-executive directors and all were recently retired members of the Blup executive board. When Karen asked about the relationship with external auditors, John said that they had an "excellent" relationship, saying that this was because the external audit practice was run by the chairman's son-in-law.

Karen said that one of the essential functions of internal audit is to provide assurance that the internal controls which underpinned financial reporting are effective. She said that effective internal controls are necessary for maintaining the integrity of financial reporting and that the new internal audit function could help with that.

Required:

(a) Discuss the importance of internal audit in a highly regulated industry such as the water industry that Blup Co operates in. (7 marks)

(b) **(i)** Criticise the ways in which Blup Co's audit committee has failed to meet best practice.

(ii) Explain why the audit committee is responsible for overseeing the internal audit function.

The total marks will be split equally between each part. (12 marks)

(c) Discuss how effective internal controls can provide assurance on the integrity of financial reporting. (6 marks)

(25 marks)

Question 3 BIGBANK

Because of a general lack of business confidence in Dubland, its major banks had severely restricted new lending. This lack of lending extended to small and large businesses, and also to individuals in society. Press statements from the banks often referred to the need to mitigate financial risks and the need to maintain capital adequacy. Over time, the lower lending produced some negative consequences in the wider Dubland economy.

Responding to these problems, the Dubland finance minister remarked that, financial risks may not only cause companies to fail but they can also cause problems in wider society. Banks, in particular, need to be more aware of their financial risks than most other sectors of the economy. They have to manage a unique set of risks and I strongly urge the directors of banks to institute robust risk management systems as part of their corporate governance.

"As finance minister, however, I also believe that banks have a vital role in supporting the economic strength of this country. They hold cash deposits and make short and long-term loans, which are vital to other businesses. Taking risks is a normal part of all business operations and our banks need to accept this risk when it comes to lending."

Ron Ng, the chief executive of BigBank, Dubland's largest bank, said that continuous and ongoing risk assessment was necessary. He said that despite the finance minister's call for higher lending, his only duty was to BigBank's shareholders and it was this duty that guided BigBank's reduced lending.

Required:

(a) Explain the meaning of "risk assessment" as used by Ron Ng and discuss, in the context of the case, the need for risk assessment to be "continuous and ongoing". (8 marks)

(b) Ron Ng believed that his "only duty" as BigBank's CEO was to the BigBank shareholders.

Required:

Describe "fiduciary duty" in the context of the case and critically evaluate the issues raised by Ron Ng's belief. (7 marks)

(c) Explain the term "financial risk" and discuss how management of these risks can be embedded in a large organisation such as BigBank. (10 marks)

(25 marks)

Question 4 BOOM CO

In early 2015, the remuneration committee of Boom Co, a listed company, met to determine the rewards for the executive directors. It was the practice of the committee to meet annually to decide on executive rewards for the forthcoming financial year. In line with best practice, the committee was made up entirely of non-executive directors.

When the remuneration committee met, its chairman, Sarah Umm, reminded those present that the committee should comply with the guidance of the relevant code of corporate governance. She read out the section that she believed was most relevant to their discussions.

"A significant proportion of executive directors' remuneration should be structured so as to link rewards to corporate and individual performance. The remuneration committee should judge where to position their company relative to other companies. But they should use such comparisons with caution in view of the risk of an upward movement of remuneration levels with no corresponding improvement in performance. Remuneration for non-executive directors should not include share options or other performance-related elements."

She explained that the committee should balance several concerns when setting rewards: the link with performance, market rates and the company's overall strategy. The strategic priority in the next few years, she explained, was to incentivise medium to long-term growth whilst retaining the existing executive board in place as long as possible.

At the end of the meeting, a new member of the committee, Sam South, asked whether there were any performance-related elements of non-executive directors' rewards. Sarah Umm explained that these were only available to executive members of the board in line with the terms of the corporate governance code.

Required:

(a)   Explain what is meant by a "code of corporate governance" and discuss the general purposes of such a code in listed companies such as Boom Co.   (7 marks)

(b)   Propose how the components of a reward package might be balanced to "incentivise medium to long-term growth whilst retaining the existing executive board in place as long as possible".   (8 marks)

(c)   Briefly explain the general roles of non-executive directors in a listed company such as Boom Co, and discuss why non-executive directors should not receive performance-related elements in their rewards as Sam South enquired.   (10 marks)

(25 marks)

DECEMBER 2013

Question 1 HIAKA ENERGY COMPANY

When the 1,000 km Hiaka pipeline in Wyland was built ten years ago, the route took it, over ground, the full length of Hiakaisland, one of Wyland's largest offshore islands. Owned and operated by Hiaka Energy Company (HEC), its construction was significantly over budget and suffered lengthy delays, but the pipeline has since become a vital source of economic growth on Hiakaisland and beyond. Its purpose is to connect the oil platforms off the north coast of the island with the deep water port of Hiakatown in the south. A land pipeline to the south is needed because sea ice in the north prevents shipping access during the winter months. The oil carried by the pipeline is loaded onto several ships each day at Hiakatown port. Most of the oil from Hiakaisland is sent to the neighbouring country of Exland, with oil from Hiakaisland representing 90% of Exland's total oil consumption. Because the contract with HEC is so important to the government of Exland, the terms of supply are subject to legal enforcement with regard to prices charged, delivery terms and the quality of the oil delivered. Because most of its output goes to export, HEC is a major source of foreign currency for Wyland.

Hiakaisland is a globally important natural habitat with a dramatic and rugged terrain. It is monitored by several international scientific agencies, some of which were very critical of the decision to build the pipeline in the first place. It is one of very few locations in which some wildlife species threatened elsewhere are still in abundance. There are healthy populations, for example, of bears, elk and otters. One well-respected international wildlife organisation (called Save Our Wilderness or "SOW") produced a report saying that the Hiaka pipeline was not environmentally sustainable and that, over time, it would deteriorate and create an unacceptable environmental risk to Hiakaisland. It said that both the company (HEC) and the government of Wyland needed to adopt longer-term time perspectives and consider the potential environmental consequences of the pipeline. The government of Exland, elected every four years, disputed this, saying that SOW's definition of sustainability was too narrow and that it should also consider the economic sustainability of Exland. The position of the board of HEC is that its operations should be "as sustainable as is economically possible".

Wyland is a developing country with few labour regulations and very little legislation on employee pay and conditions. This has enabled HEC to use a large proportion of poorly-paid immigrant labour to build and maintain the pipeline, thereby reducing its construction and operating costs. Because of the multinational nature of much of the semi-skilled workforce, there are often language difficulties, especially when conveying messages to staff working on the pipeline and on the oil platforms. HEC has a requirement that all staff should speak the language of Wyland, but this has proven to be impossible to enforce.

As the main employer on Hiakaisland, HEC employs 5,000 people including some on offshore oil platforms, others in the main southern town of Hiakatown, and others still at a number of remote locations the length of the island at strategic points situated along the pipeline. Because of the remoteness of much of the work on Hiakaisland, conditions are harsh for many of these workers. HEC employees often work in freezing temperatures and live in encampments with intermittent logistical support. Motivation and morale are often low among these maintenance employees.

There have been poor industrial relations because of this lack of support. Workers resent the company's management in Hiakatown for their harsh conditions. These poor relationships have also made it difficult for management to try to enforce the Wyland language requirement upon the immigrant labour. The remote locations and poor conditions have also meant that the company has found it difficult to recruit the skilled technical people it needs to inspect and maintain the pipeline. There is a shortage of qualified engineers and technical staff in Wyland, with many preferring to work in the cities rather than in the more difficult conditions on Hiakaisland.

HEC is one of Wyland's biggest businesses and is listed on the Wyland stock exchange. Because of the nature of the energy market, shareholders have come to expect a good annual return on investment in terms of dividends. One market analyst recently commented that a focus on short-term returns has not been good for the company's long-term strategy and that shareholders should be prepared to expect lower dividend yields as a result.

In order to address the many challenges which the company faced, HEC appointed a new chief executive and risk manager last year. Gavin Hoo was appointed chief executive and Gerry Jupp joined as risk manager. Born and educated in a highly developed country, Mr Hoo had a strong track record in the energy industry and took over at HEC on what was considered a good reward package for his home country. On Hiakaisland, however, the level of reward was very large by local standards, making him the highest paid person not just in the company, but in the entire regional economy of Hiakaisland. When the reward figure was later published in the annual report, the local press and some trade unions were angry, believing that his reward was "outrageous" and that he lived in luxury whilst unskilled immigrant workers "froze" in the maintenance parties working along the length of the pipeline. Some critics pointed to the fact that it was significantly cheaper to live on Hiakaisland than in the major cities on the Wyland mainland and that this was not reflected in Mr Hoo's rewards at all.

Meanwhile, risk manager Gerry Jupp set about examining the company's many risks. One of his first tasks was to assess some of the risks which may affect the operation of the pipeline, and he took technical advice on these to arrive at probabilities of the risks arising over the next ten years. It was recognised that there was some subjectivity involved in these measurements.

Risk 1:   Risk of terrorist attack on any part of the pipeline causing severe spillage and complete supply disruption: 10%.

Risk 2:   Risk of geological movement and/or earthquake capable of severing the pipeline in more than one place causing severe long-term supply disruption: 5%.

Risk 3:   Risk of technical failure of a joint in the pipeline causing a temporary supply disruption of a few hours but no leakage of oil: 10%.

Risk 4:   Risk of animal or natural damage to pipeline (e.g. by bears, elk or adverse weather) causing superficial damage to pipeline but no disruption to supply: 60%.

Unfortunately, Risk 4 was realised shortly after Gerry Jupp produced his calculations. At the point where it crossed the Gojo River in northern Haikaisland, the pipeline had a long and unsupported section. During a winter storm, a connection was slightly displaced resulting in a minor oil leak. Although not serious in itself and quickly repaired, the "Gojo incident" did raise concerns and showed that the pipeline was vulnerable. Seeking to protect both the pipeline and the environment on Hiakaisland, the Wyland government's industry minister wrote to CEO Gavin Hoo asking him to respond to rumours about poor internal controls in HEC and to introduce measures to reduce the chances of a repetition of the Gojo incident.

In response to the industry minister's letter, the HEC board reviewed internal controls and two resolutions were agreed. The first was that the company should establish a formal internal audit function and second, that a full review of any barriers to sound internal controls in the company should be carried out. Although a formal internal audit function was not required by statute law or any stock exchange listing rule in Wyland, the board agreed that it would be good practice, especially if the security and maintenance of the long Hiaka pipeline could be included in the scope (terms of reference) of the internal audit function to be established. It was decided that in responding to the minister, Mr Hoo should convey both the board's resolve on internal audit and also an honest review of the problems for achieving sound internal controls in the unique situation the company was in on Hiakaisland.

Required:

(a)   The term "sustainability" can be understood in different ways.

      (i)   Explain the concept of "sustainable" as used by "Save our Wilderness" (SOW) and contrast this with the concept of economic sustainability as discussed by the government of Exland.   (4 marks)

      (ii)   Using information from the case, discuss the tensions which exist between these two concepts.   (8 marks)

(b)   Assess the four risks described by Gerry Jupp and propose a suitable risk management strategy for each. Briefly explain why subjective judgement may limit the accuracy of his risk assessments.   (10 marks)

(c)   Briefly explain the meaning of "labour market conditions" in the context of executive pay and critically evaluate the decision to award Mr Hoo such a high level of reward in comparison with local rates of pay on Hiakaisland.   (10 marks)

(d)   Prepare the letter from Gavin Hoo, the chief executive of Hiaka Energy Company (HEC), to the Wyland industry minister. The letter should:

      (i)   Explain the reasons why the implementation of sound internal controls has been difficult at HEC.   (8 marks)

      (ii)   Basing your answer on the main roles of internal audit, discuss the ways in which an internal audit function might provide assurances in order to make an effective contribution to HEC.   (6 marks)

      Professional marks will be awarded in part (d) for the format, tone, logical flow and persuasiveness of the letter.   (4 marks)

(50 marks)

Question 2 SARBANES-OXLEY

The Sarbanes-Oxley legislation in the United States was introduced in 2002, partly in response to the earlier failure of the American energy company, Enron. It was decided by United States legislators that compliance should be enforceable under law rather than under listing rules. At the time it was being debated, some said that the legal enforceability of Sarbanes-Oxley would be unfair to smaller companies without the infrastructure needed to generate internal control data and to report on it. One example of this was the debate over s.404 of Sarbanes-Oxley, which mandated external reporting on the adequacy of internal controls. Before a size criterion was later introduced, this applied equally to all companies but now smaller companies are partly exempted from this requirement.

In its advice on this requirement, the United States Securities and Exchange Commission (SEC) published the following comments:

The rules we adopted in June 2003 to implement s.404 of the Sarbanes-Oxley Act of 2002 ("Sarbanes-Oxley") require management to annually evaluate whether internal control over financial reporting (ICFR) is effective at providing reasonable assurance and to disclose its assessment to investors. Management is responsible for maintaining evidential matter, including documentation, to provide reasonable support for its assessment. This evidence will also allow a third party, such as the company's external auditor, to consider the work performed by management.

Required:

(a)   Distinguish between rules and principles-based approaches to the regulation of corporate governance, and explain the disadvantages of a rules-based system such as Sarbanes-Oxley in the United States.   (7 marks)

(b)   Define "agency" in the context of corporate governance and discuss the benefits to shareholders of "maintaining a system of internal control over financial reporting" in a rules-based jurisdiction.   (10 marks)

(c)   Construct the case to exempt smaller companies from the full reporting requirements of s.404 of the Sarbanes-Oxley Act 2002.   (8 marks)

(25 marks)

Question 3 HELP-WITH-LIFE

"Help-with-life" (HWL) is a charitable organisation established ten years ago. Its stated purpose is, "to help individuals and families with social problems and related issues". Its work, in a large city with people from many countries and backgrounds, involves advising, counselling, giving practical support to service users (the people who come for help). Over the years it has been operating, HWL has realised that the best outcomes are achieved when the staff member understands and sympathises with the service users' social norms, ethical and cultural beliefs.

40% of HWL's funding comes from local government. This means that HWL has to account for its use of that portion of its funding and comply with several rules imposed by local government. One of these rules concerns demonstrating appropriate diversity amongst the managers of services such as those delivered by HWL. It requires the charity management team to involve the widest feasible range of people and to reflect the demographic make-up of the community.

HWL has recently had to replace a number of executive and non-executive members of its board. The external auditor suggested that setting up a nominations committee would help in these board appointments. The CEO, Marian Ngogo, has always stressed that all directors should share the ethical values of HWL and agree to take reduced rewards because, "every dollar we pay a director is a dollar less we are spending on service delivery". She stressed that the culture in a charity was very different from a commercial ("for profit") business and that staff and directors must share the ethical stance of HWL and had to accept a different approach to social responsibility if they joined.

Required:

(a)   Explain the roles of a nominations committee and describe how the Help-with-life (HWL) nominations committee might approach the task of nominating and appointing new directors.   (8 marks)

(b)   Explain the advantages of diversity on the board of HWL.   (8 marks)

(c)   Explain "corporate social responsibility" (CSR) and discuss the ways in which CSR and the ethical stance might differ between HWL and a commercial "for profit" business.   (9 marks)

(25 marks)

Question 4 LOBO COMPANY

A technological failure occurred at Lobo Company last year. A new computer system which was designed to control Lobo's complicated operational facility broke down shortly after it was installed. This meant that the company was unable to carry out production processes normally for several days.

The cause of the failure was later found to have been a system specification error made by Frank Bub, the operations director and a professional engineer. He had seriously miscalculated the capacity needed for the new system and had ordered a computer system which was unfit for purpose. Not only had this resulted in the loss of several days of production and a loss of loyalty and goodwill from customers and others, it also cost a large amount to repair and upgrade the system to be able to cope with the actual demands placed upon it.

Frank Bub acknowledged that he had over-ridden normal procurement procedures in purchasing the system. But he was thought by his colleagues to be such a competent engineer, it was not felt necessary for anybody else in the company to discuss the purchase with the suppliers. His fellow directors believed that Mr Bub would exercise the judgement needed to purchase and implement the new system. Because the system was needed urgently, there was no time to run it in "pilot mode" or to test it on site before it was fully installed. When he was asked about the failure, Frank Bub said that he decided to buy the system in question because an old friend had recommended it and that he saw no need to take further advice beyond that.

The non-executive directors met after the incident and collectively decided that Frank Bub, who had nine months remaining on his renewable three year contract, had lost the confidence of the board and should leave the company at the earliest opportunity. It was decided to move him to a non-critical role until such time as it was possible to remove him as cheaply as possible.

Required:

(a)   Directors may leave the service of a board in several ways.

   (i)   **Describe the main ways in which the directors of companies can leave the service of a board.**   (3 marks)

   (ii)   **Justify an appropriate way for Frank Bub to leave the board of Lobo Company, based on the circumstances of the case.**   (5 marks)

(b)   **Briefly explain "technological risk" and discuss the problems which led to the technological failure at Lobo, commenting on how these might affect shareholder confidence in the entire board.**   (8 marks)

(c)   You may assume that, as a professional engineer, Frank Bub is bound by the same fundamental principles of professional ethics as a professional accountant and must act in the wider public interest.

   Required:

   Discuss the fundamental principles of professional ethics which Frank Bub failed to observe and explain how an awareness of his duty to the public interest may have prevented his errors.   (9 marks)

(25 marks)

JUNE 2014

Question 1 WORLD JUSTICE

Several years ago, World Justice, a well-known charity, published a report on the activities of three major food companies in their marketing of manufactured baby foods in some of the poorer developing countries. The report, provocatively called "Killer Companies", said it had evidence that the three companies were "aggressively mis-selling" manufactured baby food products in these poorer countries. It was argued in the report that several problems arose with the use of these products in poorer countries which negatively affected the health of the babies, with many babies reportedly dying as a result. These problems included the use of contaminated water in the preparation of the baby food, an inability of parents to read the instructions, making up product at insufficient concentrations (thereby malnourishing the child) and aggressive selling to health facilities in those countries. Doctors often advised against the use of these products for babies because natural feeding solutions were considered safer and more beneficial in most cases.

When the "Killer Companies" report was published, it was widely reported upon and received a lot of social and political attention. Two of the three companies named in "Killer Companies" immediately decided to withdraw from the business but the third company, Xaxa Company (Xaxa hereafter), recognised what it believed to be an opportunity to take the market share left by the other two. It set about increasing its production capacity accordingly. When asked by journalists why Xaxa had not also withdrawn from the criticised business activity, the chief executive issued a press statement saying that it was a profitable business opportunity and, as the steward of shareholder value, he owed it to the shareholders to maximise their returns.

When it became widely known that Xaxa had decided to expand and develop its baby food business in poorer developing countries, Mothers Who Care (MWC), a national charity concerned with infant nutrition, organised a campaign against Xaxa. Strongly believing in the natural feeding of infants, MWC initially organised protests outside the Xaxa head office and also encouraged the public to boycott a wide range of Xaxa products in addition to the baby food products. MWC members started to use the phrase, "Xaxa kills babies" in the hope that it would become widely adopted.

As one of the country's largest companies and operating in many countries, Xaxa has a large issued share volume with the majority being held by institutional investors. Whilst the overall group profits remained strong, some shareholders began to feel concerned about the baby food issue. One prominent fund manager, Hugh Oublie, organised a meeting for institutional shareholders holding large volumes of Xaxa shares and 50 such institutional shareholders attended the meeting. The group became known as the "Oublie Group". Although all members of the Oublie Group wanted to retain their holdings in Xaxa because of the otherwise good returns, a number of questions were framed which they decided to put to the Xaxa management:

(i) could the company explain the strategic logic of pursuing the baby food business in poorer developing countries?

(ii) was the board concerned about potential reputational damage with phrases such as "Xaxa kills babies being used widely and in the media?

(iii) would the Xaxa board consider withdrawing from the baby food business in poorer developing countries because of the alleged health impacts on children in those countries?

The company issued a statement through its investor relations department, replying that the strategic logic was based on what activities provided the most profit to shareholders regardless of the effects on other claims against the company strategy. Second, the board was not concerned with reputation risks because it believed that these were "temporary concerns" which would soon be forgotten. Third, no, the board would not withdraw from the baby food market in those countries because, with the loss of two competitors, profit margins were likely to be higher and competition less. The Oublie Group expressed its dissatisfaction with this reply and said it might seek to influence the appointment of non-executive directors (NEDs) to the Xaxa board to increase the scrutiny of the executive members and their discussions on the subject.

Hugh Oublie appeared on television to say that he felt the board of Xaxa lacked balance. He said that, although profitable and a good employer in its home country, the non-executive scrutiny of company strategy had been poor for some time and the board had no meaningful sense of ethics at all. He believed that all of the executive board was dedicated to the mission to produce what he called "profit at any social cost". He further believed that none of the non-executive board members was strong enough to question the strategy and raise the problem of baby food as an ethical issue. It was this lack of non-executive scrutiny which Hugh Oublie believed was a major cause of Xaxa's unwillingness to reconsider its baby food activity. He said that he had been a long-serving observer and shareholder of Xaxa and he had noticed the company becoming more inward-looking and self-reliant in recent years. He believed this trend was very unhelpful. In addition, he expressed concerns, on behalf of the Oublie Group, about the strategic management of Xaxa and his belief that the board lacked concern for medium-term business risks brought about by the baby food marketing.

As World Justice and MWC continued their campaigns against Xaxa, some other groups became aware of the baby food situation in poorer developing countries. A television programme reported how Xaxa products were actually being used in some of the poorer countries. It claimed to confirm the problems highlighted in "Killer Companies" and it highlighted a number of other Xaxa products which consumers might stop buying if they wanted to put pressure on Xaxa's management to change their policy on baby food.

Partly in response to these pressures, the Xaxa board decided to consider two new initiatives. The first of these was to consider introducing a corporate code of ethics. By carefully drafting this and placing it prominently on its website, the board believed that it could achieve a number of favourable outcomes including improving its reputation.

The second initiative was to consider instituting a full risk audit system in response to the negative publicity it had experienced, especially from MWC, whose members were considered to be natural customers of Xaxa's other products. Private research commissioned by Xaxa showed that the baby food business was damaging Xaxa's reputation and possibly the willingness of some talented people to apply for jobs with the company. Political support for other company plans had also suffered, such that a recent planning application to set up a new factory by Xaxa, in a business area with no connection with baby food, had received opposition. Protestors, mainly local activists and MWC members, opposed the application with placards saying "Xaxa kills babies". Because the idea of risk auditing was a new initiative for Xaxa, the board has asked a local consultancy to produce guidance on the benefits of risk audit and the benefits of an external, rather than an internal, risk audit.

Required:

(a)   The underlying principles of corporate governance include transparency, judgement and reputation.

Explain these three terms and assess the Xaxa board's performance against each one.

(9 marks)

(b)   **Explain the purposes of a corporate code of ethics and examine how the adoption of such a code might make Xaxa reconsider its marketing of baby food in poorer developing countries.** *(11 marks)*

(c)   Institutional investors are potentially influential stakeholders in a company such as Xaxa.

     Required:

     (i)   **Explain why institutional investors might attempt to intervene in the governance of a company.**

     (ii)   **Discuss the reasons why the Oublie Group should attempt to intervene in the governance of Xaxa following the events described in the case.**

     Note: The total marks will be split equally between each part. *(10 marks)*

(d)   **Produce notes from the consulting company for the Xaxa board in response to its need for guidance on risk audit. The notes should address the following:**

     (i)   **Discuss, in the context of Xaxa, the stages in a risk audit.** *(8 marks)*

     (ii)   **Distinguish between internal and external risk audit, and discuss the advantages for Xaxa of an external risk audit.** *(8 marks)*

     Professional marks will be awarded in part (d) for the clarity, logical flow, style and persuasiveness of the notes. *(4 marks)*

(50 marks)

Question 2 BOB WONG

Bob Wong was fortunate to inherit some money and decided he wanted to invest for the long term in one or more investments so he would have a higher income in retirement. He was not a specialist in accounting and had little understanding of how investments worked.

Bob studied an investment website which suggested that he needed to be aware of the level of risk in an investment and also that he needed to know what his basic attitude to risk would be. This meant he needed to decide what his risk appetite was and then select investments based on that.

When Bob studied share listings in newspapers, he noticed that they were subdivided into sectors (e.g. banks, pharmaceuticals, mining, retail). He noticed that some sectors seemed to make higher returns than others and he wanted to know why this was. One website suggested that risks also varied by sector and this was partly explained by the different business and financial risks which different sectors are exposed to.

One website said that if a potential investor wanted to know about any given company as a potential investment, the company's most recent annual report was a good place to start. This was because, it said, the annual report contained a lot of voluntary information, in addition to the financial statements. Bob could use this information to gain an understanding of the company's strategy and governance. The website suggested that the contents of the corporate governance section of the annual report would be particularly helpful in helping him decide whether or not to buy shares in a company.

Required:

(a)   **Explain "risk appetite" and "risk awareness", and discuss how Bob's risk appetite might affect his choice of investments.** *(8 marks)*

(b)   Explain "business risk" and "financial risk" and discuss why risks might vary by sector as the website indicated.   (8 marks)

(c)   Distinguish, with examples, between mandatory and voluntary disclosure in annual reports, and assess the usefulness of corporate governance disclosure to Bob in selecting his investments.   (9 marks)

(25 marks)

Question 3 DEETOWN

Hum and Hoo is an established audit practice in Deetown and has a large share of the audit services market among local businesses. Because Deetown is a relatively isolated area, many clients rely on Hum and Hoo for accounting and technical advice over and above the annual audit. This has meant that, over time, Hum and Hoo has also developed expertise in compliance advice, tax, strategy consulting and other professional services.

Because non-audit work is important to Hum and Hoo, staff have "business growth" criteria strongly linked with bonuses and promotion. This means that many of the professional accountants in the firm actively seek to increase sales of non-audit services to businesses in the Deetown area, including from audit clients. The culture of the firm is such that everybody is expected to help out with any project which needs to be done, and this sometimes means that staff help out on a range of both audit and non-audit tasks. The lines between audit and non-audit services are sometimes blurred and staff may work on either, as workload needs demand. Managing partner Cherry Hoo told staff that the non-audit revenue is now so important to the firm that staff should not do anything to threaten that source of income.

Cherry Hoo said that she was thinking of beginning to offer a number of other services including advice on environmental reporting and the provision of environmental auditing services. She said she had spoken to local companies which were looking to demonstrate their environmental sustainability and she believed that environmental reporting and auditing might be ways to help with this. She said she was confused by the nature of environmental reporting and so was not sure about what should be audited.

Required:

(a)   Explain "ethical threat" and "ethical safeguard" in the context of external auditing, and discuss the benefits of effective ethical safeguards for Hum and Hoo.   (8 marks)

(b)   Explain "environmental audit" and assess how environmental reporting and auditing might enable companies to "demonstrate their environmental sustainability" as Cherry Hoo suggested.   (8 marks)

(c)   Some corporate governance codes prohibit audit firms such as Hum and Hoo from providing some non-audit services to audit clients without the prior approval of the client's audit committee. This is because it is sometimes believed to be against the public interest.

   Required:

   Explain "public interest" in the context of accounting services and why a client's audit committee is a suitable body to advise on the purchase of non-audit services from Hum and Hoo.   (9 marks)

(25 marks)

Question 4 TZO COMPANY

Mahmood is a junior employee of Tzo Company (a large, listed company). Tzo is a processor of food labelled as containing only high quality meat. The company enjoys the trust and confidence of its customers because of its reputation for high quality products. One day, when passing through one area of the plant, Mahmood noticed some inferior meat being mixed with the normal product. He felt this must be unauthorised so he informed his supervisor, the factory manager, who told Mahmood that this was in fact a necessary cost reduction measure because company profits had been declining in recent months. Mahmood later found out that all stages of the production process, from purchasing to final quality control, were adapted in order to make the use of the inferior meat possible.

The factory manager told Mahmood that the inferior meat was safe for humans to eat and its use was not illegal. However, he told Mahmood that if knowledge of the use of this meat was made public, it would mean that customers might stop buying the products. Many jobs could be lost, probably including Mahmood's own. The factory manager ordered Mahmood to say nothing about the inferior meat and to conduct his job as normal. Mahmood later discovered that the main board of Tzo was aware of the use of the inferior meat and supported its use in seeking to reduce costs and maintain profits. In covering up the use of the inferior meat, the factory produced a fraudulent quality control report to show that the product was purely based on high quality meat when the company knew that this was not so.

When Mahmood heard this, he was very angry and considered telling an external source, such as the local newspaper, about what he had seen and about how the company was being dishonest with its customers.

Required:

(a) **Explain how Mahmood might act, in each case, if he were to adopt either conventional or post-conventional ethical assumptions according to Kohlberg's definitions of these terms. Your answer should include an explanation of these two terms.** (8 marks)

(b) **Construct an ethical case for Mahmood to take this matter directly to an external source such as a newspaper.** (8 marks)

(c) Some jurisdictions have a compulsory regulatory requirement for an auditor-reviewed external report on the operation and effectiveness of internal controls (such as s.404 of Sarbanes Oxley).

Required:

Explain how such a requirement may have helped to prevent the undisclosed use of the inferior meat at Tzo Company. (9 marks)

(25 marks)

Answer 1 PRIVATE, LISTED AND PUBLIC GOVERNANCE

(a)   **Main principles**

Corporate governance is a key element in improving economic efficiency and growth as well as enhancing investor confidence. It involves a set of relationships between a company's management, its board, its shareholders and other stakeholders and also provides the structure through which the objectives of the company are set, and the means of attaining those objectives and monitoring performance are determined.

Good corporate governance should provide proper incentives for the board and management to pursue objectives that are in the interests of the company and its shareholders and should facilitate effective monitoring. The presence of an effective corporate governance system, in an individual company and across an economy as a whole, helps to provide a degree of confidence that is necessary for the proper functioning of a market economy.

Governance is achieved through a variety of ways (e.g. legal requirements placed on all firms, listing requirements and separate "best practice" codes) usually to be applied by listed companies. Where legal procedures are relatively weak, the respective corporate governance code would normally be more detailed.

The OECD principles, for example, detail a number of elements:

■ The protection and facilitation of the exercise of shareholders' rights.

■ Ensuring the equitable treatment of all shareholders, including minority and foreign shareholders with the opportunity to obtain effective redress for violation of their rights.

■ Recognising the rights of stakeholders established by law or through mutual agreements and encouraging active co-operation between corporations and stakeholders in creating wealth, jobs, and the sustainability of financially sound enterprises.

■ Ensuring that timely and accurate disclosure is made on all material matters regarding the corporation, including the financial situation, performance, ownership, and governance of the company.

■ Ensuring the strategic guidance of the company, the effective monitoring of management by the board, and the board's accountability to the company and the shareholders.

In a number of jurisdictions, some of the above principles (e.g. protection of shareholder rights and disclosure of information) are already enshrined in corporate law.

Tutorial note: *Using another basis (e.g. the UK Code) would obtain the marks just as well.*

(b)   **State owned enterprises and the public sector**

The Commonwealth Association for Corporate Governance (CACG) issued a set of Guidelines in 1999 wherein it was stated that most of the largest and economically significant industries in many jurisdictions are state-owned and that many of their directors are not independent as their appointments are often politically motivated. The guidelines also noted that there was a severe shortage of skilled individuals to act as company directors.

State-owned entities differ from public companies in that the directors of these concerns have a duty to the taxpayers and to the community as a whole, compared to the fiduciary relationship between shareholders and the board of directors in private companies.

The guidelines also suggested that sound corporate governance in state-owned enterprises is of particular importance in developing economies because they provide a role model for companies in the growing private sector to encourage a more ethical manner of corporate governance.

However, with the growth of "best practice" in the private sector, many governments are taking a lead in applying similar governance requirements on state owned enterprises. Even if such enterprises are not in direct competition with private companies, their stakeholders (e.g. the taxpayers) are demanding stronger leadership, transparency and accountability from such enterprises.

Many governments are also introducing corporate best practice into the general areas of public services (e.g. local authorities, health service and transport). The UK's Seven Principles of Public Life (Nolan Report) are a good example of implementing corporate governance in the public service. The principles cover:

- **Selflessness** – holders of public office should act solely in terms of the public interest. They should not do so in order to gain financial or other material benefits for themselves, their family, or their friends.

- **Integrity** – holders of public office should not place themselves under any financial or other obligation to outside individuals or organisations that might seek to influence them in the performance of their official duties.

- **Objectivity** – in carrying out public business, including making public appointments, awarding contracts, or recommending individuals for rewards and benefits, holders of public office should make choices on merit.

- **Accountability** – holders of public office are accountable for their decisions and actions to the public and must submit themselves to whatever scrutiny is appropriate to their office.

- **Openness** – holders of public office should be as open as possible about all the decisions and actions that they take. They should give reasons for their decisions and restrict information only when the wider public interest clearly demands.

- **Honesty** – holders of public office have a duty to declare any private interests relating to their public duties and to take steps to resolve any conflicts arising in a way that protects the public interest.

- **Leadership** – holders of public office should promote and support these principles by leadership and example.

A further example is the report by the Independent Commission for Good Governance in Public Services where six principles of good governance were identified:

(1) Focusing on the organisation's purpose and outcomes for citizens and service users.
(2) Performing effectively in clearly defined functions and roles.
(3) Taking informed, transparent decisions and managing risk.
(4) Developing the capacity and capability of the governing body to be effective.
(5) Engaging stakeholders and making accountability real.

(6)   Promoting values for the whole organisation and demonstrating the values of good governance through behaviour.

In conclusion, the above examples show that the principles of good corporate governance can just as easily be applied to public services as to private and listed companies.

(c)   Agency and stakeholders in the public sector

In a private sector company, agents are usually the company's directors with the company's shareholders being the principals. The directors have a fiduciary duty to maximise the long-term value of the business to the benefit of the shareholders. The shareholders set the directors the objective of maximising their return.

Within the public sector there are no shareholders, but there are individuals and other participants that provide the equivalent financing (i.e. corporate and individual taxpayers through direct or indirect taxation). In the majority of cases, the taxpayers are also the users of the services provided by the public sector. Just as in the private sector, shareholders are stakeholders, so taxpayers and service users are stakeholders within the public sector.

Private sector directors have a fiduciary duty based around generating profits and investing wisely. For the public sector, profits are not the key objective but the delivery of appropriate services efficiently, effectively and economically (the "3Es") are.

Efficiency is about delivering an agreed (acceptable to stakeholders) level of service for less cost, time or effort. It is about the action taken.

Effectiveness concerns delivering a better (continually improving) service or getting a better "return" for the same amount of expense, time or effort of the resources used. It is about achieving results.

Economy is the careful use of resources to save expense, time or effort. This will be about the delivery of a service within the appropriate constraints.

Public sector value for money can often lead to conflicting views, very often based upon political stances. First of all the social purpose and social contract has to be agreed. Some stakeholders, through their stakeholder claims, will agree a particular service is needed, others will not. Some will consider the service to be value for money (e.g. the public funding of a high speed railway link) others will consider such extravagance to be a total waste of money and that the money could have been more effectively used in other areas (e.g. education or health).

Although the concepts of agency and stakeholders are easily understood for public services at a basic level they are far more complex in practice.

Answer 2 PUBLIC SECTOR GOVERNANCE ARRANGEMENTS

(a)   National, subnational and supranational level of public services

National

Typically a national government, usually based in the country's capital city, is divided into various departments (e.g. treasury, interior ministry, foreign office, defence ministry, health service, education and social services).

In terms of primary governance, these departments are led by a political minister (e.g. Sunny Xhengj, Emland's health minister) from the governing political party, supported by a permanent staff of career civil servants who rarely change on the appointment of a new government. The senior civil servants will act as advisors and policy implementers to their minister, but on a non-political basis.

On a change of government (and therefore ministers) each department's policies will more than likely change to reflect the proposals and promises made by the new government during the election.

This structure is important in democratic countries as the policies adopted by the various departments affect the entire population of the country as well as, perhaps, populations of other countries (e.g. through trading and foreign aid) and it is critical that they are subject to political change when the electorate changes a government at an election.

This process is an example of the application of a "social contract" between the people and the government (i.e. the state only exists to serve the will of the people and the people are the source of all political power enjoyed by the state). The people can choose to give or withhold this power.

Subnational

Some countries are organised or subdivided at a "below" (i.e. "sub-") national level, into regional authorities, which variously called regional assemblies, federal states, cantons, departments, municipalities, local authorities or similar.

Some selected powers are devolved down to these sub-national bodies by national government in the belief that these selected powers are either best handled by local people (to meet specific local needs) or that service delivery to the regions will be more efficient or cost effective.

Typical powers devolved down to the sub-national level include planning (e.g. roads and new housing permissions), utilities (e.g. energy and water), policing, local schools, housing, support of vulnerable communities, rubbish collection, etc.

In many cases, sub-national public sector organisations are led by elected representatives in a way that is similar to national governments. These are supported by permanent officials in a similar manner to civil servants in national governments. In other cases, those who run the sub-national authority are directly appointed by and are responsible to, the national government often in a "power-vertical" arrangement.

Supranational

Supranational bodies are formed by a grouping of national governments ("locally" or worldwide) for a shared purpose. They are often subject to significant pressures as the larger the grouping of governments, the greater the potential for conflicts and disagreements (e.g. pressure from each country's own people to prefer one outcome to another).

Typical examples include:

■ The European Union, with offices in Strasbourg and Brussels. Similar bodies for trading and/or political reasons exist elsewhere in the world.

- The United Nations (UN) expresses the collective opinion of many countries on a range of international issues (in 2014, 192 nation states were members). The UN employs many thousands of people, at its headquarters in New York as well as around the world through its various agencies (e.g. the World Health Organisation, refugee agency, environmental programme, etc).

- The World Trade Organisation (WTO, formerly the General Agreement on Tariffs and Trade), the International Monetary Fund (IMF), World Bank and the International Court of Justice at The Hague.

(b)   **Principles**

Public sector governance comprises the arrangements (including political, economic, social, environmental, legal and administrative structures and processes) put in place to ensure that the intended outcomes for stakeholders are defined and achieved.

The fundamental function of good governance in the public sector is to ensure that entities achieve their intended outcomes while acting in the public interest at all times.

Acting in the public interest requires:

- Behaving with integrity, demonstrating strong commitment to ethical values and respecting the rule of law – tone at the top, embedded public interest culture, codes of conduct, core values, separation of executive from the judicial system, avoid corruption and misuse of power.

- Ensuring openness and comprehensive stakeholder engagement – maintain public trust, open access to relevant information, stakeholder consultations and stakeholder partnerships.

In addition achieving good governance in the public sector also requires effective arrangements for:

- Defining outcomes or impacts in terms of sustainable economic, social, and environmental benefits. For example, levels of taxation, service delivery, infrastructure maintenance, management of assets and debt.

  Tutorial note: *Sustainability in this context is defined as the capacity of an individual entity, community or global population to continue to survive successfully in meeting its intended (economic, environmental, and social) outcomes within its resource limits.*

- Determining the actions necessary to optimise the achievement of the intended outcomes (e.g. full information, objective analysis, strategic planning, risk analysis, budgetary systems, value for money and KPIs).

- Developing the entity's capacity, including the capability of its leadership and the individuals within it. This incorporates the "capitals" (e.g. financial, manufactured, intellectual, human and natural) leadership skills, diversity, succession planning, learning and development, service-orientated culture, and engaged and competent workforce.

- Managing risks and performance through robust internal control and strong public financial management. For example, embedded risk management framework (e.g. COSO), audit committee, internal audit, integrated monitoring and reporting.

■   Implementing good practices in transparency, reporting and audit, to deliver effective accountability. For example, open and accessible, regular reporting (internal and external), integrated reporting and external assurance reporting.

Tutorial note: *The above principles are from "The International Framework: Good Governance in the Public Sector" (IFAC, CIPFA July 2014). Credit would also be given for answers based on the Seven Principles of Public Life (Nolan Principles) or the report by the Independent Commission for Good Governance in Public Services*

(c)   **Arrangements**

Sunny's assertion that a "one size fits all" approach to implementing corporate governance in the public sector would not work is perfectly correct. She has, however, failed to recognise that the "one size fits all" approach to corporate governance, more commonly referred to as a rules-based approach, is just one option. The corporate governance approach most commonly used is the principles-based approach such as the UK's Corporate Governance Code and South Africa's King Code III.

As Sunny correctly points out, within the public sector there are many variations on organisational structures, objectives and arrangements. Although there are no shareholders or profit drivers, a national government or supranational government (e.g. the European Union) will:

■   have a far larger stakeholder base than any one international company (i.e. the entire national/supranational population);

■   deal with far larger budgets and far more complex "business" relationships than a single national or international company.

Because of these variations, any governance arrangements/codes for the public sector must be based on principles similar to those briefly described above.

A good governance structure contributes to the effective performance of the public sector that:

■   must be accountable to the public for the proper use and stewardship of the funds and other assets with which they are entrusted. Good governance and appropriate checks and balances serve to gain and maintain that trust;

■   must rely on the continuing support and confidence of their stakeholders including, as the case may be, customers, employees, lenders, suppliers and business partners. These stakeholders need to be assured of the quality and the ethical standards of the public bodies with which they deal; and

■   is expected by the community to set an example in terms of transparency, openness, accountability, and organisational and personal integrity, in relation to matters such as human resources, procurement, remuneration and disclosure policies.

In the public sector, specific user groups, those directly responsible for funding and the community at large (i.e. those from which resources are ultimately derived and to whom services are delivered) assume a greater importance as stakeholders. However, the pivotal role of the "governing board" and the issues of transparency and accountability are as relevant to the public sector as they are to the private sector.

Governance arrangements within the public sector can often mirror those found within private and listed companies, but the major difference will be that there is no market mechanism for measuring performance (as found with listed companies). Depending on the nature of the public service entity, it can be relatively straight forward to apply sound governance arrangements modelled on those for listed companies, provided the political will is strong.

Every public sector entity needs one or more individuals who are explicitly responsible for providing strategic direction and oversight while being accountable to its stakeholders.

The simplest form of governance may well be that used by Sunny; a single minister running a governmental department with civil servants as advisors and managers reporting to her. At the subnational level, local senior managers will be delegated the task of running local operations. Oversight of this model could be provided by the board of government ministers, referred to as "the Cabinet" in the UK. However, this may not provide appropriate public interest accountability; only government interest accountability.

In some countries, oversight of government roles is provided by various public standing committees comprising cross-party elected members of the national elective body (e.g. Parliament in the UK). They would be supported in their task by independent auditors (e.g. the National Audit Office in the UK) whose role would include scrutinising public spending and the application of specific governance codes and principles. Minutes of the standing committees and the reports of the auditors would be in the public domain.

Beyond the "single" model, many public sector bodies are able to apply the corporate governance model of the business world:

- There would be a main board comprising a chief executive, chairman, executive officers and independent non-executives.

- In some cases, the non-executives would form the oversight board, separating the governing and management functions. This oversight board is often referred to as a board of trustees.

- Care must be taken to ensure that appointments to the board are open and transparent, as they are often made by government officials.

As for listed company governance, public sector boards could also have specific sub-committees (e.g. finance and budgeting, audit and nominations). It is possible that the remuneration of most executives would be set by government guidelines. However, where an executive's remuneration is based entirely on market factors, non-executives would agree the compensation (as for listed companies).

The roles of the sub-committees and the non-executives would be very similar to those of the committees and NEDs in a listed company (i.e. strategy, scrutiny, risk and people).

At the level of a local entity (e.g. a school in a local education authority) the oversight body may be a board of governors comprising:

- the head teacher;
- a teachers' union representative (usually a teacher at the school);
- elected parents; and
- a local education authority representative.

Regular governors meetings would be held with full reports being made to parents. Parents would have formal access to the chairman of the governors and informal access to any of the governors (e.g. meeting in a local shop) as well as the head teacher and other teachers.

A key feature of business corporate governance is the use of investors' websites and social media to enhance openness, transparency and communication. Many public sector bodies have also incorporated similar e-systems into their governance arrangements to provide, for example, information on their services to the general public and a forum to lodge or discuss complaints. In addition, many public services can now be provided electronically.

In summary, Sunny's assertion cannot be proven. The principles of corporate governance are equally applicable to the public sector as they are to companies. The only true barrier is the political will to implement governance arrangements and provide true public interest services.

Answer 3 HORACE HOI

(a)   **Charities and public listed companies**

Differences between these organisations

(1)   *Regulation:* Listed companies are subject to all the provisions of company law plus any listing rules that apply. Listing rules (e.g. the need to adopt the UK Corporate Governance Code in the UK) impose a number of obligations on listed companies such as non-executive directors (NEDs), committee structures, a range of reporting requirements, etc. Charities, in contrast, must receive recognition by a country's charity authority to operate and they then receive the concessions that charitable status confers. This often involves favourable tax treatment and different reporting requirements. Because charities are not public companies they are not subject to listing rules although, depending upon the country's rules, they may be subject to audit and have some reporting requirements.

(2)   *Strategic purpose* of the organisation: Listed companies exist primarily to make a financial return for their investors (shareholders). This means that they employ and incentivise people, including directors, to maximise long-term cash flows. Value is added by the creation of shareholder wealth and this is measured in terms of profits, cash flows, share price movements and price/earnings. For a charity, the strategic purpose is to support the charitable cause for which the organisation was set up. It is likely to be a social or benevolent cause and funds are donated specifically to support that cause and this expectation places a different emphasis on the purpose of governance.

(3)   *Stakeholders and societal expectations*: Society typically expects a business to be efficient in order to be profitable so that, in turn, it can create jobs, wealth and value for shareholders. Society expresses its support for a business by participating in its resource or product markets (i.e. by supplying its inputs (including working for it) or buying its products). A charity's social legitimacy is tied up with the charity's achievement of benevolent aims. Stakeholders in a business often have an economic incentive to engage with the organisation whereas most stakeholders in a charity have claims more concerned with its benevolent aims.

How differences affect governance structures

There can be a number of substantive differences between the governance structures of public companies and charities. In a public company, a board consisting of executive directors and NEDs is accountable to the shareholders of the company. The principals are able to hold the board accountable through AGMs (annual general meetings) and GMs (general meetings) at which they can vote on resolutions and other issues to convey their collective will to the board. In a charity, the operating board is usually accountable to a board of trustees. It is the trustees who act as the interpreters and guarantors of the fiduciary duty of the charity (because the beneficiaries of the charity may be unable to speak for themselves). The trustees ensure that the board is acting according to the charity's stated purposes and that all management policy, including salaries and benefits, are consistent with those purposes.

Tutorial note: *The term "extraordinary" general meeting was removed from company law in England and Wales by the Companies Act 2006. Now, any meeting of the shareholders other than the AGM is simply a "general meeting".*

(b)   **Transparency**

Definition

Transparency is usually defined in terms of openness and adopting a default position of information provision rather than concealment. This means that unless there is an overwhelming reason not to disclose information of any kind (perhaps for reasons of commercial sensitivity) then information should be disclosed or made available upon request to any interested stakeholder.

The case for greater transparency in governance of HHO

Transparency is an important principle in corporate governance, including at HHO, for a number of reasons.

In general, transparency has the effect of *reassuring investors* that their funds are being responsibly stewarded and used for worthwhile investments. In the case of a charity, such as HHO, without shareholders in the conventional sense, donors give money to support the charity's stated aims and purposes. With the relief of suffering to animals being a prominent reason any donors give to HHO, the amount of money diverted for other purposes, such as salaries, would be information of considerable interest.

Transparency would *inform and placate HHO's critics*, including the journalists who are investigating it. Public commentators like journalists are capable of causing damage to HHO's reputation and this in turn can affect donations and support for the organisation.

There are a number of potentially *damaging allegations* made against Mr Hoi including the likelihood of large payments to himself and some profligacy in the purchase of the private jet. These allegations could be rebutted if the organisation were to make the accounts public and explain the case for the purchase of the jet. For a charity receiving money from "well-meaning individuals that care greatly about animal suffering", the allegations have the potential to do much reputational damage to the charity.

The *publication of the financial data is an inadequate expression of transparency* and appears to be a poor attempt to give the appearance of providing information whilst providing no useful detail at all. This would not meet any stakeholder's information needs and fails to address any of the concerns raised about HHO. It does not give any absolute financial figures, for example, in terms of income and costs. Such a truncated summary actually gives the impression, to any informed observer, of an attempt at concealment and this provides a strong reason to provide a full financial statement.

(c)   **Audit committee and internal control deficiencies**

There are a number of apparent internal control deficiencies, although the case does not permit definite and specific allegations of internal control deficiencies to be made or to conclude that a complete lack of governance structure exists at HHO. However, any such organisation would benefit from having an audit committee with wide-ranging powers and responsibilities when reviewing internal controls. With regard to the situation at HHO, the most important areas for audit committee attention are monitoring the adequacy of internal controls, checks for compliance with relevant regulation and codes, checking for fraud and reviewing existing internal control statements for accuracy.

Monitoring the adequacy of internal controls involves analysing the controls already in place to establish whether they are capable of mitigating risks. In the case of HHO, there are internal risks that the controls need to be capable of controlling.

The risk of fraud and the risk of compliance failure are relevant internal risks.

To check for compliance with relevant regulation and codes refers to HHO's compliance with its legal and other regulatory constraints. It is likely that HHO has a number of regulatory constraints as a result of its charitable status. It may also have voluntary codes it seeks to abide by, perhaps made public through its marketing or reporting literature, and the audit committee could also test for compliance with these.

Checking for fraud is also within the remit of an audit committee and this would, at first glance, be a priority at HHO. There are grounds for believing that inadequate remuneration policies exist at HHO and grounds for suspecting some financial dishonesty. There also seems to be a lack of accountability for the behaviour and actions of Horace Hoi, especially if the claims about his lavish lifestyle are accurate. The misuse of donations for personal enrichment would be outside of what is allowed under his charitable status and this could be reviewed by the audit committee.

Finally, an audit committee could play a more supervisory role if necessary, for example reviewing major expenses and transactions for reasonableness. This might include measuring transactions against its regulatory regime and the reasonable expectations of its trustees and donors.

Answer 4 STAKEHOLDERS, DIRECTORS AND FIDUCIARY DUTIES

(a)   **Stakeholder groups**

The range of stakeholders includes many diverse groupings (e.g. shareholders, directors/managers, lenders, employees, suppliers (materials and services), customers, governments, communities and the environment).

Tutorial note: *Only FIVE were asked for. If more than five were listed, ensure you only discuss, as below, five. Marks will only be awarded based on five.*

These groups are likely to share in the wealth and risk generated by a company in different ways and thus conflicts of interest are likely to exist. Conflicts also exist not just between groups but within stakeholder groups. This might be because sub groups exist (e.g. preference shareholders and equity shareholders). Alternatively it might be that individuals within a group have different preferences (e.g. to risk and return, short term and long term returns). Good corporate governance is partly about the resolution of such conflicts.

Stakeholders' financial and other objectives may be identified as follows:

Shareholders

Shareholders are normally assumed to be interested in wealth maximisation. This, however, involves consideration of potential return and risk. Where a company is listed this can be viewed in terms of the share price returns and other market-based ratios using share price (e.g. price earnings ratio, dividend yield, earnings yield).

Where a company is not listed, financial objectives need to be set in terms of accounting and other related financial measures. These may include, for example, return of capital employed, earnings per share, gearing, growth, profit margin, asset utilisation, market share. Many other measures also exist which may collectively capture the objectives of return and risk.

Shareholders may have other objectives for the company and these can be identified in terms of the interests of other stakeholder groups. Thus, shareholders, as a group, might not only be interested in wealth maximisation but also profit maximisation (to be reinvested in the business rather than distributed) the welfare of their employees or the environmental effects of the company's operations.

Directors and managers

While directors and managers are in essence attempting to promote and balance the interests of shareholders and other stakeholders it has been argued that they also promote their own interests as a separate (internal) stakeholder group regardless of their fiduciary duties.

This arises from the divorce between ownership and control where the behaviour of managers cannot be fully observed giving them the capacity to take decisions which are consistent with their own reward structures and risk preferences. Directors may thus be interested in their own compensation package including payment for losing their job in the event of a takeover or early retirement.

In a non-financial sense, they may be interested in building empires, exercising greater control, or positioning themselves for their next promotion. Non-financial objectives are sometimes difficult to separate from their financial effects.

Lenders

As connected stakeholders, lenders are concerned to receive payment of interest and ultimate re-payment of capital.

They do not share in the upside of very successful organisational strategies as the shareholders do. They are thus likely to be more risk averse than shareholders, with an emphasis on financial objectives that promote liquidity and solvency with low risk (e.g. gearing, interest cover, security, cash flow).

Non-financial interests are few, but a typical semi-financial interest is the kudos attached to the sponsorship of a major event (e.g. Wimbledon tennis tournament, test cricket matches, Formula One).

Employees

The primary interest of employees (as internal stakeholders) is their salary/wage and security of employment. To an extent there is a direct conflict between employees and shareholders as wages are a cost to the company and a revenue to employees.

Performance-related pay based on financial or other quantitative objectives may, however, go some way toward drawing the divergent interests together.

Non-financial interests of employees would cover the workplace environment and perhaps the status of working for a particular organisation.

Suppliers and customers

Suppliers and customers are external stakeholders with their own set of objectives (profit for the supplier and, possibly, customer satisfaction from the goods or services received) that, within a portfolio of businesses, are only partly dependent on the company in question.

Nevertheless it is important to consider and measure the relationship in terms of financial objectives relating to quality, lead times, volume of business, price and a range of other variables in considering any organisational strategy.

(b) **Fiduciary duties**

A fiduciary duty is one that is imposed on certain persons because of the position of trust and confidence in which they stand in relation to another. The duty is more onerous than generally arises under a contractual or tort relationship. It requires full disclosure of information held by the fiduciary, a strict duty to account for any profits received as a result of the relationship, and a duty to avoid conflicts of interest.

Under English law, for example, the fiduciary duties of directors (as derived under common law) to the company include:

- To act in good faith in the best interests of the company and promote the success of the company;

- To act within the powers conferred by the company's constitution and exercise powers for proper purposes;

- Not to restrain discretion (must use independent judgement on the company's behalf);

- To avoid conflicts of interest and conflicting duties;

- Not to make a secret profit (includes accepting benefit or bribes from third parties);

- To exercise due skill and care in the performance of their duties.

A director must act in a way that they consider, in good faith, would be most likely to promote the success (i.e. long-term increase in value) of the company for the benefit of its members as a whole. This duty adds a focus of "enlightened shareholder value" which must take (at least) into account:

- the likely consequence of any decision in the long term;

- the interests of the company's employees;

- the need to foster the company's business relationships with suppliers, customers and others;

- the effect of the company's operations on the community and the environment;

- the desirability of the company maintaining a reputation for high standards of business conduct; and

- the need to act fairly as between the members of the company.

This appears to be moving agency fiduciary duties into the realm of stakeholder theory.

(c) **How good corporate governance procedures can help manage the problems**

Corporate governance is the system by which organisations are directed and controlled.

Where the power to direct and control an organisation is given, then a duty of accountability exists to those who have devolved that power. Part of that duty of accountability is discharged by disclosure both of performance in the normal financial statements but also of the governance procedures themselves.

The UK Corporate Governance Code is an example of a principles based code. Although it has mandatory application for companies listed on the London Stock Exchange, there is an overall "comply or explain" provision. Thus any divergence from the requirements of the code must be explained.

In deciding on which of the divergent interests should be promoted, the directors have a key role. Much of the corporate governance regulation in the UK (including the Corporate Governance Code) has therefore focused on the control of this group and disclosure of its activities. This is to assist in controlling their ability to promote their own interests and make more visible the incentives to promote the interest of other stakeholder groups.

A particular feature of the UK is that Boards of Directors are unitary (i.e. executive and non-executive directors sit on a single board). This contrasts to Germany for instance where there is more independence between the groups in the form of two-tier boards (where directors on a management board report to the non-executive directors of a supervisory board).

Particular corporate governance features in the UK'S Corporate Governance Code include:

- independence of the board with no covert financial reward;

- adequate quality and quantity of independent non-executive directors to act as a counterbalance to the power of executive directors (at least 50% of the board);

- remuneration committee (to decide on the remuneration of executives) that is 100% independent non-executives;

- appointments committee (to recommend appointments to the board) comprising a mix of executive and independent non-executives with no one group being able to dominate;

- audit committee, comprising 100% non-executive directors, responsible for overseeing the financial integrity of the company and financial statements (including external auditors, their work and fees and internal auditors);

- separation of the roles of chairman and chief executive to prevent concentration of power;

- full disclosure of all forms of director remuneration including shares and share options;

- dialogue with institutional shareholders and encouraging private investors to participate in the annual general meeting (AGM); and

- maintaining a sound system of internal control (based on risk assessment) to safeguard shareholders' investment and the company's assets.

Overall, the visibility given by corporate governance procedures goes some way toward discharging the directors' duty of accountability to stakeholders and makes more transparent the underlying incentive systems of directors.

Answer 5 ROSH & CO

(a) **Defining and explaining agency**

Agency is defined in relation to a principal. A principal appoints an agent to act on his behalf. In the case of corporate governance, the principal is a shareholder in a joint stock company and the agents (that have an agency relationship with principals) are the directors. The directors remain accountable to the principals for the stewardship of their investment in the company. In the case of Rosh, 60% of the shares are owned by shareholders external to the Rosh family and the board has agency responsibility to those shareholders.

Criticisms of Rosh's CG arrangements

The corporate governance arrangements at Rosh and Company are far from ideal. Five points can be made based on the evidence in the case.

There are several issues associated with the non-executive directors (NEDs) at Rosh. It is doubtful whether two NEDs are enough to bring sufficient scrutiny to the executive board. Some corporate governance codes require half of the board of larger companies to be non-executive and Rosh would clearly be in breach of such a requirement.

Perhaps of equal concern, there is significant doubt over the independence of the current NEDs as they were recruited from retired executive members of the board and presumably have relationships with existing executives going back many years. Some corporate governance codes (such as the UK Corporate Governance Code) specify that NEDs should not have worked for the company within the last five years. Again, Rosh would be in breach of this provision.

Succession planning for senior positions in the company seems to be based on Rosh family membership rather than any meritocratic approach to appointments (there does not appear to be a nominations committee). Although this may have been acceptable before the flotation when the Rosh family owned all the shares, the flotation introduced an important need for external scrutiny of this arrangement. The lack of NED independence makes this difficult.

There is a poor (very narrow) diversity of backgrounds among board members. Although diversity can bring increased conflict, it is generally assumed that it can also stimulate discussion and debate that is often helpful.

There is a somewhat entrenched executive board and Mary is the first new appointment to the board in many years (and is the first woman). Although experience is very important on a board, the appointment of new members, in addition to seeding the board with talent for the future, can also bring fresh ideas and helpful scrutiny of existing policies.

There is no discussion of strategy and there is evidence of a lack of preparation of strategic notes to the board. The assumption seems to be that the "best" option is obvious and so there is no need for discussion and debate. Procedures for preparing briefing notes on strategy for board meetings appear to be absent. Most corporate governance codes place the discussion and setting of strategy as a high priority for boards and Rosh would be in breach of such a provision.

There is no evidence of training for Mary to facilitate her introduction into the organisation and its systems. Thorough training of new members and on-going professional development of existing members is an important component of good governance.

(b) **Nominations committees**

General roles

- Advises on the balance between executives and independent non-executive directors and establishes the appropriate number and type of NEDs on the board. The nominations committee is usually made up of NEDs.

- Establishes the skills, knowledge and experience possessed by current board and notes any gaps that will need to be filled.

- Acts to meet the needs for continuity and succession planning, especially among the most senior members of the board.

- Establishes the desirable and optimal size of the board, bearing in mind the current size and complexity of existing and planned activities and strategies.

- Seeks to ensure that the board is balanced in terms of it having board members from a diversity of backgrounds so as to reflect its main constituencies and ensure a flow of new ideas and the scrutiny of existing strategies.

Application to Ross

In the case of Rosh, the needs that a nominations committee could address are:

- To recommend how many directors would be needed to run the business and plan for recruitment accordingly. The perceived similarity of skills and interests of existing directors is also likely to be an issue.

- To resolve the issues over numbers of NEDs. It seems likely that the current number is inadequate and would put Rosh in a position of non-compliance with many of the corporate governance guidelines pertaining to NEDs.

- To resolve the issues over the independence of NEDs. The closeness that the NEDs have to existing executive board members potentially undermines their independence and a nominations committee should be able to identify this as an issue and make recommendations to rectify it.

■ To make recommendations over the succession of the chairmanship. It may not be in the interests of Rosh for family members to always occupy senior positions in the business.

(c) **Retirement by rotation**

Definition

Retirement by rotation is an arrangement in a director's contract that specifies his contract to be limited to a specific period (typically three years) after which he must retire from the board or offer himself (being eligible) for re-election. The director must be actively re-elected back onto the board to serve another term. The default is that the director retires unless re-elected.

Importance

Retirement by rotation reduces the cost of contract termination for underperforming directors. They can simply not be re-elected after their term of office expires and they will be required to leave the service of the board as a retiree (depending on contract terms).

It encourages directors' performance (they know they are assessed by shareholders and reconsidered every three years) and focuses their minds on the importance of meeting objectives in line with shareholders' aims.

It is an opportunity, over time, to replace the board membership while maintaining medium-term stability of membership (one or two at a time).

Application to Rosh

Retirement by rotation would enable the board of Rosh to be changed over time. There is evidence that some directors may have stayed longer than is ideal because of links with other board members going back many years.

Answer 6 DING COMPANY

(a) **Director's induction programme**

The overall purpose of induction is to minimise the amount of time taken for the new director to become effective in his new job. There are four major aspects of a director's induction.

To convey to the new starter, the organisation's norms, values and culture. This is especially important when the new employee is from a different type of culture. Because Sam moved from a different country to join Ding Company, he had to adjust to a new national culture as well as a new corporate culture. There is evidence from the case that he misunderstood some of the cultural norms in that it was alleged that he made what he considered normal but what was perceived as an inappropriate remark to a young female employee. An induction programme including content on culture and norms may have prevented this situation from occurring.

To communicate practical procedural duties to the new director including company policies relevant to a new employee. In Sam's case this would involve his orientation with his place in the structure, his reporting lines (up and down), the way in which work is organised in the department and practical matters. In the case scenario, Sam made a simple error in the positioning of his office furniture. Again, this is an entirely avoidable situation had the induction programme provided him with appropriate content on company policy in this area.

To convey an understanding of the nature of the company, its operations, strategy, key stakeholders and external relationships. For a new director, an early understanding of strategy is essential and a sound knowledge of how the company "works" will also ensure that he adapts more quickly to the new role. In the case of a financial controller such as Sam, key external relationships will be with the company's auditors and banks. If Sam is involved in reporting, the auditor relationship will be important and if he is involved in financing, the banks and other capital providers will be more important.

To establish and develop the new director's relationships with colleagues, especially those with whom he will interact on a regular basis. The importance of building good relationships early on in a director's job is very important as early misunderstandings can be costly in terms of the time needed to repair the relationship. It is likely that Sam and Annette will need to work together to repair an unfortunate start to their working relationship as it seems that one of her first dealings with him was to point out his early misunderstandings (which were arguably due to her failure to provide him with an appropriate induction programme).

(b) **Critically evaluate Annette's belief**

Countries differ in their employment of various types of board structure. Companies in the UK and US have tended towards unitary structures while Japanese companies and some European countries have preferred two–tier or even multi-tier boards. The distinction refers to the ways in which decision-making and responsibility is divided between directors.

In a unitary structure, all the directors have a nominally equal role in board discussions but they also jointly share responsibility (including legal responsibility) for the outcome of those discussions.

On a two tier board, the senior board acts as a "kitchen cabinet" in which decisions are concentrated while other directors, typically departmental managers, will be on the "operating board" and brought into board discussions where the senior (upper tier) board deem it appropriate.

There are some arguments in favour of the adoption of a two-tier structure in turbulent environments. As the case implies, turbulent and dynamic environments change often and strategic leadership is partly about continually adjusting strategy to optimise the company's fit with its environment. A smaller board can act quick and decisively in a way that larger and more cumbersome boards cannot. This is because meetings of larger numbers of people require excessive consultation, discussion and debate before a decision can be reached.

When a decision needs to be taken quickly, this can be inconvenient. The meeting of a small number of people is therefore easier, cheaper and quicker to arrange because there are fewer diaries to match. As these arguments focus on both the efficiency and effectiveness of strategic decision-making, Annette has a strong case for supporting two-tier boards.

The arguments against two-tier boards are as follows:

■   In any complex situation where finely balanced judgments are made, such as making strategic decisions in turbulent environmental conditions, input from more people is likely to provide more views on which to make the decision. Where, say, technical, detailed financial or operational details would be of benefit to the decision then a larger board would be likely to provide more feedback into the decision making process.

- The second reason is that decisions taken by a corporate board with little or no consultation with the operating board may not enjoy the full support of those key departmental directors who will be required to implement the decision. This, in turn, may cause friction, discord and resentment that will hinder good relations and thus impede the implementation of the strategy.

- Additionally, without a full understanding of operations, an inappropriate decision may be taken by the corporate board and unworkable procedures implemented.

- Finally, Annette is quite an autocratic personality and the two-tier board may be little more than a device to grant her excessive powers over company strategies and activities.

(c) **Arif Zaman's understanding of his role**

The first observation to make is that, overall, Arif Zaman has a poor understanding of his role as chairman and poorly represents the interests of Ding's shareholders. He does not seem to understand his role as intended by Cadbury, Sarbanes Oxley and other influential codes on corporate governance.

It appears from the case that he cedes too much power to Annette. One of the purposes of having a separate chairman is to avoid allowing the chief executive to operate without recourse to the chairman. The chairman, along with the non-executive directors, should hold the chief executive to account.

Arif allowed Annette's views to take effect on matters such as board structure. Arif is legally head of the board and not Annette. Ding's shareholders have a reasonable expectation that Arif will personally ensure that the strategic oversight of the board will be a matter for the chairman who is, notionally at least, an independent non-executive director.

Being old friends with Annette threatens Arif's independence as chairman. Is he acting as a representative of the shareholders or as Annette's friend? He seems to be doing the job as a favour to Annette and seems to see no intrinsic value in his role in terms of acting to provide checks and balances on the activities of the executive board and the chief executive in particular.

Arif seems to view the chairing of board meetings as optional. He said that he saw his role as "mainly ceremonial" and that he "chaired some board meetings when he was available". Both of these attitudes are inappropriate and demonstrate an underestimation of the importance of the chairman in leading the company and its strategy.

Answer 7 KK

(a) **"Conflict of interest"**

A conflict of interest is a situation in which an individual has compromised independence because of another countervailing interest which may or may not be declared. In the case of non-executive directors, shareholders have the right to expect each NED to act wholly in the shareholders' interests while serving with the company. Any other factors that might challenge this sole fiduciary duty are likely to give rise to a conflict of interest. Does the director pursue policies and actions to benefit the shareholders or to benefit himself in some other way?

Application to the case

John has a longstanding and current *material business relationship with KK* as CEO of its largest supplier. This creates an obvious incentive to influence future purchases from Soria Supplies over and above other competitor suppliers, even if the other suppliers are offering more attractive supply contracts as far as KK is concerned. It is in the interests of KK shareholders for inputs to be purchased from whichever supplier is offering the best in terms of quality, price and supply. This may or may not be offered by Soria Supplies. Similarly, a conflict of interest already exists in that Susan Schwab, KK's finance director, is a NED on the board of Soria Supplies. Soria has a material business relationship with KK and Susan Schwab has a conflict of interest with regard to her duty to the shareholders of KK and the shareholders of Soria Supplies.

His appointment, if approved, would create a *cross directorship with Susan Schwab*. As she was appointed to the board of Soria Supplies, any appointment from Soria's board to KK's board would be a cross directorship. Such arrangements have the ability to create a disproportionately close relationship between two people and two companies that may undermine objectivity and impartiality in both cases. In this case, the cross directorship would create too strong a link between one supplier (Soria Supplies) and a buyer (KK) to the detriment of other suppliers and thus potentially lower unit costs.

John's brother-in-law is Ken Kava, the chief executive of KK. Such a close *family relationship* may result in John supporting Ken when it would be more in the interests of the KK shareholders for John to exercise greater objectivity. There should be no relationships between board members that prevent all directors serving the best interests of shareholders and a family relationship is capable of undermining this objectivity. This is especially important in public listed companies such as KK.

(b) **Advantages of appointing non-executives to KK's board**

The case discusses a number of issues that were raised as a result of the rapid expansion. An effective NED presence during this period would expect to bring several benefits.

In the case of KK, the NEDs could provide essential input into two related areas: monitoring the strategies for suitability and for excessive risk. In *monitoring the strategies for suitability*, NEDs could have an important scrutinising and advising role to fulfil on the "aggressive" strategies pursued by KK. All strategy selection is a trade-off between risk and return and so experience of strategy, especially in risky situations, can be very valuable.

NEDs could also *monitor the strategies for excessive risk*. The strategy role of NEDs is important partly because of increasing the collective experience of the board to a wide range of risks. With KK pursuing an "aggressive" strategy that involved the "increasingly complex operations", risk monitoring is potentially of great importance for shareholders. There is always a balance between aggression in a growth strategy and caution for the sake of risk management. The fact that some of the other executive directors are both new to the company (resulting from the expansion) and less experienced means, according to the case, that they may be less able and willing to question Mr Kava. Clearly, an effective non-executive presence would be able to bring such scrutiny to the board. They may also place a necessary restraint on the strategic ambitions of Mr Kava.

They could *provide expertise on the foreign investments including*, in some cases, country-specific knowledge. It is careless and irresponsible to make overseas investments based on incomplete intelligence. Experienced NEDs, some of whom may have done business in or with the countries in question, could be very valuable. Experienced NEDs capable of offering specific risk advice, possibly through the company's committee structure (especially the risk committee) would be particularly helpful.

Investors are reassured by an effective non-executive presence on a board. The fact that investors have expressed concerns over the strategy and risk makes this factor all the more important in this case. An experienced and effective NED presence would provide shareholders with a higher degree of confidence in the KK board so that when large overseas investments were made, they would be more assured that such investments were necessary and beneficial.

Finally, through an effective nominations committee, the NEDs could have *involvement in the recruitment and appointment of executive and non-executive directors* through the nominations committee structure. Specifically when the business is growing the need for new people is at its height and the *appointment of specialists at board level in such periods is strategically important.* Through the use of contacts and through the experience of recruiting directors for many years, experienced NEDs could make a worthwhile contribution.

Tutorial note: *This is a case analysis task. The four roles: people, strategy, risk, scrutiny would not gain marks unless clearly used to analyse the case.*

(c)   **Typical contents of a "best practice" corporate governance report**

Tutorial note: *Several corporate governance codes of practice prescribe the content for a report as part of an annual report. Although these vary slightly, the following are prominent in all cases.*

Information on the *board and its functioning.* Usually seen as the most important corporate governance disclosure, this concerns the details of all directors including brief biographies and the career information that makes them suitable for their appointment. Information on how the board operates (e.g. frequency of meetings and how performance evaluation is undertaken) is also included in this section. This section is particularly important whenever unexpected or unanticipated changes have taken place on the board. Investors, valuing transparency in reporting, would always expect a clear explanation of any sudden departures of senior management or any significant changes in personnel at the top of the company. Providing investor confidence in the board is always important and this extends to a high level of disclosure in board roles and changes in those roles.

The *committee reports* provide the important non-executive input into the report. Specifically, a "best practice" disclosure includes reports from the non-executive-led remuneration, audit, risk and nominations committees. In normal circumstances, greatest interest is shown in the remuneration committee report because this gives the rewards awarded to each director including pension and bonuses. The report on the effectiveness of internal controls is provided based in part on evidence from the audit committee and provides important information for investors.

There is a section on *accounting and audit issues* with specific content on who is responsible for the accounts and any issues that arose in their preparation. Again, usually a matter of routine reporting, this section can be of interest if there have been issues of accounting or auditor failure in the recent past. It is often necessary to signal changes in accounting standards (that may cause changes in reporting) or other changes such as a change in a year-end date or the cause of a restatement of the previous accounts. These are all necessary to provide maximum transparency for the users of the accounts.

Finally there is usually a section containing *other papers and related matters* which, although appearing to be trivial, can be a vital part of the accountability of directors to the shareholders. This section typically contains committee terms of reference, AGM matters, NED contract issues, etc.

Meeting Fin Brun's information needs

Fin Brun is voicing a reasonable and realistic concern to Mr Kava because it is usually difficult to determine the contributions of individual directors (unless there has been some other publicity, positive or negative, throughout the year). The *bonuses awarded to each director* are, however, disclosed in the report of the remuneration committee and this gives an indication of the committee's view on each director's performance. The biographies of all directors, including NEDs, is *included in a best practice disclosure and that can also provide information* on the type of person the director is and an indication of his or her fitness for the job.

Tutorial note: *The examiner instructed markers to "allow for variations in the expression of ideas".*

Answer 8 LUM CO

(a)   **Family and listed company governance**

There are a number of differences between the governance arrangements for a privately-owned family business like Lum and a public company which Lum became after its flotation.

In general, governance arrangements are much more formal for public companies than for family businesses. This is because of the need to be accountable to external shareholders who have no direct involvement in the business. In a family business that is privately owned, shareholders are likely to be members of the extended family and there is usually less need for formal external accountability because there is less of an agency issue.

Linked to this, it is generally the case that larger companies, and public companies in particular, are more highly regulated and have many more stakeholders to manage than privately-owned, smaller or family businesses. The higher public visibility that these businesses have makes them more concerned with maintaining public confidence in their governance and to seek to reassure their shareholders. They use a number of ways of doing this.

For example, public companies must comply with regulations that apply to their stock market listing (listing rules). Although not a legal constraint in a principles-based jurisdiction, listing rules require listed companies to meet certain standard of behaviour and to meet specific conditions. These sometimes include using a unitary board structure and thus, in the case, would require a change in the governance arrangements at Lum.

The more formal governance structures that apply to public companies include the requirement to establish a committee structure and other measures to ensure transparency and a stronger accountability to the shareholders. Such measures include additional reporting requirements that do not apply to family firms.

Crispin's view

It is likely that the flotation will bring about a change in the management culture and style in Lum. Flotations often cause the loss of the family or entrepreneurial culture and this contains both favourable and unfavourable aspects. Whether the company loses the freedom to manage as they wish will depend upon a number of factors:

- Whether Gustav Lum's "wishes" (such as the values and beliefs) are known and trusted by the shareholders. The need for returns to meet shareholder expectations each year often places cost pressures on boards and this, in turn, sometimes challenges a paternalistic management style (such as at Lum) which some investors see as self-indulgent and costly.

- The company will become subject to requirements of listing rules (e.g. relating to corporate governance) and, because of its higher visibility on the stock market, a range of other societal expectations may be placed upon the company. This will have an effect on all aspects of the company's internal systems and norms, including its prior management style. Because of these things, the family will no longer be able to choose how to act in a number of ways, which supports Crispin's view.

- The board of Lum will be subject to influence from institutional investors. They will demand an effective investor relations department, information on a number of issues throughout the year, briefings on final year and interim results and sound explanations whenever performance or behaviour is below expectation. This places the management of Lum in a very different environment to when it was privately owned.

- The board will be under pressure to produce profits against targets each year, which may militate against the company's previous long-term and sustainable commercial approach. If, for example, the long-term approach may have meant taking less profit from a particular operation in one year to leave liquidity or cash in place for a future period, this may become more difficult for a listed company, which can sometimes be under pressure to achieve short-term financial targets such as a dividend payment.

(b)   **Induction and CPD**

Induction for the new NEDs

Induction is a process of orientation and familiarisation that new members of an organisation undergo upon joining. It is designed to make the experience as smooth as possible and to avoid culture or personality clashes, unexpected surprises or other misunderstandings. In the case of the problems with NEDs at Lum, an effective induction programme will enable the new NEDs to gain familiarisation with the norms and culture of Lum. This might be more important for Lum, being at flotation stage and having a deep-seated family culture.

They will be able to gain an understanding of the nature of the company and its business model. This will, as with the culture and norms, be especially relevant for a company like Lum emerging from a long period as a private company with little need to explain its business model to outside parties.

Induction will help NEDs in building a link with people in Lum and other directors. The building of good quality interpersonal links is important in NEDs working effectively. This applies to their relationships with other executive and non-executive directors, and also with relevant people in the company itself. This is especially important in NEDs populating the board committees.

Induction will enable the new NEDs to gain an understanding of key stakeholders and relationships including those with auditors, regulators, key competitors and suppliers. In order to understand the business model operated by Lum, NEDs need to understand its external relationships and how these support the company's operation.

CPD for the existing executives

The purpose of any programme of CPD is to update skills and knowledge as relevant to the professional situation. This will typically involve content on regulation and law, best practice, new developments, etc. Directors should undergo CPD regularly to keep these areas up to date and to ensure they do not "fall behind" on key skills.

In the case of the changes at Lum, another specific benefit of CPD will be learning about working with NEDs and the new board procedures that apply to listed companies. For Lum this involved creating a new unitary board, employing NEDs and generally taking a more consultative approach to decision-making.

They would also benefit from learning about compliance requirements as a listed company. Legal and regulatory frameworks differ between private and public companies. The listing rules that will be imposed by the stock exchange may be seen as an imposition, especially the need to comply with the corporate governance code. This is likely to necessitate a lot of internal change in governance and reporting behaviour and the CPD will help to provide the directors with this support.

After the flotation, the board of Lum gained a number of shareholders other than the Lum family. This would have created a new governance environment and so learning about coping with the expectations of shareholders would also be a benefit of the CPD. This would include, for example, learning about investor relations, dealing with shareholders at an AGM and similar.

(c)   Unitary and two-tier boards

In a unitary board, all directors, including all executive and non-executive directors, are members. All directors are of equal "rank" in terms of their ability to influence strategy and they also all share the collective responsibility in terms of legal and regulatory liability. There is no distinction in constitution or law between strategic oversight and operational management.

In a two-tier board, responsibilities are split between a supervisory or oversight board (chaired by the company chairman), and an operational board (usually chaired by the chief executive). The supervisory board decides on strategic issues and the operational board becomes responsible for executing the strategy determined by the supervisory board.

Responsibilities between the boards are clearly demarcated with the supervisory board responsible for many legal and regulatory compliance issues (e.g. relating to financial reporting). Directors on the lower tier (operational board) do not have the same levels of responsibility or power as those on the supervisory board.

Difficulties for the Lum family

The family will lose the tight control they enjoyed prior to the flotation. In a unitary board, all strategic decisions need to be taken by a full board including the NEDs. It is precisely to prevent small groups of powerful executives from making decisions on their own that the counterweight of the non-executive board was introduced. This may lead to frustration in the family members, which may affect the objectivity of some decisions.

The company will lose the capacity for fast decision-making in the family supervisory board because of the need to involve everybody. Large boards generally meet regularly but on fixed dates. NEDs and other executive directors are likely to seek explanations for decisions taken outside the main board discussions and can act against any members, including family members as the Lum family only controls 20% of the shares.

The change in culture brought about by the governance changes are difficult for the family to manage and the movement to a unitary board is likely to add to the difficulty of this adjustment. The need to consult widely (on a larger board) and to seek consensus are likely to be significant changes for the family. For those used to the family way of managing the company, these changes are likely to be difficult to deal with.

Answer 9 SONIA TAN

(a) **Agency costs**

An agency cost is a cost incurred by the shareholder in monitoring the activities of company agents (i.e. directors). Agency costs are normally considered as "over and above" existing analysis costs and are the costs that arise because of compromised trust in agents (directors). In this case, the increased agency costs that arise are the increased monitoring and "policing" costs that Sentosa House (Sonia) will incur because of the irregular behaviour described in the case.

The first problem identified is Eastern's non-compliance with relevant codes/requirements in respect of non-executive directors and committee structure. There are an insufficient number of NEDs to form the normal committee structure for a public company which means that Sentosa may consider itself to have to monitor some of the risks to Eastern that otherwise the risk committee would undertake.

The investor relations department shows evidence of being unhelpful and uninformed – an unfortunate combination of failings. The chairman appears to be arrogant and potentially untrustworthy (he saw no need for risk committee and dealt very abruptly with Sonia when she called). Finally, the company is pursuing risky strategies with no obvious explanation as to why such strategies are necessary.

In this situation, then, Sentosa House has the choice of selling its holding in Eastern or incurring increased monitoring costs to ensure that its own investors' interests, in turn, are adequately represented.

(b) **Institutional investor intervention**

Intervention by an institutional investor in a company whose stock it holds is usually considered to be radical step and normally represents a step change in agency costs for the investor. This caveat notwithstanding, it is an important "last resort" for institutional investors to have available to them as they seek to adequately represent the interests of their own investors.

There are a number of conditions under which it would be appropriate for institutional investors to intervene in a company whose shares it is holding:

■ Concerns about strategy in terms of products sold, markets serviced, expansions pursued or any other aspect of the company's overall strategic positioning.

■ Its operational performance may give rise, especially if there are one or more segments that have consistently underperformed without adequate explanation.

■ When non-executive directors do not hold executive management to account. There may, for example, be evidence of unaccountable "kitchen cabinets" or curious executive decisions that are not adequately challenged by nonexecutive directors.

■ Consistent or serious failure in internal controls would justify intervention, although this, in turn, may become evident through operational underperformance. On-going or unaddressed failures in, for example, quality assurance, health and safety, environmental emissions, budgetary control or information systems might justify intervention.

■ Failing to comply with the relevant code, laws or stock market rules is the next situation. If the company is listed in a rules-based jurisdiction, it is a matter of law but in a principles-based country, compliance is only "optional" under the stock market's "comply or explain" rules. Consistent or unexplained non-compliance is like to be penalised by the market.

■ Inappropriate remuneration policies, if extreme or obviously self-serving, might attract intervention. Such a situation would normally also signify a failure of the remunerations committee which would make it a double cause for concern.

■ A poor approach to social responsibility is a condition for possible intervention, especially if there is publicly-available evidence that might adversely affect the reputation of the company.

With reference to the case, Eastern Products fail on three counts that might encourage institutional shareholder intervention:

(1)   its failure to comply with relevant code (particularly on number of non-executive directors and lack of risk committee);

(2)   the NEDs are not holding executives to account because there is an insufficient number of them;

(3)   there are concerns about strategy (which is considered to be very risky).

(c)   Risk committee

Risk committees are considered best practice by most corporate governance regimes around the world for a number of reasons. Sonia has, for good reason, doubts over the competence and good faith of the management of Eastern Products and a risk committee made up of non-executive directors could help her confidence in a number of ways.

In the first instance, the information systems put in place to provide information for the risk committee. This would generate awareness of and facilitate review of all relevant risks for discussion by the risk committee, including those arising from the "very risky" strategy.

It would review and assess the effectiveness of internal controls on risk. A committee made up of independent, non-executive directors would bring scrutiny to Thomas on two fronts. There is evidence that Thomas may be relatively inexperienced, having been in post for only two years, and the way that he dealt with Sonia's entirely legitimate enquiry shows some evidence of immaturity and/or impatience. Non-executive presence would be able to challenge and act as a counterweight to this failing. Non-executive directors would also bring scrutiny of Thomas's leadership over strategy, especially (in the context of the risk committee) the wisdom of his "very risky" strategies.

(d)   **Principles-based jurisdiction**

The opinion shows confusion over the meaning of the term "compulsory". Although, in a principles-based jurisdiction, compliance is not legally compulsory, it is required for the stock market listing. Therefore, compliance is effectively compulsory if the company wishes to enjoy the benefits of its listing. Companies in principles-based jurisdictions are subject to "comply or explain" in that non-compliance needs to be explained in terms of specific areas of non-compliance and the reason for noncompliance.

Compliance is also necessary for market confidence in the Eastern Products stock in that the market would be likely to devalue a stock that was a consistent non-complier. Finally, shareholders and stock markets are entitled to challenge the explanation for non-compliance if they are not satisfied with the explanation given in the annual report.

Answer 10 HAITCHLAND

(a)   **CEO's reward package**

Purposes

Reward packages are generally considered to have three purposes: to attract, retain and motivate. To attract means that they must be set at a level adequate to ensure that people with suitable skills will find the post attractive. If the salary is too high, a number of people with the wrong skill levels will be attracted and if it is too low, too few suitable applicants will be attracted.

Retention means ensuring that the level is adequate to prevent a good chief executive from seeking employment elsewhere in order to find a level of reward more suited to his skills and experience. Finally, rewards serve to motivate. This means that there must be enough reward to provide loyalty and a desire to achieve in the role. This is often done by providing a part of the reward in the form of a variable payment linked to corporate performance.

Influencing factors

The market rate is the first factor that influences the reward level. This is what the case meant when it said "commensurate with the importance of the job and in line with other public companies of similar size". The market rate is the transfer value of Mrs Evans if she were to move to a comparable position in another company. In the case, it is evident that the remuneration committee believes this to be double the previous salary she was paid when the gas supplier was owned by the state.

Legal, fiscal or regulatory constraints are relevant in many situations. Public servants, including those employed by state monopolies, are sometimes constrained in their earnings by legislation or maximum differentials (i.e. a compulsory multiple between the highest and lowest paid in an organisation). Mrs Evans's salary had previously been limited because of "government constraints on the salaries of public servants", but the privatisation meant she was now free of this limitation.

The third influencing factors are previous performance in the job (if relevant) and the outcomes of performance reviews. The recommendation of the remuneration committee has clearly based its value of Mrs Evans on her past performance. Based on this, it has not only decided to recommend her retention in post but also the substantial pay increase. The knowledge of her strategic and communications skills is based upon observing her in post when she worked for the nationalised company and, based on these, there is a belief she will perform well in future.

Fourth, stakeholder opinion and ethical considerations are also relevant factors in some situations. Where a CEO is highly visible or in charge of a politically-sensitive organisation, the opinions of stakeholders are sometimes a constraint on what can be paid. This might apply to charities, for example, non-governmental organisations (NGOs) and similar organisations. In the case, Dale Gas appears to be seeking to pay Mrs Evans the increased salary despite the concerns of some in society.

(b)   **"Market risk"**

Definition

Market risk concerns potential losses on capital markets from changes in the value or volatility of a share price or other security. A number of factors give rise to market risk, sometimes referred to as "market or price sensitive" factors including a range of external opportunities and threats. In the case of Dale Gas, an internal factor, the potential loss of a trusted CEO, is thought, by Tom Nwede, to be a source of market risk because her loss would cause a devaluation of Dale Gas shares.

Justification for Tom Nwede's belief the remark

In the context of the case, Mr Nwede was referring to the increased market risk and loss of shareholder value that may arise were the experienced Mrs Evans to be replaced because of the public concern. Increased volatility or a reduction in share price could result in a lower company value and a lower return on investment for the clients of XY Investments and other shareholders in Dale Gas.

Mr Nwede is clearly of the view that Mrs Evans is important for the stability of Dale Gas after its privatisation and for the mitigation of market risk. He is saying that it was important that the protestors and opposing small shareholders did not win in opposing the salary increase as that increase was, he felt, important in retaining and motivating Mrs Evans in the important period ahead.

Shareholders greatly value competent leadership in the companies they invest in, and Mrs Evans was clearly held in high regard by XY Investments and other institutional shareholders. The case highlights her excellent strategic and communication skills, both of which are valued by shareholders. The company will be strategically repositioned because of the privatisation and her communication skills will be necessary in managing the business and in conveying information to shareholders and others.

There were several board changes resulting from the privatisation. This would have meant that some new members were unfamiliar with the gas industry and would need to learn their new roles at a strategically important time for the company. Market uncertainty and hence market risk will be reduced by the continuing presence of an experienced and trustworthy CEO. This would, accordingly, be valued by shareholders in that she would be a source of valuable experience, continuity and stability.

She was respected by, and had the trust of, employees meaning that necessary internal changes could be made. These would be more difficult were a new and less trusted CEO to be brought in (although in other cases, a new CEO can have a positive effect). These changes are deemed necessary and so future shareholder value is likely to depend upon them being competently and fully implemented.

(c) **"Proxy voting"**

Definition

A proxy is a substitute or "other person" that can be nominated to attend a company meeting to exercise the votes of shareholders unable or unwilling to attend in person. The proxy can be the company chairman (where the shareholder agrees with the directors' recommendation on a particular vote) or another person so nominated. It requires the completion of a "proxy form" transferring the shareholder's voting right to the proxy person. A proxy other than the chairman will almost always have highly specific instructions of how to vote on each motion in the meeting. The validity and the number of votes for each proxy are essential in calculating the outcome of each vote.

Advantages

The advantages of the appointment of a proxy include a lower agency cost if fund managers do not need to attend each AGM in person. This becomes more important as the number of individual stocks in a fund increases. Where votes are routine and uncontested, there is no need for fund managers to attend in person and proxy voting (where the proxy is a company officer, such as the chairman) facilitates this absence. In addition, the use of proxies in the case means that fund managers would not need to face the added pressure of being confronted by the smaller shareholders' protest. These are likely to be seen as an irritation by Mr Nwede with no possibility of them changing his voting were he to attend in person.

Answer 11 GEELAND

(a) **Rules and principles-based approaches to corporate governance**

Distinction

There are two broad approaches to the regulation of corporate governance provisions: rules-based and principles-based. In a rules-based country (jurisdiction), all provisions are legal rules, underpinned by law, transgression against which is punishable in law. Often characterised as a "box ticking" approach, full compliance is required by all companies at all times (excepting where dispensations are granted, again, under the provisions of the law).

In a principles-based jurisdiction, legal force applies to the provisions of company laws but additional listing rules are enforced on a "comply or explain" basis. It is important to note that compliance is not voluntary in that the provisions can be ignored, but that provisions may not be complied with in full, usually for a limited period if the full reason for non-compliance is explained to the shareholders. This allows for the market to judge the seriousness of the non-compliance and to potentially re-appraise or revalue the company as a result.

Critical evaluation of stock exchange guidance

The remark in the Geeland Code strongly argues in favour of a principles-based approach to corporate governance. In particular, it is critical of rules-based codes that would, for example, place a blanket ban on combining the roles of chairman and chief executive. In order to allow for differences between circumstances, it is arguing for flexibility and "common sense".

Arguments for

In most cases, compliance with general principles is cheaper than compliance with a detailed "box ticking" regime. A common criticism of rules-based approaches is the expense of compliance including the establishment of information systems to meet reporting requirements (for example on internal controls), consultancy costs, increased management costs and reporting costs. Where some flexibility is possible, the principles-based approach allows some "common sense" to be employed in the extent of detailed compliance.

A principles-based approach is flexible and allows companies to develop their own approach, perhaps with regard to the demands of their own industry or shareholder preferences. This places the emphasis on investor needs rather than legal demands. There may be no reason, for example, why companies in lower risk industries should be constrained by the same internal control reporting requirements as companies in higher risk industries. As long as shareholders recognise and are satisfied with this, the cost advantages can be enjoyed.

An example of the flexibility afforded by a principles-based approach is that it allows for transitional arrangements and unusual circumstances. Details such as the contract terms of directors may need to be varied to meet individual needs or the notice periods might similarly be varied. In the event of a sudden, unexpected change such as a death in service, a company can enter a phase of technical non-compliance but, with suitable explanation of the reason for non-compliance, most shareholders will nevertheless be satisfied.

It avoids the need for expensive and inconvenient monitoring and support structures, the costs of which are ultimately borne by the companies themselves (through stock market or regulatory bodies) or by the taxpayer. The costs and inconvenience of policing compliance with rules has been shown to be material in some situations, especially in smaller companies. Similarly, the costs of a large national "watchdog" to monitor and enforce detailed compliance are considerable.

Arguments against

There may be confusion over what is compulsory under law and what is principles-driven under listing rules. A lack of clarity might be present, especially where compliance expertise is not available to management (such as in some smaller companies) between legally-required compliance and listing rules which are subject to comply or explain. This may confuse some management teams and cause non-compliance borne of lack of advice and information.

A principles-based approach assumes that markets are capable of understanding the seriousness of any temporary or lengthier periods of non-compliance and of revaluing the shares as a result. Non-specialist shareholders may not understand why a given provision is not complied with nor appreciate the potential consequences of the non-compliance. Cleverly-worded comply or explain statements might mislead shareholders.

A "box ticking" approach offers the advantage of gaining full compliance at all times (i.e. all boxes are actually ticked) whereas a principles-based approach allows some bad practice to continue. A full compliance regime is likely to provide a greater overall confidence in regulation and this, in turn, will further support long-term shareholder value.

A rules-based approach provides standardisation and prevents any individual companies gaining competitive or cost advantages with lower levels of compliance. This creates a "level playing field" in which all competitors in an industry understand what is required.

(b)   Separation of roles of chairman and chief executive

The strongest and most common reason for the separation of these roles is to avoid the dangers of unfettered power that may arise when power is concentrated in a single, powerful individual. The original proposition for the separation of roles was in the UK's Cadbury Report in 1992 which was itself a response to a number of corporate "scandals", similar to those in Geeland, involving unfettered power and the abuse of shareholder wealth as a result.

Accountability is better served by the separation of roles because the chief executive has a named person, in addition to the non-executive directors (NEDs), to whom he must account for the company's performance and his own behaviour. This serves to protect against conflicts of interest where chief executives may be tempted to act in their own self-interest rather than to serve the best interests of the shareholders.

Third, both roles are complex and demanding. In large companies, it is likely that the two roles cannot be carried out effectively by one person. By gaining the advantages of a separation of duties (and hence a division of labour), the performance of the company's management in total will be enhanced. The two roles are materially different in terms of their skills, and it enhances organisational effectiveness for one to chair the board (chairman) and another, with different skills, to manage the strategy of the company. It is usual for the chairman role to be undertaken by a NED, whilst the chief executive is an executive director. Having this distinction at the top of the company allows the chief executive to be hands on and directly involved in the management of the company, whilst the chairman can adopt a more supervisory position.

Finally, it is considered best practice because it provides a reassurance to investors and ensures compliance with relevant codes. Investor confidence in company management is very important and this is enhanced by having a transparent and clear separation of roles. Where codes specify separation and this can be demonstrated, unlike at Anson Company, unqualified comply or explain statements can be issued thereby promoting investor confidence.

(c)   Assessment of "comply or explain" statement

The statement clearly identifies the one area of non-compliance and represents a full discharge of the company's reporting obligation to comply or explain. In a principles-based jurisdiction, this statement is required under listing rules and involves informing shareholders of the level of compliance and also specifying any areas of non-compliance, which the company has done in this case.

It is clear and free of ambiguity in what it says. Clearly though, one area of non-compliance is explained. The area of non-compliance is identified and the individual is named. The naming of William Klunker may be material because if he is known and trusted by shareholders, the breach may be less important than if he were less known and less trusted.

It does not provide a good reason for the non-compliance other than saying that it was "benefiting from having Mr Klunker in control" which might be seen as weak by some investors. The reasons for combining the roles in July 2009 are not given and so it could probably be argued that this is not a full explanation.

It does, however, provide a date for returning to full compliance against which management can be held accountable for failure. This will reassure investors that its period of non-compliance is temporary and the default position of the company is to remain in full compliance with the relevant code.

Answer 12 ZOGS COMPANY

(a)   **Independence of NEDs**

Independence is a quality possessed by individuals and refers to the avoidance of being unduly influenced by a vested interest. This freedom enables a more objective position to be taken on issues compared to those who consider vested interests or other loyalties.

Independence of non-executive directors (NEDs) can be threatened by over-familiarity with the executive board, which is why many corporate governance codes have measures in place to prevent this. These include restrictions on share option schemes for NEDs, time-limited appointments and bans on cross-directorships. Other restrictions, depending on jurisdiction and code, include salaries being set at an appropriate level, a compulsory number of years after leaving the service of a company before being eligible for a NED role with that company (if ever), a similar requirement relating to business relationships, and no close personal relationships between executives and non-executives.

Consideration of NED independence

In the case of the independence of non-executive directors, Mr Louse is arguing that those with no previous contact with the other members of the board and who come from outside the industry that Zogs is in, will be more independent than those who may have some form of vested interest. In this he is only partly accurate: whilst succession to a NED role from an executive position in the same company is likely to threaten independence, appointments to NED positions from other companies within the same sector are quite common and still provide industry knowledge to a board. The benefits of greater independence include:

- Independent people brought in as NEDs are less likely to have prior vested interests in terms of material business relationships that might influence judgments or opinions. Such vested interests may involve friendships with other board members or past professional relationships. Past or current equity holdings in companies within the industry may encourage unhelpful loyalties (many CG codes restrict NEDs from holding shares or share options in companies they are on the boards of).

- Independent people are likely to have fewer prejudices for or against certain policies or individuals as working relationships will not have been built up over a number of years. Accordingly, they are likely to start from the "ground up" in seeking clarifications and explanations for each area of discussion. Previous rivalries, alliances or embedded ideas would not frustrate discussions and this may allow for more objective discussions.

- Independent non-executive directors are more likely to challenge the established beliefs of less independent people (such as executive directors). This is a more effective way of scrutinising the work of board committees and of increasing their effectiveness. This has the advantage of challenging orthodoxy and bringing fresh perspectives to committee discussions.

On the other hand, some NEDs are appointed because of their connections with the existing board, either through prior industry involvement, prior executive membership or prior service on another board with one or more other directors. These are considered by Mr Louse to be less independent.

There are, however, a number of advantages when NEDs have some familiarity with a company and board they are joining. A key non-executive role, including in board committees, is providing strategic advice. This can often arise from a thorough knowledge of the strategic issues in a company or industry. Retired executive directors, like Mr Louse, sometimes serve as NEDs in the same company and are thus able to bring their experience of that industry and company to bear on committee discussions (although in some countries, there are time restrictions on executives becoming NEDs in the same company).

A prior connection is advantageous when some level of technical knowledge is required. Therefore, Mr Louse's comment about independence depending upon NEDs' needing to be from a different industry background or sector is not quite appropriate. When serving on an appointments committee, for example, knowledge of the industry and the technical aspects of a company's operations will increase effectiveness. This might apply in electronics, chemicals, accounting services and financial services, for example. When serving on a risk committee in, for example, a bank, a technical knowledge of key risks specific to that particular industry can be very important.

The contacts and personal networks that a NED with industry experience can bring may be of advantage, especially for informal discussions when serving on a nominations committee, for example.

(b)   **Risk committees**

Five general roles

(1)   Agreeing and approving the organisation's risk management strategy, including strategies for strategic risks. This is likely to be drawn up in discussion with other parts of the organisation, including the main board.

(2)   Reviewing reports on key risks prepared by departments on operational risks. These might be reports from operations (e.g. production), finance or technical departments on risks that specifically may affect them.

(3)   Monitoring overall risk exposure and ensures it remains within the limits established by the main board. Exposure is generally defined as the totality of losses that could occur and the acceptable exposure will vary according to the risk strategy. Some organisations accept a higher exposure than others because of their varying risk appetites.

(4)   Assessing the effectiveness of risk management systems and policies. This is usually based on past data, where a risk has materialised, or "stress testing" of systems where the risk has not yet materialised.

(5)   Approving and agreeing any statements or disclosures made to internal or external audiences, such as risk reporting to analysts or in the annual report. Shareholders have the right to expect accurate and relevant reports on the risks in their investments, and so any reports issued outside the company need to be approved by the risk committee.

Mr Louse has a weak understanding of the roles and purposes of a risk committee, for example "stopping risks affecting" companies is not within the remit of a risk committee. Some risks affect everybody including businesses; others apply because of industry membership, geographical location, business activity, strategic positioning or business strategy. The role of a risk committee is to identify, review and construct a strategy for managing those risks.

He also complained that the risk committee was "always asking for more information, which was inconvenient". Gathering information is a crucial part of a risk committee's role and it is in the company's overall interest to ensure that information supplied to the risk committee is accurate, current and complete.

He misunderstands the nature of the committee's role if he perceives it to be "gloomy and pessimistic". This is an understandable but unfair criticism. Risks are, by their nature, things that might go wrong or potential liabilities, but the reason why risks need to be understood is to ensure the ongoing success and prosperity of Zogs Company, and that is a very positive thing.

Finally, he wrongly believed that all material risks were external risks and so the risk committee should be looking outwards and not inwards. Risks can be internal or external to the company and many internal risks can be highly material such as financial risks, liquidity risks, operational risks, etc.

(c)   **Risk in small v large companies**

Small companies exist in different strategic environments to large companies and because of this, a number of differences apply when it comes to corporate governance systems. There are a number of compliance issues, for example, where large companies are required to comply with provisions that smaller companies are not. Some of the differences in regulation and shareholder expectations are driven by differences in the legal status of the organisation (e.g. whether incorporated, whether listed, where domiciled, etc).

In the case of risk management systems in smaller companies, there will be a lower overall (aggregate) loss to shareholders than in a large company in the event of a major risk being realised. In larger companies, especially listed companies, a major event can affect markets around the world and this can affect the value of many investment funds (e.g., pension funds). This is unlikely to be the case in any given smaller company.

Many smaller companies, including SmallCo, are privately owned and they are therefore not subject to listing rules and, in some cases, other legal regulations. In many smaller companies, any loss of value when a risk is realised is a personal loss to owners and does not affect a high number of relatively "disconnected" shareholders as would be the case in a large public company.

Risk probability and impact is often correlated with size. Smaller companies have fewer risks because of their lower profiles, fewer stakeholders and less complex systems than larger organisations. Accordingly, the elaborate risk management systems are less necessary in smaller companies and could be a disproportionate use of funds. This is not to say that smaller companies do not face risks, of course, but that the impacts, say to shareholders or society, are less with a smaller rather than a larger company because of the totality of the losses incurred.

The costs of risk monitoring and control may often outweigh the impacts of losses being incurred from risks, if not in a single financial period then maybe over a period of years. There are substantial set-up fixed costs in establishing some risk management systems and, in some cases, variable costs also (e.g. linked to production output). With fewer total risks, there could be less value for money in having risk controls.

In summary, risk committees and risk mitigation systems are more important in larger companies than in smaller companies. However it is good practice for all companies, however small, to carry out some form of risk monitoring in order to remain competitive in their environment.

Tutorial note: *Notice the parallels between small and large firm implementation of corporate governance codes.*

Answer 13 OLAND

(a) **Sound corporate governance**

Corporate governance is the system by which organisations are directed and controlled. A sound system of corporate governance, whether rules or principles-based, is capable of reducing company failures in a number of ways:

- It addresses issues of management, management succession and alignment of board interests with those of shareholders. This reduces the agency problem and makes it less likely that management will promote their own self-interests above those of shareholders. By promoting longer-term shareholder interests over personal or short-term interests, companies are less likely to come under the types of pressures that might lead to failure.

- A sound system of corporate governance helps to identify and manage the wide range of risks that a company can face, some of which will be capable of causing the company to fail. These might arise from changes in the internal or external environments, and most codes specify a strict set of management procedures for identifying and controlling such risks.

- An effective code will specify a range of effective internal controls that will ensure the effective use of resources and the minimisation of waste, fraud, and the misuse of company assets. Internal controls are necessary for maintaining the efficient and effective operation of a business, whereas weak or absent controls are more likely to lead to the conditions that could threaten its survival.

- Effective codes encourage reliable and complete external reporting of financial data and a range of other voluntary disclosures. By using this information, investors can establish what is going on in the company and will have advanced warning of any problems. This need to report creates an accountability of management to shareholders and restricts the types of actions and behaviours likely to threaten company survival.

- Compliance with a code underpins investor confidence and gives shareholders a belief that their investments are being responsibly managed. This confidence extends to other stakeholders such as tax authorities, industry regulators and others, some of whom can cause a great deal of trouble for the company if they believe the company is being poorly managed.

- Sound corporate governance will encourage and attract new investment of share capital and also make it more likely that lenders will extend credit and provide increased loan capital if needed. This could help some companies survive in difficult times in terms of cash flow and capital requirements when companies with poorer corporate governance reputations may receive less of such support.

(b) **Rules and principles based approaches**

In a rules-based approach to corporate governance, provisions are made in law and a breach of any applicable provision is therefore a legal offence. This means that companies become legally accountable for compliance and are liable for prosecution in law for failing to comply with the detail of a corporate governance code or other provision.

A principles-based approach works by (usually) a stock market requiring compliance with a detailed code a condition of listing. Shareholders are then encouraged to insist on a high level of compliance in the belief that higher compliance is more robust than lower compliance. When, for whatever reason, a company is unable to comply in detail with every provision of a code, the listing rules state that the company must explain, usually in its annual report, exactly where it fails to comply and the reason why it is unable to comply. The shareholders, and not the law, then judge for themselves the seriousness of the breach. This is what Martin Mung meant by markets punishing bad practice.

Comply or explain is intended to allow latitude in compliance with details of corporate governance provision, but is not "optional" in the usual meaning of the term. Listing rules insist on compliance with codes in many countries with "comply or explain" allowed when compliance with detail is not possible or desirable, usually in the short to medium term. If the shareholders are not satisfied with the explanation for lack of compliance, they can punish the board by several means including holding them directly accountable at general meetings, by selling shares (thereby reducing the value of the company) or by direct intervention if a large enough shareholder.

Comply or explain

Comply or explain is seen as an alternative to a rigid "rules-based" approach and is effective for the following reasons:

- It enables the policing of compliance by those who own the entity and have a stronger vested interest in compliance than state regulators who monitor compliance in a legal sense. This places the responsibility for compliance upon the investors who are collectively the legal owners of the company.

- It makes the company accountable directly to shareholders who can decide for themselves on the materiality of any given non-compliance.

- It reduces the costs of compliance and recognises that "one size" does not fit all. There may be legitimate reasons for temporary or semi-permanent non-compliance with the detail of a corporate governance code, perhaps because of size or the company adopting its own unique approach for highly specific and context-dependent reasons.

- It avoids the need for inflexible legislation, which, itself, is sometimes also ineffective. Whereas the effectiveness of a "comply or explain" principles-based approach relies on the ability and willingness of shareholders and capital markets to enforce compliance, rules-based approaches rely on the effectiveness of law enforcement officials.

(c)   **Accountability**

Boards of directors are accountable to the shareholders of the company. This means they are answerable to them in that they can be called to give an account for their behaviour and actions as agents of the shareholders.

In the context of the corporate governance code, it is recognised that boards do not always fully reflect the wishes and needs of shareholders and this can represent a failure of accounting from the board to the shareholders. The measures proposed aim to close that gap and make it less likely that unqualified or ill-equipped people will be appointed to, or remain on, the board.

Re-election of directors

Corporate governance codes have had provisions for the retirement of directors by rotation for some time. This is when a fixed period of time is set for directorships, after which the default position is that the director retires or leaves the service of the company unless actively re-elected by the shareholders to serve another term in office. Enhancing accountability to shareholders is a key objective of any corporate governance code. The shortening of service contracts from three years to one year may result in greater accountability for the following reasons:

It will enable shareholders to remove underperforming directors much more quickly and to impose their will upon a board with less delay than previously. Rather than paying for underperforming directors to remain in post, with possible damage to the company as a result, or by paying out severance costs, they can simply decide not to re-elect them at the end of the one-year service contract.

It will enable shareholders to rebalance or refresh a board in the light of environmental changes or changes in strategy, rather than waiting for a period of time for the three-year terms of previously re-elected directors to elapse. This would make the company more responsive to the wishes of shareholders and reduce the feeling that any director has a "right" to be on the board at any point. However, a shorter period may leave the board under greater pressure to demonstrate short term success and that could be at the expense of longer term prosperity.

The availability of biographical details will enable shareholders to clearly see the experience of a candidate and decide for themselves whether they are likely to add value at a given point. The effect of this will be to act as a "check and balance" against vested interests that may exist between and among directors. It also places a responsibility upon candidates seeking election or re-election to a board to actively demonstrate their suitability rather than just expecting it as an entitlement.

Answer 14 CORPORATE SOCIAL RESPONSIBILITY

(a) **Term**

The unprecedented growth in power of corporations over the last half century, together with an informed and educated general public, created a real threat to the legitimacy of the corporation within society, which the concept of corporate social responsibility (CSR) has sought to counteract.

Exactly what "social responsibility" means varies according to the industry, company and location. But whether it was reforestation or cutting down on pollution or increasing diversity in the workforce, social responsibility was the term used to capture those activities of a corporation that were beneficial to society.

According to Carroll, CSR encompasses the economic, legal, ethical and philanthropic expectations placed on organisations by society at a given point in time. Ashridge College in the UK considers CSR to be "the obligation that organisations have to act responsibly towards the social and environmental context in which they operate. This means at least the need to protect society and the environment from harm and perhaps the need to actually add value in these areas – it's a move away from just considering profit and shareholder value into broader awareness of the role of business in society"

CSR is the consciousness of businesses in a free enterprise world that business is not merely for profits, but also with promoting desirable social ends like providing employments, elimination of promotion, avoiding pollution and whatever good that will benefit society.

These words were however rejected by economists like Adam Smith and Milton Friedman who felt that the doctrine of social responsibility is not so much as market mechanisms but more a political process.

(b) **Company activities**

Examples of activities that could be described as showing awareness of CSR are:

- Provision of social and sporting facilities for workers and the local community.

- Supporting specific charities through resource donations including money, materials, supplies and manpower.

- Making donations to relief work especially to natural disasters cause by flooding, earthquakes and many other types of relief works for famine, droughts and hunger.

- Capital expenditures approved for building pollution and environmental preventive systems or constructions to safe guard people around the company's factory or project sites (such expenditures may not necessarily be required by any laws or regulations).

- Providing safety and protective clothing and equipment to workers and employees in work places that are deemed high risk to health beyond the requirements of law or regulations.

- Providing educational and medical facilities to the local communities of third world suppliers.

- Developing specific drugs to assist in aid programs and delivering them at cost or for free (e.g. river blindness).

(c) **Argument for**

Directors of a company, as agents, must act in the interests of the owners of the company, the shareholders. They have a fiduciary duty to act in good faith in the best interests of the company. But in maximising the wealth of shareholders, directors cannot afford to ignore the effect of stakeholders (stakeholder theory).

Milton Friedman argued that a society determines and meets its needs and wants through the market place where the self-interest pursuit by business happens to result in society getting what it wants. Corporations have no responsibilities other than making a profit for shareholders through economic and legal means. Only human beings have moral responsibility for their actions. Social issues are the province of the state and not corporations, thus corporate social responsibility is not appropriate – "The business of business is …. business".

However, with the development of corporate governance and stakeholder awareness and activism, companies engage in CSR as they perceive doing so will improve their profits (e.g. ethical buyers will only buy from ethical companies).

In selecting CSR issues, a company's board should avoid reacting to external pressures (or the latest "fads") unless by doing so, value is added to the business. Only those issues that create business value and can be linked to the company's core business and sustainability in the long-run should be considered.

Swanson (1995) suggested that there were three main types of motivation for CSR:

- the utilitarian perspective (an instrument to help achieve performance objectives);

- the negative duty approach (compulsion to adopt socially responsible initiatives to appease stakeholders); and

- the positive duty view (businesses self-motivated regardless of social pressures).

In either case, adapting CSR is crucial for good corporate governance as:

- Organisations that are seen as ethically and morally sound attract better business (e.g. customers, suppliers, additional finance). Those considered unsound are boycotted.

- Employees are more attracted to work for, and are more committed to, socially responsible companies.

- Positive contribution to society will be a long-term investment in a safer, better educated and more equitable community creating a more stable context in which to do business.

- Companies are motivated to involve stakeholders in their decision-making and to address social challenges. Stakeholders are increasingly aware of the importance and effect of corporate decisions on society and the environment and thus need to judge the company on its CSR.

- Differentiating the company in the marketplace based on its corporate responsibility strategy and commitments;

- Maintaining a (social) license to operate with the public or specific stakeholders;

- Attracting favourable financing conditions as financial markets wake up to ESG (environmental, social, and governance) issues and demand better information on social and environmental performance;

- Encouraging innovation through a better understanding of stakeholder needs or future risks;

- Enhancing reputation by providing truthful and robust information on tough issues

All the above will result in greater long-term wealth being generated by the organisation.

(d) **Corporate social responsibility and integrated reporting**

Integrated reporting refers to a reporting process based on integrated thinking. Integrated thinking is the active consideration by an organisation of the relationships between its various operating and functional units and the capitals that the organisation uses or affects.

Integrated thinking leads to integrated decision-making and actions that consider the creation of value over the short, medium and long term.

Integrated reporting can be viewed as a development in response to the greater focus worldwide on corporate social responsibility.

- The integrated reporting process helps an organisation communicate how it is socially responsible to a broad range of stakeholders including employees, customers, suppliers, business partners, local communities, legislators, regulators and policy-makers.

- The integrated report helps to communicate social responsibility by recognising that value is created through relationships with stakeholders.

- The integrated report communicates social responsibility because it reports how the capitals (financial, manufactured, intellectual, human, social and relationship, and natural) of an organisation interact with the external environment.

- The integrate report helps to communicate social responsibility because it provides information on the resources and relationships affected by the organisation.

Answer 15 SHAREHOLDERS AND ANNUAL GENERAL MEETINGS

(a)   **Private and institutional shareholders**

Tutorial note: Candidates are not expected to know a lot about private equity and venture capital but should be sufficiently familiar with private and institutional investors to obtain at least a pass mark.

Private shareholders are individual persons or entities investing in a listed company. Private investors are not, themselves, members of the financial community but hold shares in a private and individual capacity. The vast majority of private personal shareholders will only individually hold a small fraction of the shares issued within any one company.

However, in some situations individuals may hold a controlling shareholding within an entity. Where the controlling interest is owned by another company, then a group situation arises.

Institutional shareholders are organisations that hold, invest and trade large volumes of shares and securities in their own right. They include mutual funds, hedge funds, pensions, insurance companies, trusts, banks, governments and fund managers of various other investment companies that hold shares in a listed company. Such investors may hold between 1% and 5% (or more) of a company's share capital and account for the significant majority of daily trades on stock exchanges.

An institutional private shareholder variant is private equity and venture capital. This is the finance provided in return for an equity stake in potentially high growth unlisted companies. Instead of going to the stock market and selling shares to raise capital, private equity firms raise funds from sources such as pension funds, endowments, and high net worth individuals. Private equity firms use these funds, along with borrowed money, to invest in underperforming companies that have the potential for high growth.

Venture capital is a specific component of the private equity industry and refers to when funds are used to invest in companies in the seed (concept), start-up (within three years of the company's establishment) and early stages of development. In general venture capital funds invest in companies at an early stage in their development when they often have little or no track record and are cash-hungry. In contrast, private equity funds invest in more mature companies with the aim to eliminate inefficiencies and drive growth.

(b)   **Treatment of minority shareholders**

In general terms a minority shareholder is one who is not a majority shareholder (i.e. one entitled to the rights of not less than 50% of a class of equity shares). A minority shareholder clearly does not have voting control.

More specifically, in many jurisdictions (for legal and tax purposes) a minority shareholder is a shareholder (individual or company) holding less than a specified percentage of paid-up capital of company (typically 5%). Above this benchmark a shareholding may then be regarded as "substantial". Minority shareholders hold such small percentages that they have little stakeholder power in annual general meetings, unless they are able to effectively organise themselves into a pressure group.

Without legal or corporate governance protection, majority shareholders are most likely to treat minority shareholders unfairly by oppressing or suppressing them. For example, suggestions of minorities may be ignored or they may not be given the chance even to give their views and opinions (e.g. at general meetings).

Oppressive conduct is an expansive term that covers a multitude of situations dealing with improper conduct. Courts may determine according to the facts of a particular case, whether the acts complained of serve to frustrate the legitimate expectations of minority shareholders, or whether the acts are of such severity as to warrant the relief requested.

Typical examples of unfair treatment of minority shareholders by majority shareholders include:

- refusal to declare dividends;

- refusal to distribute earnings as bonuses or retirement benefits;

- siphoning off earnings through exorbitant salaries and bonuses to management shareholders;

- termination of employment (equivalent to a denial of dividends or any return on investment);

- removal as directors or officers (or effectively depriving minority shareholders any active voice or meaningful role in management and operation of the company);

- issuing shares to majority nominees thus diluting minority holdings;

- deliberate withholding of information (e.g. of shareholder meetings) or manipulation of company books and records;

- holding shareholder meetings at inconvenient locations for, or refusing entry to, minority shareholders

Squeeze-out techniques, as above, are used to "lock in" a minority shareholder for two reasons:

- to force a sale of a minority interest at less than a fair price; and
- to "freeze out" the minority of a fair return on investment.

(c)   **Rights and equitable treatment**

The OECD principles contain the following provisions relating to the rights and equitable treatment of shareholders:

Rights

- Secure methods of ownership, registration, and transfer of shares.

- Shareholders to receive relevant information on the corporation on a timely and regular basis including the voting procedures that govern general shareholder meetings.

- To participate in, and to be sufficiently informed on, decisions concerning fundamental corporate changes including effective participation in general shareholder meetings.

Equitable treatment

- All shareholders have effective redress for violation of their rights.

- All shareholders of the same series of a class are treated equally.

- Minority shareholders are protected from abusive actions of the majority holders.

- Any changes in voting rights are approved by those classes of shares which are negatively affected.

- Processes and procedures for general shareholder meetings allow for equitable treatment of all shareholders.

- Insider trading and abusive self-dealing prohibited.

- Members of the board and key executives disclose to the board whether they, directly, indirectly or on behalf of third parties, have a material interest in any transaction or matter directly affecting the corporation.

(d) **Recommendations for AGM**

The Malaysian Code on Corporate Governance, for example, recommends that the quality of AGMs could be improved in the following ways:

- giving shareholders sufficient time to present their views and opinions on matters that concern them;

- encouraging, rather than suppressing, their participation in enquiring into the company's affairs, particularly the financial and other transactions of the company;

- ensuring all directors (executive and non-executive) and management are present and that relevant questions be directed to the director concerned; and

- providing answers to shareholders' questions raised at the AGM at a later date, if they were not answered at the AGM.

As noted above, the OECD recommends that:

- processes and procedures for general shareholder meetings allow for equitable treatment of all shareholders.

In the UK, shareholders are protected by significant requirements enacted within company law including the need to give adequate notice of meetings, full agenda and details of resolutions, ability to place resolutions on the agenda (usually requires a minimum holding or number of supporters), suitable premises to allow easy access and accommodation of expected number of shareholders.

Because of the extensive legal requirements, the UK Corporate Governance Code primarily concentrates on the use of proxy voting that allows any shareholder to cast their vote without the need to attend the meeting and the need for all directors to attend the AGM.

Answer 16 GLUCK AND GOODMAN

(a)　　**Internal control and audit**

(i)　　*General objectives of internal control*

An internal control system comprises the whole network of systems established in an organisation to provide reasonable assurance that organisational objectives will be achieved.

Specifically, the general objectives of internal control are as follows:

To ensure the orderly and efficient conduct of business in respect of systems being in place and fully implemented. Controls mean that business processes and transactions take place without disruption with less risk or disturbance and this, in turn, adds value and creates shareholder value.

To safeguard the assets of the business. Assets include tangibles and intangibles, and controls are necessary to ensure they are optimally utilised and protected from misuse, fraud, misappropriation or theft.

To prevent and detect fraud. Controls are necessary to show up any operational or financial disagreements that might be the result of theft or fraud. This might include off-balance sheet financing or the use of unauthorised accounting policies, inventory controls, use of company property and similar.

To ensure the completeness and accuracy of accounting records. All accounting transactions must be completely and accurately recorded, assets and liabilities correctly identified and valued and all costs and revenues accounted for.

To ensure the timely preparation of financial information which applies to statutory reporting (e.g. year end accounts) and also management accounts, if appropriate, to facilitate effective management decision-making.

(ii)　　*Factors affecting the need for internal audit and controls*

Tutorial note: *This answer is based partly on Turnbull guidance.*

The nature of operations within the organisation arising from its sector, strategic positioning and main activities.

The scale and size of operations including factors such as the number of employees. It is generally assumed that larger and more complex organisations have a greater need for internal controls and audit than smaller ones owing to the number of activities occurring that give rise to potential problems.

Cost/benefit considerations. Management must weigh the benefits of instituting internal control and audit systems against the costs of doing so. This is likely to be an issue for medium-sized companies or companies experiencing growth.

Internal or external changes affecting activities, structures or risks. Changes arising from new products or internal activities can change the need for internal audit and so can external changes such as PESTEL factors.

Problems with existing systems, products and/or procedures including any increase in unexplained events. Repeated or persistent problems can signify the need for internal control and audit.

The need to comply with external requirements from relevant stock market regulations or laws. This appears to be a relevant factor at Gluck & Goodman.

(b) **Criticisms**

The audit committee is chaired by an executive director. One of the most important roles of an audit committee is to review and monitor internal controls. An executive director is not an independent person and so having Mr Chester as chairman undermines the purpose of the committee as far as its role in governance is concerned.

Mr Chester, the audit committee chairman, considers only financial controls to be important and undermines the purpose of the committee as far as its role in governance is concerned. There is no recognition of other risks and there is a belief that management accounting can provide all necessary information. This viewpoint fails to recognise the importance of other control mechanisms such as technical and operational controls.

Mr Hardanger's performance was trusted without supporting evidence because of his reputation as a good manager. An audit committee must be blind to reputation and treat all parts of the business equally. All functions can be subject to monitor and review without "fear or favour" and the complexity of the production facility makes it an obvious subject of frequent attention.

The audit committee does not enjoy the full support of the non-executive chairman, Mr Allejandra. On the contrary in fact, he is sceptical about its value. In most situations, the audit committee reports to the chairman and so it is very important that the chairman protects the audit committee from criticism from executive colleagues, which is unlikely given the situation at Gluck and Goodman.

There is no internal auditor to report to the committee and hence no flow of information on which to make control decisions.

Internal auditors are the operational "arms" of an audit committee and without them, the audit committee will have little or no relevant data on which to monitor and review control systems in the company.

The ineffectiveness of the internal audit could increase the cost of the external audit. If external auditors view internal controls as weak they would be likely to require increased attention to audit trails, etc that would, in turn, increase cost.

(c)   **Market risk**

Definition of market risk

Market risks are those arising from any of the markets that a company operates in. Most common examples are those risks from resource markets (inputs), product markets (outputs) or capital markets (finance).

Tutorial note: *Alternative definitions of market risk would be acceptable. IFRS 7, for example, offers a technical definition: "Market risk is the risk that the fair value or cash flows of a financial instrument will fluctuate due to changes in market prices. Market risk reflects interest rate risk, currency risk, and other price risks".*

Why non-compliance increases market risk

The lack of a fully compliant committee structure (such as having a non-compliant audit committee) erodes investor confidence in the general governance of a company. This will, over time, affect share price and hence company value. Low company value will threaten existing management (possibly with good cause in the case of Gluck and Goodman) and make the company a possible takeover target. It will also adversely affect price-earnings and hence market confidence in Gluck and Goodman's shares. This will make it more difficult to raise funds from the stock market.

Answer 17 TREADWAY COMMISSION

(a)   **Distinction between rules-based and principles-based approaches**

This case refers to compliance relating to internal control systems in particular but rules and principles are the two generic approaches to corporate governance and depend on the nature of regulation. Rules-based control is when behaviour is underpinned and prescribed by statute of the country's legislature. Compliance is therefore enforceable in law such that companies can face legal action if they fail to comply.

In a principles-based jurisdiction, compliance is required under stock market listing rules but non-compliance is allowed based on the premise of full disclosure of all areas of non-compliance. It is believed that the market mechanism is then capable of valuing the extent of non-compliance and signalling to the company when an unacceptable level of compliance is reached.

Benefits to an organisation of a principles-based approach

There are four main benefits:

(1)   It avoids the need for strict compliance with inflexible legislation which, typically, fails to account for differences in size and the risk profiles of specific companies or sectors.

(2)   This means that compliance is less burdensome in time and expenditure for the organisation as the minutiae of general legislation can be interpreted in context rather than obeyed in detail.

(3)   It allows companies to develop their own sector and situation-specific approaches to internal control challenges. These will typically depend on each company's interpretation of its own internal control challenges. For example, physical controls over cash will be vital to some businesses and less relevant or not applicable to others.

(4)   This, in turn, allows for flexibility and temporary periods of non-compliance with relevant external standards on the basis of "comply or explain", a flexibility that would not be possible in a rules-based jurisdiction.

(b)   **Non-industry specific (i.e. general) advantages of internal controls**

The advantages and benefits of internal controls are partly as described in COSO's reasons. The case describes these benefits in terms of enjoying "greater internal productivity and producing higher quality reporting". In addition, internal control underpins investor confidence, ensures compliance with internal and external control measures and facilitates the provision of management reports as needed.

Mr Rogalski is incorrect in his view that controls need to be industry sector specific to be effective. The effective and efficient performance of businesses of all kinds rest on the observance of well-designed and tightly-monitored internal controls. Waste in the form of lost time, wasted resources, faults and other costs are avoided. Efficiency is increased by conformance to standards designed to support productivity. However, the types of controls in place and the systems supporting them will differ from sector to sector.

The information gained from compliance with internal control measures is used in the preparation of content for internal and external reporting. This is especially applicable to the external reporting on internal controls such as under Sarbanes Oxley s.404 which is mandatory in the US. Other national codes have similar provisions.

Where compliance with agreed standards is an important part of the business, internal control data allows for this. This can be industry sector-specific but the general principles of effective control apply to all types of organisations: internal control data is needed to demonstrate compliance. Examples of sector specific internal controls (for managing sector-specific risks) include measures in financial services or those complying with certain ISO standards in their products or processes (e.g. ISO 14000).

Internal controls underpin and cultivate shareholder confidence which is relevant in any industry setting. Acceptable returns on shares rest on conformity with systems to ensure adequate levels of efficiency, effectiveness, security, etc and the avoidance of waste and fraud.

Internal control systems enable the provision of reports and other information as needed by either external agencies or internal management. Although some industries are likely to have a need for external reporting (e.g. nuclear, oil and gas), internal report provision is necessary in any industry.

Tutorial note: *Credit would be given for other relevant points (e.g. from F8 Audit and Assurance).*

"Unmonitored controls tend to deteriorate over time"

This statement refers to the need to establish which controls need to be monitored to support a sound system of internal controls and how to monitor those controls. Once a control system is designed and responsibilities for its management allocated, only those targets and controls that are made a part of someone's job or performance measurement will be monitored and thereby maintained. Any metrics that are not a part of this control regime will go unchecked and may not remain within compliance limits as circumstances change over time. The main roles of internal audit are to provide information to management on the relevance and effectiveness of internal control systems and to provide the evidence to demonstrate why those controls are effective or not. This requires the identification of which controls to monitor and developing effective ways of monitoring those controls.

The complexity of the control regime is also relevant. There is a balance between having a sufficient number of controls in place and having too many. In this context, "too many" means that control systems must be actually useable. Over-complex controls are likely to deteriorate over time if their monitoring is not possible within reasonable cost limits and this could also cause operational inefficiencies.

Furthermore, an organisation is not static and so different controls will be needed over time. As activities change as a result of changes in organisational strategy, the controls that need to be monitored change and the tolerances of those controls may also change (they may become tighter or looser). Constant updating of controls is therefore necessary, especially in frequently changing business environments.

(c)   **Internal audit testing**

This is the internal assessment of internal controls using an internal auditor or internal audit function applying audit techniques to controls based on predetermined measures and outcomes. It is a management control over the other internal controls in an organisation and ensures the levels of compliance and conformity of the internal controls in an organisation.

Roles of internal audit in ensuring effective internal controls

Internal audit underpins the effectiveness of internal controls by performing several key tasks.

Internal audit reviews and reports on the controls put in place for the key risks that the company faces in its operations. This will involve ensuring that the control (i.e. mitigation measure) is capable of controlling the risk should it materialise. This is the traditional view of internal audit. A key part of this role is to review the design and effectiveness of internal controls. Many organisations also require internal audit staff to conduct follow-up visits to ensure that any weaknesses or failures have been addressed since their report was first submitted. This ensures that staff take the visit seriously and must implement the findings.

Internal audit may also involve an examination of financial and operating information to ensure its accuracy, timeliness and adequacy. In the production of internal management reports, for example, internal audit may be involved in ensuring that the information in the report is correctly measured and accurate. Internal audit needs to be aware of the implications of providing incomplete or partial information for decision-making.

It will typically undertake reviews of operations for compliance against standards. Standard performance measures will have an allowed variance or tolerance and internal audit will measure actual performance against this standard. Internal compliance is essential in all internal control systems. Examples might include safety performance, cost performance or the measurement of a key environmental emission against a target amount (which would then be used as part of a key internal environmental control).

Internal audit is used to review internal systems and controls for compliance with relevant regulations and externally-imposed targets. Often assumed to be of more importance in rules-based jurisdictions (e.g. the US) many industries have upper and lower limits on key indicators and it is the role of internal audit to measure against these and report as necessary. In financial services, banking, oil and gas, etc, legal compliance targets are often placed on companies and compliance data is required periodically by governments.

Tutorial note: *Again credit would be given for relevant content from earlier papers, particularly F8.*

Answer 18 YAYA COMPANY

(a)   Ineffective internal controls

Well-designed internal controls (IC) systems can be ineffective for a number of reasons.

Costs outweighing benefits

This is when an IC system provides poor value for money or it provides more assurance than is needed (i.e. the control is over-specified). In such a situation, the control will not be supported or trusted by those working alongside or within the control, and this will reduce its effectiveness.

Failures in human judgement

Can occur when assessing a control, or fraud in measuring or reporting a control. Where a control relies upon human measurement, error is always a possibility either through lack of training, incompetence, wilful negligence or having a vested interest in control failure (e.g. Jane Goo believed she could gain financially by a product failing to pass successfully through a quality control standard).

Collusion between employees

Often happens where there is vested interest to misapplying or circumventing a control. The risk of this is greater when two or more people believe they may gain by it. It could be, for example, a sales team misquoting sales figures against a budget or directors misreporting accounting data to increase their bonuses or maintain a higher share price before exercising share options. The collusion between Jane Goo and John Zong (who received part of the payment) was one of the factors that may have led to the failure of QC controls being effective at Yaya.

Non-routine or unforeseen events

These can render controls ineffective if they are intended to monitor a specific process only. Most internal controls are unable to cope with extraordinary events and so need to be adapted or circumvented when such events occur.

Obsolete

Previous or existing controls can become obsolete because they are not updated to meet changed conditions. A control introduced to monitor a process or risk that has changed, reduced or been discontinued will no longer be effective. Changes to key risks, for example, need to be modified if they are to continue to remain effective in controlling the risk.

(b)   Deficiencies at Yaya

Jane Goo was fraudulently entering compliance reports with no-one required to countersign them or confirm her checks. The system did not require a second signature and no-one saw the product compliance reports after completion, so Jane had no one to review, confirm and assure that her QC measurements were true or accurate. She believed herself to be poorly paid and this may have increased the incentives for her to carry out the deceit.

Additionally, it appears she was left to "destroy" the goods that failed QC, allowing her to sell the goods externally. Segregating the disposal of the goods from the creation of the reports would also have helped prevent this fraud occurring.

Linked to this, there was collusion between Jane Goo and John Zong, who received part of the proceeds for his complicity in the fraud. This meant that the both of the people in the QC department were involved and the isolation of the laboratory made the discovery of their activities less likely.

There was no control capable of automatically signalling to management that the failure rate had increased. The fact that the rate rose gradually and not in a steep change seems to have made the change less visible, but a maximum acceptable failure rate with an appropriate measurement system would have triggered a signal to management that the rate had risen above it.

The way the QC department was viewed by the company meant that its activities would have received less scrutiny than other parts of the business. The QC department was marginalised and located away from other activities and the combination of these factors made it unlikely that they would often be disturbed. The fact that there was no automatic reporting link between QC and Mr Janoon was perhaps symptomatic of the marginalisation and this contributed to the problem.

The operations director Ben Janoon was negligent as a manager and had little control over the process. He rarely visited the QC lab, failed to monitor product failure rates, and failed to spot a fourfold increase in product failure rates. It was he that designed the system and with such a large number of weaknesses in the system, he must bear some of the responsibility for the lack of control, if not for the actual fraud itself.

(c) **Qualities of information**

Useful information has a number of general qualities that distinguishes it from less-than-useful information. This is a very important element of an internal control system, as evidenced by a lack of information flow to Ben Janoon at Yaya Company. Information flowing to Mr Janoon should be relevant, reliable, timely, understandable and cost-beneficial.

Relevant means that anything that Jane Goo feels should be brought to Mr Janoon's attention should be included in the information. Any changes to the overall quality of finished goods should be voluntarily reported, for example, any issues that would prevent the QC lab performing its important function or any changes to product failure rates.

Reliable refers to the trustworthiness of the information and whether or not it is a faithful representation of what is being conveyed. It concerns the assumption that it is "hard" information, that it is complete, correct, that it is impartial, unbiased, accurate and complete. Mr Janoon needs to know that the information he receives from Jane Goo is a true reflection of what is actually the case in the QC lab and that, for example, the reported failure rates are not understated for her personal gain.

Timely refers to the fact that information has a time value. Information that is late, for example, may be completely useless to the receiver. Information should arrive so that it can be processed effectively by the receiver and used for decision-making as it was intended.

Understandable in that Mr Janoon does not understand the science behind the QC processes and it is therefore important that any information from the QC lab is understandable by him. Because Jane Goo and John Zong had relevant scientific qualifications, it was important that information fed to Mr Janoon was free of jargon and in a form that is meaningful to him as a non-scientist.

Cost beneficial means that the cost incurred to generate the information does not outweigh its benefit. Simple reports on QC compliance at Yaya would probably be very cost-beneficial, for example, but in other situations, special reports can be expensive to produce and have little consequence to end users.

Mr Janoon could receive more frequent reports, maybe weekly or monthly, on QC failure rates. The fact that two years went by without him noticing the increased failure indicated that he had no effective information flow on the problem. A reliable flow of key QC metrics would enable him to plot these metrics over time, thereby highlighting any changes over time. Providing a predetermined format for Jane Goo to complete would ensure that he obtained the necessary information and it would place the information flow in his hands rather than with Jane Goo.

The information he receives could be of a higher quality, with more detail and possibly "drilled down" data on product compliance against specific metrics. The "drilled down" data would have detected the fact that Jane Goo had failed products that should, according to the product specification, have passed, and this could also have detected the fraud earlier.

Regular routine physical contact with QC employees, especially the QC manager. The fraud was partly caused by the environment within Yaya that saw QC as marginal and inconvenient, and partly by Jane Goo, believing that her work was unaccountable and unmonitored. By moving the QC lab closer to the main operations or establishing a clearer formal reporting regime from the QC manager to the operations director, the quality of information flows would be improved, and opportunity for fraud diminished.

Answer 19 BELIK

(a)   **"Whistleblowing"**

"Whistleblowing" is a term to describe a reporting system whereby:

- a person of lesser authority and power is able to inform another party (not necessarily their immediate superior) of a malpractice, fraudulent misconduct and a breach of trust; and

- positive actions will be taken by higher authorities to uncover such a misdeed, without taking any retaliatory actions against the person of lower rank who made the report.

It is a voluntary procedure (in that it is not compulsory to report) made by the employee who takes the misconduct or malpractice seriously without fear of penalty or punishment.

The concept is important in building integrity into a system of corporate governance. It further assists in strengthening the confidence of shareholders and investors.

However, a properly thought out system should be implemented to ensure it is not abused and that whistleblowing is genuinely carried out in the organisation.

In the context of the scenario, the internal auditor correctly reported her concerns to her immediate superior. However, having discovered that nothing was done, she is unsure of what to do next as there appears to be no whistleblowing guidelines in place. In reporting to the CEO or the CFO she may be reporting to an individual who has sanctioned what she believes to be the inappropriate transactions. Should she therefore go outside of her normal reporting lines and report to the audit committee – that is the guidance she requires.

(b) **Best practice**

A good policy on "whistle blowing" will only be effective only if it has the confidence of the employees, (who are the intended users). Employees' representatives (e.g. trade unions) should be involved in establishing the procedure and the monitoring of its implementation.

An appropriate guide should deal, for example, with the following:

- the procedure should be documented and a copy given to every employee;

- key aspects of the procedure should be set out (e.g. the person to whom the employee should report suspicions and concerns);

- a statement to the effect that the employer takes malpractices or misconduct seriously and management is committed to a culture of openness and transparency and that employees should be assured of secrecy and confidentiality;

- assurance to employees that there will be not be retaliation or reprisal where they report "in good faith" and they should not fear penalty or punishment;

- the need for a whistle-blower to provide a certain level of proof to substantiate their allegations;

- the need for an external route to be offered as well as an internal reporting procedure; and

- the procedure by which an allegation will be investigated should also be set out.

(c) **Audit committee**

The main roles and responsibilities of the audit committee under the UK Corporate Governance Code, in relation to the financial statements, internal audit and whistleblowing are to:

- monitor the integrity of the financial statements of the company including reviewing significant financial reporting judgements used within them (also covers formal announcements relating to the company's financial performance);

- review the company's internal financial controls;

- review internal control and risk management systems (if not dealt with by a separate risk committee or the Board);

- monitor and review the effectiveness of the company's internal audit function. If there is no internal audit, consider if there is a need and recommendation to the board accordingly;

- report to the board, identifying any matters in respect of which it considers that action or improvement is needed and making recommendations as to the steps to be taken;

- review arrangements by which staff of the company may, in confidence, raise concerns about possible improprieties in matters of financial reporting or other matters ("whistle blowing"). There is a need to ensure that arrangements are in place for the proportionate and independent investigation and for appropriate follow-up action.

In the Sarbanes-Oxley Act employees and auditors are also guaranteed protection against the company if they disclose confidential information to parties involved in a fraud claim.

Answer 20 FRANKS & FISHER

(a)   **Internal audit**

There is an obvious cost involved in setting up internal audit in an organisation and so it is typical to ask what factors signify the need for internal audit before one is established. Several factors influence the need for internal audit:

The scale, diversity and complexity of the company's activities. The larger, the more diverse and the more complex a range of activities is, the more there is to monitor (and the more opportunity there is for certain things to go wrong).

The number of employees. As a proxy for size, the number of employees signifies that larger organisations are more likely to need internal audit to underpin investor confidence than smaller concerns.

Cost-benefit considerations. Management must be certain of the benefits that will result from establishing internal audit and it must obviously been seen to outweigh the costs of doing so.

Changes in the organisational structures, reporting processes or underlying information systems. Any internal (or external) change is capable of changing the complexity of operations and, accordingly, the risk.

Changes in key risks could be internal or external in nature. The introduction of a new product, entering a new market, a change in any of the PEST/PESTEL factors or changes in the industry might trigger the need for internal audit.

Problems with existing internal control systems. Any problems with existing systems clearly signify the need for a tightening of systems and increased monitoring.

An increased number of unexplained or unacceptable events. System failures or similar events are a clear demonstration of internal control weakness.

The case on Franks & Fisher highlights three factors that would underpin its need to establish internal audit.

There has been growth in number of products, activities and (presumably) processes in recent times, thereby complicating the internal environment and introducing more opportunity for internal control failure.

There have been problems with internal control systems (the line stoppage and Mr Kumas's comment that, "problems with internal control in a number of areas").

Finally, there was an unacceptable event (the line stoppage) that was attributed to poor internal control. Mr Kumas confirmed this with his opinion about a "great need" for internal audit.

(b)   **Appointment**

In practice, a decision such as this one will depend on a number of factors including the supply of required skills in the internal and external job markets. In constructing the case for an external appointment, however, the following points can be made. Primarily, an external appointment would bring detachment and independence that would be less likely with an internal one.

Firstly, then, an external appointment would help with independence and objectivity (avoiding the possibility of auditor capture). He would owe neither personal loyalties nor "favours" from previous positions. Similarly, he would have neither personal grievances nor conflicts with other people from past disputes or arguments.

Some benefit would be expected from the "new broom" effect in that the appointment would see the company through fresh eyes. He would be unaware of vested interests. He would be likely to come in with new ideas and expertise gained from other situations.

Finally, as with any external appointment, the possibility exists for the transfer of best practice in from outside – a net gain in knowledge for Franks & Fisher.

(c)   **Reporting to finance director**

The first thing to say is that Mr Kumas's belief is inappropriate and it would be an unacceptable idea for the internal auditor to report to a divisional director who might be the subject of an internal audit.

The reasons put forward in favour of his request are spurious. All Mr Kumas's information and expertise would be available to the internal auditor in any event, with or without his oversight of the function.

Reporting to Mr Kumas would be a clear threat to the independence of the internal auditor as he/ she would not be objective in auditing the accounting and finance department.

The advice from relevant codes and guidelines would also strongly counsel against My Kumas's proposal. The Cadbury code is typical where, point (g) under the "role of the internal audit committee" emphasised the independence of the internal audit function from management. Mr Kumas's request should be refused.

(d)   **Objectivity**

Objectivity is a state or quality that implies detachment, lack of bias, not influenced by personal feelings, prejudices or emotions. It is a very important quality in corporate governance generally and especially important in all audit situations where, regardless of personal feeling, the auditor must carry out his task objectively and with the purpose of the audit uppermost in mind.

The IESBA (IFAC) Code of Ethics explains objectivity in the following terms (Introduction, clause 16): "… fair and should not allow prejudice or bias, conflict of interest or influence of others to override objectivity."

It thus follows that characteristics that might demonstrate an internal auditor's professional objectivity will include fairness and even-handedness, freedom from bias or prejudice and the avoidance of conflicts of interest (e.g. by accepting gifts, threats to independence, etc).

The internal auditor should remember at all times that the purpose is to deliver a report on the systems being audited to his principal. In an external audit situation, the principal is ultimately the shareholder and in internal audit situations, it is the internal audit committee (and then ultimately, shareholders).

Answer 21 AGREX

The following checklist is based on the Turnbull Guidance for the board to consider (as a minimum) as part of its review process when preparing the annual statement on internal controls.

Risk assessment

- Does the company have clear strategic and operational objectives?

- Have the objectives been fully communicated to provide effective direction to employees on risk assessment and control issues?

- Are the significant internal and external operational, financial, compliance and other risks identified and assessed on a continuous basis?

- Is there a clear understanding by management and others within the company of what risks are acceptable to the board?

Control environment and control activities

- Does the board have clear strategies and policies for dealing with and managing the significant risks that have been identified?

- Do the company's culture, code of conduct, human resource policies and performance reward systems support the business objectives, risk management and internal control system?

- Does senior management demonstrate, through its actions as well as its policies, the necessary commitment to competence, integrity and foster a climate of trust within the company?

- Are authority, responsibility and accountability defined clearly such that decisions are made and actions taken by the appropriate people?

- Are the decisions and actions of different parts of the company appropriately co-ordinated?

- Does the company communicate to its employees what is expected of them and the scope of their freedom to act?

  - Customer relations.
  - Service levels for both internal and outsourced activities.
  - Health, safety and environmental protection.
  - Security of tangible and intangible assets.
  - Business continuity issues.
  - Expenditure matters.
  - Accounting, financial and other reporting.

- Do people in the company (and in its providers of outsourced services) have the knowledge, skills and tools to support the achievement of the company's objectives and to manage effectively risks to their achievement?

- How are processes/controls adjusted to reflect new or changing risks, or operational deficiencies?

Information and communication

■ Do management and the board receive timely, relevant and reliable reports on progress against business objectives (quantitative and qualitative) and the related risks?

– Key performance reports and benchmarking key performance indicators.
– Variance analysis and indicators of change.
– Regulatory reports, customer satisfaction and employee attitudes.

■ Do they use such reports for decision-making and management review purposes?

■ Are information needs (thus related information systems) reassessed as objectives and related risks evolve and as reporting deficiencies are identified?

■ Are periodic reporting procedures, including half-yearly and annual reporting, effective in communicating a balanced and understandable account of the company's position and prospects?

■ Are there established channels of communication for individuals to report suspected breaches of law or regulations or other improprieties (whistle-blowing)?

Monitoring

■ Are there on-going processes embedded in the company's overall business operations which monitor the effective application of the policies, processes and activities related to internal control and risk management?

– Control self-assessment and confirmation by personnel of compliance with policies and codes of conduct
– Internal audit reviews and specific management reviews

■ Do these processes monitor the company's ability to re-evaluate risks and adjust controls effectively in response to changes in its objectives, its business, and its external environment?

■ Are there effective follow-up procedures to ensure that appropriate change or action occurs in response to changes in risk and control assessments?

■ Is there appropriate and timely communication to the board (or board committees) on the effectiveness of the monitoring processes on risk and control matters?

■ Are there specific arrangements for management monitoring and reporting to the board on risk and control matters of particular importance?

– Actual or suspected fraud.
– Illegal or irregular acts.
– Matters that could adversely affect the company's reputation.
– Matters negatively impacting financial position.

Answer 22 ULTRA-UBER

(a) **"Liquidity risk"**

Liquidity risk refers to the difficulties that can arise from an inability of the company to meet its short-term financing needs (i.e. its ratio of short-term assets to short-term liabilities). Specifically, this refers to the organisation's working capital and meeting short-term cash flow needs. The essential elements of managing liquidity risk are, therefore, the controls over receivables, payables, cash and inventories.

Manufacturing has historically had a greater challenge with the management of liquidity risk compared to some other sectors (especially low inventory businesses such as those in service industries like those that Bob Ndumo is NED for). In the case of UU, this is for three reasons:

(1) Manufacturing usually requires higher working capital levels because it buys in and sells physical inventory, both on credit. This means that both payables and receivables are relatively high. It also, by definition, requires inventory in the form of raw materials, work-in-progress and finished goods, and therefore the management of inventory turnover is one of the most important management tasks in manufacturing management. In addition, wages are paid throughout the manufacturing process, although it will take some time before finished goods are ready for sale.

(2) Manufacturing has complex management systems resulting from a more complex business model. Although other business models create their own liquidity problems, the variability and availability of inventory at different stages and the need to manage inventories at different levels of completion raises liquidity issues not present in many other types of business (e.g. service-based business).

(3) UU has a number of weaknesses that amplify its structural liquidity position as a manufacturer. Its ineffective credit control department and its voluntary 20 day supplier payment policy both increase the short-term cash pressure and thereby increase the likelihood of liquidity risks becoming realised.

(b) **Risk embeddedness**

Risk embeddedness refers to the way in which risk awareness and management are interwoven into the normality of systems and culture in an organisation. These two twin aspects (systems and culture) are both important because systems describe the way in which work is organised and undertaken, and culture describes the "taken-for-grantedness" of risk awareness and risk management within the organisation.

The methods by which risk awareness and management can be embedded in organisations are as follows:

Aligning individual goals with those of the organisation and building these in as part of the culture. The need for alignment is important because risk awareness needs to be a part of the norms and unquestioned assumptions of the organisation. Training of staff at all levels is essential to ensure risk is embedded throughout the organisation.

Including risk responsibilities with job descriptions. This means that employees at all levels have their risk responsibilities clearly and unambiguously defined.

Establishing reward systems that recognise that risks have to be taken (thus avoiding a "blame culture"). Those employees that are expected to take risks (e.g. those planning investments) should have the success of the projects included in their rewards.

Establishing metrics and performance indicators that monitor and feedback information on risks to management. This would ensure that accurate information is always available to the risk committee and/or board, and that there is no incentive to hide relevant information or fail to disclose risky behaviour or poor practice. A "suggestion box" is one way of providing feedback to management.

Communicating risk awareness and risk management messages to staff and publishing success stories. Part of the dissemination of, and creating an incentive for, good practice, internal communications is important in developing culture and continually reminding staff of risk messages.

(c) **Obstacles to embedding liquidity risk management at UU**

The case draws attention to three aspects of working capital management at UU: payables, receivables and inventory. All of these are necessary issues in the management of liquidity and hence the reduction of liquidity risk. Specifically, however, it identifies four potential obstacles to embedding the management of liquidity risk. Primarily, however, the individual managers of the company are all acting in isolation and not working together for the good of the company.

The *sales manager's desire to have high levels of finished goods* for maximum customer choice. It is quite reasonable for a sales manager to support high levels of finished goods inventory but there is an inventory-holding cost associated with that which increases the amount of money tied up in working capital. A wider recognition of the overall liquidity pressures on the business would be a very helpful quality in the sales manager and this is a potential obstacle.

The same points apply to the *manufacturing director's desire to have high raw material levels*. Clearly, his effectiveness as head of manufacturing is partly measured by the extent to which the factory fulfils orders and avoids the disruptions to production that arise through inventory "stock-outs". He prefers having raw materials in stock rather than having to order them with a supplier's lead time but this, of course, leads to a greater exposure to liquidity risk.

The *ineffective credit control department*. According to the manufacturing director, the credit control department, responsible for the timely payment of receivables, was poor. The vulnerability to liquidity risk is clearly influenced by days receivables and so an ineffective credit control department is a major obstacle.

Finally, the *CEO's desire to pay payables early* as part of the company's social responsibility efforts. Brian Mills is clearly of the view that offering a voluntary prompt payment of payables is an important component of the company's social responsibility and that is costing the company an average of 10 days payables on most accounts. Over the course of a year that will place a great deal of arguably unnecessary pressure on working capital. The fact that it is the CEO himself that holds this view might make it difficult to change.

(d) **Voluntary supplier payment policy**

Supplier payment disclosures have become increasingly popular in recent years in some countries as a signal of intent to suppliers that larger buyers will not exploit the economic advantage that they sometimes have over smaller suppliers. It is usual for these statements to announce that all payments will be made in line with the supplier's terms and so UU's intention to voluntarily pay within 20 days is more generous that would usually be expected.

In terms of criticism as a means of demonstrating social responsibility, the case says that the purpose of the policy is to "publicly demonstrate our social responsibility". A key limitation of the policy is, however, that the policy *only focuses on one stakeholder* (suppliers) and apparently ignores other groups. Given the information in the case, the social responsibility policy is apparently aimed at one single stakeholder which is an ineffective overall strategy.

Secondly, however, it is unlikely that this policy is the best use of resources *if the desire is to "publicly demonstrate" social responsibility*. Measures aimed more at customers or more charitable causes would be likely to attract more publicity if that is the intention.

The policy is *very costly to UU in terms of cash flow*. So much so that the finance director has questioned whether it can actually be afforded, especially at times of a lack of short-term credit, particularly during the global economic recession. It is, of course, a matter of ethical debate as to how committed UU should be to its social responsibility in terms of resources.

Finally, the policy *does not enjoy the support of the other directors* and is thus hard to maintain as an on-going commitment. This means it is vulnerable and susceptible to change if the CEO is the only person who really believes in it. As a part of the company's overall strategic positioning, the components of social responsibility must enjoy widespread support, especially among the senior officers in the company, and arguably most importantly, it must enjoy the support of the finance director.

Answer 23 YGT

(a)   **Risk assessment**

Raz Dutta's beliefs

Raz is wrong in both of her assertions. The belief that risks do not change very much is only true in static environments. In reality, the changeability of risks depends upon the organisation's place on a continuum between highly dynamic and completely static. The case mentions changes in some of YGT's risks and this suggests that there is some dynamism in its environment. Clearly then, her belief is very difficult to defend.

Her belief that risks "hardly ever" materialise may be historically true (but this is also unlikely) but the risk assessment highlighted at least two "likely" risks which could well materialise. Risk D was assessed as "highly likely" and Risk B was also likely with a high potential impact. Neither of these variables would be known were it not for intelligence gained as part of the risk assessment. Importantly, Risk B was a "high/high" risk meaning that it is a likely risk with a high impact once it materialised. Being unaware of this could have caused great damage to the organisation.

Why risks are dynamic and need to be assessed regularly

Risk assessment is a dynamic management activity because of changes in the organisational environment and because of changes in the activities and operations of the organisation which interact with that environment. At YGT, the case describes Risk C as arising from a change in the activity of the company: a new product launch. The new product has obviously introduced a new risk that was not present prior to the new product. It may be a potential liability from the use of the product or a potential loss from the materials used in its production, for example.

Changes in the environment might include changes in any of the PEST (political, economic, social, technological) or any industry level change such as a change in the competitive behaviour of suppliers, buyers or competitors. In either case, new risks can be introduced, existing ones can become more likely or have a higher impact, or the opposite (they may disappear or become less important). The case describes Risk D as arising from a change in legislation which is a change in the external environment.

(b)   **TARA – Strategies for managing each risk assessment**

Risk A is **accept**. This means that the likelihood is low and the impact is low such that even if the risk materialised, it would not have a high severity. The case says that the activity giving rise to Risk A is capable of making good returns so given that both likelihood and severity are low, there is no obvious reason to pursue any of the other strategies with regard to this risk.

Risk B is **avoid**. When the likelihood and impact are high, it would be irrational to accept the risk and so the risk should be avoided. This may involve changing behaviour or discontinuing a certain activity. The case says that the activity giving rise to Risk B is capable of making good returns, but importantly, it is not strategically vital. Given this, and because the case information does not mention the possibility of viably transferring the risk, there is no reason to bear the risk unless the potential return is very large and the company has a high risk appetite.

Risk C is **transfer**. YGT says that the activity giving rise to the risk must not be discontinued (so avoidance is not an option) and specifies that it can be transferred ("alternative arrangements for bearing the risks are possible"). To transfer risk is to share it with another party. The most common way to do this is to insure against losses or to outsource or licence the activity to a third party thereby transferring that risk to that third party.

Risk D is **reduce**. The case emphasises that the risk cannot be transferred (by insurance or outsourcing) but that the activity that gives rise to the risk can be reduced. Reduction involves reducing the risk exposure by carrying out the activity in a different way, doing less of the activity that gives rise to the risk or adopting behaviour that, whilst still exposing the company to the risk, results in a lower impact if the risk is realised.

(c)   **Related risks and positive correlation**

Related risks are risks that vary because of the presence of another risk. This means they do not exist independently and they are likely to rise and fall in importance along with the related one. Risk correlation is a particular example of related risk.

Risks are positively correlated if the two risks are positively related in that one will fall with the reduction of the other and increase with the rise of the other. They would be negatively correlated if one rose as the other fell. In the case of environmental risks and reputation risk, they may be positively correlated for the following reasons.

Environmental risks involve exposure to losses arising from an organisation's consumption of resources or impacts through its emissions. Where an environmental risk affects a sensitive situation, (be it human, flora, fauna or other), this can cause negative publicity which can result in reputation damage. These two risks can have a shared cause (i.e. they can arise together and fall together because they depend upon the same activity). They are considered separate risks because losses can be incurred by either of both of the impacts (environmental or reputational).

Activities designed to reduce environmental risk, such as acquiring resources from less environmentally-sensitive sources or through the fitting of emission controls, will reduce the likelihood of the environmental risk being realised. This, in turn, will reduce the likelihood of the reputation risk being incurred. The opposite will also hold true: a reduction of attention to environmental risk will increase the likelihood of reputation loss.

(d)   **Culture of risk awareness advice**

Explanation

Risk awareness is a *capability of an organisation* to be able to recognise risks when they arise, from whatever source they may come. A culture of risk awareness suggests that this capability (or competence) is present throughout the organisation and is woven into the *normal routines, rituals, ways of thinking and is taken-for-granted* in all parts of the company and in all employees.

Assessment

Risks can arise in any part of the organisation and at any level. Not all risks are at the strategic level and can be captured by a risk assessment. A culture of risk awareness will help ensure that all employees are capable of identifying risks as and when they arise.

Risks are dynamic and rise and fall with changes in the business environment and with changes in the company's activities. With changes to the company's risk profile occurring all the time, it cannot be assumed that the risks present at the most recent risk assessment will remain the same. Being prepared to adapt to changes is a key advantage of a culture of risk awareness.

A lack of risk awareness is often *evidence of a lack of risk management strategy* in the organisation. This, in turn, can be dangerous as the company could be more exposed to risk than it need be because of the lack of attentiveness by staff. A lack of effectiveness of risk management strategy leaves the company vulnerable to unrecognised or wrongly assessed risks.

Answer 24 .JH GRAPHICS

(a)   **Normative-instrumental**

The normative-instrumental distinction describes two different approaches or underlying ethical motivations. Often applied to the ways in which organisations behave towards stakeholders, it can be applied to any situation in which ethical motivations are relevant.

In the case, Jenny Harris is demonstrating a normative approach to adoption of the corporate code of ethics. It is evident from what she says that she is internally motivated. She described herself as personally driven by high ethical values and appears to see ethical behaviour as an end in itself. She tends not to take the business implications of the proposed code into account and thereby tends towards the altruistic rather than the strategic. Her attitude is informed primarily by internal motivation rather than the pursuit of external reward.

Alan, by contrast, demonstrates instrumental characteristics. He appears to be primarily motivated by business performance and sees the ethical code as a means to further other objectives (not as an end in itself). His attitude to the code of ethics is underpinned by questions about what can be gained, for the business, of the code's adoption. Accordingly, he is strategic rather than altruistic in him motivation.

(b) **Kohlberg**

This question draws on two of Kohlberg's three levels of moral development. In particular, it asks how the decision on possible apology for and withdrawal of the image would vary depending on whether Jenny, as the chief executive of JH Graphics ("JHG"), makes conventional and pre-conventional ethical assumptions.

The conventional ethical level views the moral "right" according to whether it is compliant with the existing legal and regulatory frameworks and/or norms of the society or culture in which the decision is taking place. If the image was generally acceptable and offensive only to the religious group in question, it can probably be assumed that it was otherwise culturally inoffensive. It was certainly not illegal as no laws were broken. From the conventional level, therefore, there is no case for withdrawing the image.

The pre-conventional moral development level views the moral right as that which attracts the least punishment and the most reward. Whereas in the case of personal morality, such rewards and punishments are likely to be made at the personal level, the issues involved are more complex for organisations.

Pre-conventional morality might ask, for example, whether the company is likely to be rewarded or punished by keeping or withdrawing the image. In this context, rewards or punishments are likely to be viewed in economic terms or in terms of boycotts or increased business arising from the publicity.

(c) **Response**

This is a complicated ethical situation and the board of JHG will be considering several factors in attempting to come to a decision over what to do with the offending image.

One factor likely to be considered is the possible effects of the dispute on the reputation of company. It is not at all certain that the row will be damaging. In some industries, possibly including graphic design, to be seen to be capable of producing provocative and challenging imagery could be advantageous whereas in other situations it may be adverse.

The company will also be likely to take into account the level and direction of public/political opinion and support. The case mentions that the controversy was a major news story and it would be necessary to find out whether the independent coverage of the issue was generally critical or generally favourable of JHG. If the majority of public opinion was against JHG and supportive of the religious critics, that may be influential in JHG considering the withdrawal of the image.

Consideration should also be given to the economic importance of the advertisement/client to JHG. The case says that the client is happy with the image (and presumably untroubled by the religious controversy) but from JHG's point of view, the question concerns how much they could possibly lose if they unilaterally withdrew the rights to use the image and thereby upset the client.

The board would also be likely to consider the possible direct influence of offended religious groups on JHG. The Mendelow map, which measures the influence of a stakeholder by considering its power and interest, may be helpful in determining how influential the religious group is likely to be on the wellbeing of JHG. Is it, for example, large and potentially influential (e.g. in terms of mobilising opinion) or small and unlikely to have an effect?

The directors should also assess the value of all the unexpected publicity to JHG? Mr Leroy is clearly of the view that is "was bringing the company free publicity and that was good for the business". Although such a profile-raising controversy might be damaging to JHG, it might also be advantageous, especially if being seen as being willing to "push the boundaries" of taste and decency is a potential source of competitive advantage. The publicity received is obviously far more than the company could afford in terms of buying publicity but this needs to be weighed against whether the publicity is good for JH or adverse.

The national culture in which the decision is taking place could have an influence on the outcome. The intensity of the debate over the importance of not causing offence will vary depending on the national culture, which can, in turn, influenced and underpinned by historical and religious culture.

(d)   **Stakeholder legitimacy**

This question touches on the debate over stakeholder recognition and the limits of corporate accountability and responsibility. It is in the nature of any stakeholder that they make a "claim" on the activities of the organisation. The debate is over whether that claim is recognised and whether, accordingly, the nature of the claim is taken into account in decision-making.

In this instance, it is relatively uncontroversial to recognise the religious group as a stakeholder (Freeman's definition defines a stakeholder as an entity that can "affect or be affected by..."). The perceived legitimacy of the claim depends on where the limit of accountability is drawn and the reasonableness of the claim.

There is a continuum of legitimacy with, perhaps, shareholders being "entirely legitimate" in making a claim at one extreme and terrorists as "entirely illegitimate" at the other. The legitimacy of the religious group's claim (they are unlikely to have a direct economic relationship with JHG) depends on where that line is drawn. It might also be pointed out that offence taken by a stakeholder does not necessarily imply a responsibility towards the stakeholder.

Answer 25 RAILWAY DEVELOPMENT COMPANY

(a)   **Tucker and Route A**

Is the decision to choose Route A profitable?

Yes. This will be cheaper for the company (RDC) because it avoids the need to make the compulsory purchase of Mr Krul's farm. This will save the company $1 million and enable a profit to be made, over 10 years, of $5 million. The equivalent 10-year profit figure for Route B would, accordingly, be $4 million.

Is it legal?

The case says that both routes (A and B) had been given planning permission, so there is no difference between them on matters of legality. Route A is a legally allowable option as it has planning permission from the local government authority.

Is it right?

This depends upon the ethical perspective adopted. Route A would deliver a higher profitability for RDC and also preserve important local social and economic benefits by keeping Mr Krul's farm. The farm supports local jobs, perhaps has an important role in the local community and, being a farm, provides a source of local food. If these benefits are seen as more important than the future of the birds, then it is right to choose Route A. If the claim of the birds and their impact on the local ecosystem is more important than the profitability of the project and the benefits provided by the farm, then it was wrong to choose Route A.

Is it fair?

This depends upon how the legitimate and reasonable claim of Mr Krul to remain on his land is weighed against the claim of the colony of birds to survive. The choice of Route A ignores the claim of the birds' right to gain access to their feeding site and because the birds are endangered, it may threaten their future. It is fair to Mr Krul, but unfair to the colony of birds. Mr Krul, however, employs people who would otherwise lose their jobs, potentially having a negative impact on them and their families. In addition, the farm has been in Mr Krul's family for four generations and that may also be a relevant factor when considering the fairness of the decision.

Is it sustainable and/or environmentally acceptable?

Route A was probably the less environmentally-sustainable of the two options. Because Route A was chosen, it will mean destroying the important feeding site for the colony of threatened birds. This will threaten the population of these birds and the case suggests that this may represent a threat to the environmental sustainability of local ecosystems. The loss of the feeding ground and the birds may therefore have other unforeseen environmental consequences. Whichever route is chosen, an environmental benefit may accrue because of the replacement of car journeys with increased rail travel.

Summary

The company chose to prioritise cost-savings and the impact of the farm on the local community over the negative environmental impact that Route A entailed. This may have something to do with Eddie Krul having a louder "voice" than the birds and so more able to express his claim than the voiceless birds (the pressure group did not speak up until after the decision was made). RDC essentially had two choices which would both have had negative effects on some of the stakeholders. It chose to take the decision that was less sustainable but more favourable to shareholders and the stakeholders in the farm.

(b)   Stakeholder recognition

A decision such as the selection of a new route for a major construction project is bound to create "winners" and "losers". In most projects it is important to identify and recognise the claims of all of the stakeholders for several reasons:

■   It is necessary to gain an understanding of the sources of potential risk and disruption. "Save the Birds", for example, has threatened to disrupt the construction of Route A as it seeks to protect the birds' feeding ground. Mr Krul, similarly, threatened to bring legal action in the event that Route B was chosen.

■   It is important in terms of assessing the sources of influence over the objectives and outcomes for the project (such as identified in the Mendelow model). Stakeholder influence is assessed in terms of each stakeholder's power and interest, with higher power and higher interest combining to generate the highest influence.

The local government authority, for example, had no view on which was chosen but as a high power stakeholder (capable of granting or withholding legal permission), it could have been very influential had it expressed a view either way.

- It is necessary to identify potential areas of conflict and tension between stakeholders, especially relevant when it is likely that stakeholders of influence will be in disagreement over the outcomes.

  A survey of the stakeholders in a rail-building project such as this, once mapped in terms of influence, would signal which stakeholders are likely to cause delays and paralysis by disagreement and whose claims can then be studied for ways to reduce disagreement.

- There is an ethical and reputational case for knowledge of how decisions affect stakeholders, both inside the organisation or external to it. Society can withdraw its support from organisations that it perceives as unethical or arrogant. This can affect organisational performance by reducing their reputations as employers and suppliers of future services.

  RDC may acquire a reputation for environmental damage and this could mean they lose public trust on future projects of this type. A "deep green" perspective would take an unfavourable view of companies that failed to recognise some stakeholder claims.

(c)   **Stakeholder claim**

A stakeholder is any person or entity that can affect or be affected by the actions or policies of an organisation. In the case of RDC, two "affected" stakeholders are Eddie Krul and the colony of endangered birds. The local government authority is both affected by the decision and can also have an influence over the decision. A claim is the outcome sought or the outcome that would provide most benefit or do least harm to a given stakeholder. It is what that particular stakeholder "wants" or would want, if it were able to understand and voice its claim.

Assessment of the claims

Mr Krul was seeking to maintain his house and land by getting RDC to choose Route A. His claim is based partly on his family having been on the same land for four generations and that he employs a number of local people. As a "vocal" critic, he is able to clearly articulate his views and lobby for his preferred option. He clearly understands what would happen to him if Route B was chosen and can clearly voice that concern to decision-makers.

The only concerns of the local government authority were making sure the investment went ahead with the benefits it believed would accrue to the local region. Its claim is to ensure that the investment and jobs are attracted and in pursuit of that, takes no view on the competing claims of Mr Krul and the colony of birds. It could be criticised for being passive in this decision and for assuming that RDC could evaluate such a decision adequately themselves, in both economic and ethical terms.

The colony of birds is a "voiceless" stakeholder, although it does now have "Save the Birds" claiming to speak on its behalf. The bird colony does not understand that its feeding ground is threatened but it will incur material loss when Route A is developed. Because it does not have an effective voice (other than the "outrage" of "Save the Birds" after the decision was taken), it was unable to contribute to the debate over the choice of route. The local government authority did not prioritise one stakeholder over the other when granting RDC permission to develop either route.

Answer 26 ESKADA

(a)   **Corporate governance issues**

As with Enron, Eskada appears to be applying all the necessary requirements of good corporate governance (as required at the time). The scenario shows that the role of the CEO and Chairman are separated, there is an audit committee and remunerations committee duly composed of independent non-exec directors, the risk manager reported to the audit committee (although this was later changed with the new risk manager reporting directly to the CEO) and there appears to be communication with the institutional shareholders. It thus appears that Eskada is applying the letter, but not the spirit, of corporate governance.

The UK Corporate Governance Code states that every company should be headed by an effective board, which is collectively responsible for the success of the company. The board's role is to provide entrepreneurial leadership of the company within a framework of prudent and effective controls which enables risk to be assed and managed. Decisions should be taken objectively in the interest of the board.

It is clear from the scenario that the board failed to effectively control the CEO and the company. David had built up an atmosphere of fear to ensure his policies were carried through with very little opposition or challenge. His style seemed to be that if anyone upset him, they would be moved sideways, disciplined or sacked. Thus fellow executives were probably in fear for their jobs (which would have been well paid and with good bonuses for achieving targets) and would thus not wish to challenge David.

As part of their role as members of a unitary board, NEDs should constructively challenge and help develop proposals on strategy. They should challenge any aspect of strategy they see fit and offer advice or input to help to develop successful strategy; they are required to represent the shareholders' interests against the possibility that agency issues arise to reduce shareholder value and they need to ensure that the company has an adequate system of internal control and risk management.

The Tyson report identified four personal attributes required by NEDs in order to carry out the responsibilities of their role:

- Integrity and high ethical standards;
- Sound judgement;
- Ability and willingness to challenge and probe;
- Strong interpersonal skills

Although they follow the requirements of good corporate practice, the NEDs singularly failed in their responsibilities as detailed above. They showed little willingness, integrity or ethical standards to challenge the actions of David and his methods to increase profits. No action appears to have been taken by the audit committee (or the non-exec directors as a group) when bringing to the attention of the board the concerns of the risk manager only to have them ignored by David. The lack of challenging David over the sacking of the risk manager and changing the reporting line of the new risk manager shows a similar lack of sound judgement.

Lastly, the non-executive directors on the remuneration committee completely failed to hold David accountable for the disastrous acquisition of BCM. By negotiating the terms of his leaving the bank, they seemed to have shown weak interpersonal skills (e.g. negotiating, being assertive) in accepting his terms and thus rewarding him for failure. It would be well within the rights of the remuneration committee to have recommended to the board for David to have been dismissed for gross misconduct.

(b)   Problems of personal ethics

Although corporate governance codes may be considered as being best practice, that practice can easily be negated by directors (either singularly or as a group) who do not uphold good moral and ethical standards. Laws and regulations, including Codes of Corporate Governance, can never be enough on their own. Good corporate governance practice requires high personal ethics on the part of directors including the non-executive directors and executive managers.

Individuals must adhere to strict ethical conduct in their personal decision making in business as well as in private life for corporate governance to be truly effective. True ethical conduct would be a behaviour that is in accordance with an unwritten code of ethics and set of moral values. If directors carried out their duties in accordance with acceptable ethical and moral norms, there is an argument that written corporate governance codes, corporate social responsibility and similar practice would not be necessary.

There are several ways of considering the moral and ethical development of David. As he has progressed through his career, David's moral development does not appear to have risen beyond Kohlberg's Level 1, pre-conventional morality. He may have seen that as he gained greater power he was able to judge right or wrong in terms of the expected rewards. Greater power within the boardroom would allow him to only be concerned with greater rewards, with minimal fear of failure and punishment. His approach has become instrumentalist – what's in it for me? Aspects of fairness, reciprocity and equality are interpreted in physical or practical terms rather than in terms of loyalty, gratitude or justice.

David has a very high internal locus of control. He has developed a strong belief in his ability to determine his own life and destination. He does not however appear to consider the moral consequences on others of the actions he takes and therefore his personal integrity may be considered as low. This also reflects his moral imagination – it seems not to stretch beyond ways of making profits.

As a career banker, he will have been exposed to a culture of high rewards, bonuses and compensation – often earning more than his fixed salary in bonuses. Basing rewards on set criteria and benchmarks (e.g. sales made, share price, contracts won, strength of the statement of financial position) will always run the risk that managers and employees will engage in unethical (and often illegal) practices in order to meet or exceed expectations. This will be compounded where the unethical practice is accepted (and not punished) by senior management so that it becomes accepted practice within the organisation. David's treatment of his executive managers implies that he encourages such behaviour so long as it is making profits.

Finally, his approach reflects teleological egoism. He is very self-centred and his actions reflect this self-interest. He uses the bank to pursue his own aims and interests rather than to please others. Even when he decides to move on he fails to recognise his faults and aims to derive the greatest benefit from events.

(c)   Integrated thinking

Integrated thinking is the active consideration by an organisation of the relationships between its various operating and functional units and the capitals that the organisation uses or affects.

Integrated thinking leads to integrated decision-making and actions that consider the creation of value. David clearly did not engage in the practice of integrated thinking with other people in governance of Eskada. This is especially evidenced by his dismissal of those who did not agree with him.

Integrated reporting is based on a business environment in which integrated thinking is embedded in mainstream business practice and places value on the organisation's relationship with its stakeholders. Integrated thinking in the business environment and the adoption of integrated reporting cannot force a change in behaviour but does not facilitate the type of aggressive and controlling behaviour exhibited by David.

The phrase "tone at the top" is often used to describe the environment and culture internal to a business which is set by those in governance of an organisation. Integrated thinking and reporting encourages the "tone at the top" to be one which is inclusive of others and considers the opinions of others. Integrated reporting encourages those in governance to reflect and consider how decisions and actions will impact the business, its stakeholders, and the external environment.

Integrated reporting often uses key performance indicators of financial and non-financial information to communicate the creation of value for an organisation. In the case of Eskada, these key performance indicators could have included a measurement of employee morale and dissatisfaction with management. The measurement of these attitudes could have been an early indication that the organisation was not creating value through human capital. David's sole reliance on financial targets, aggressive selling of the bank's products and dismissal of staff who disagreed with him were strong indicators of the "negative" culture at the bank.

Integrated reporting shifts the focus of decision making to consider how the decisions create value over the short, medium, and long term and not just in the short term.

While integrated reporting is not guaranteed to fix issues like those seen at Eskada, the process does encourage a business environment and the development of key relationships that are in contrast to an environment where one individual can monopolise decision making.

Answer 27 BIGGO

(a)   **Rights and responsibilities**

The comment by Albert Doo identifies rights and responsibilities as being two essential characteristics of citizenship, be it human or organisational in nature. In the same way that individuals have rights and responsibilities in society, so do business organisations such as Biggo. The question asks about rights and responsibilities in the context of Biggo.

A right is an expectation of the benefits that Biggo can receive, by virtue of citizenship, from society. Biggo can expect the right to have the freedom to conduct business by engaging in resource and product markets, to enjoy the protection of the law and the goodwill of other members of society in supporting the right of the organisation to exist, to innovate and grow. Biggo had the right, for example, to expect fair treatment under law in respect of its planning application (and in fact received this permission).

A responsibility is a duty owed, by the citizen (in this case, Biggo), back to society as a quid pro quo for the extension of rights. These are owed by virtue of the citizen's membership of society. In most societies, responsibilities extend to compliance with all relevant laws and regulations, including the payment of taxes, and compliance with the behavioural norms of that society. Biggo, along with all other businesses, has a number of legal and ethical responsibilities but it is the extent to which the ethical responsibilities are recognised that is the subject of dispute along the Gray, Owen & Adams continuum.

Interpretation at the two ends of Gray, Owen & Adams "continuum"

Gray, Owen & Adams described seven possible positions that can be adopted on a company's relations with its stakeholders. These concern the ethical assumptions of the roles of a business in society and are as follows: the pristine capitalist, the expedient, the social contractarian, the socialist, the social ecologist, the radical feminist and the deep green. The range of views along this continuum are primarily characterised by the ways in which they interpret the rights and responsibilities of business.

Broadly speaking, the nearer to the pristine capitalist end of the continuum, the greater the rights of shareholders and the fewer their responsibilities to a wider constituency. Conversely, the nearer the "deep green" end of the continuum, the fewer the perceived rights and the greater the responsibilities of the company and its agents to a more widely defined group of stakeholders.

At the "pristine capitalist" end of the continuum, rights and responsibilities are understood principally in terms of economic measures. The company has the right to pursue its legal business activity and to develop that business with the support of society and the governing authorities. In return, its responsibilities are limited to the profitable production of goods and services and, accordingly, the generation of profits that are entirely attributable to shareholders. It is not the responsibility of businesses to pursue any other social, environmental or benevolent end. In this context, it is clearly not the company's responsibility to use shareholders' money to contribute to the new children's play area.

At the socialist-to-green end of the continuum, it is argued that businesses like Biggo have fewer (and contestable) rights and much greater responsibilities. According to positions at the deep green end, Biggo, does not, for example, have the right to consume non-sustainable resources "simply" for the purposes of wealth creation. They may not have the moral right, even if they have a legal right, to build on the community's play area. At the same time, Biggo has a wide responsibility to society and to the environment that might seriously constrain their behaviour and activities.

(b)   **Which positions are best described?**

Robert Tens

Robert is closest to the expedient position. The expedient position is one in which social responsibility is seen in terms of what return can be gained from social responsibility policies and actions. In other words, it may be expedient to adopt social responsibility actions but only if by doing so, it furthers its strategic interests. The expedient position does not recognise any implicit social responsibility as such and social policies are therefore only pursued if a clear strategic rationale can be identified for them.

His comment considers the actions towards the community in terms of cultivating current and future employees: it is an exercise of specific stakeholder management with the key stakeholder being the local community. By engaging in activities that give the appearance of being socially responsible (i.e. making the requested donation) other economically advantageous ends can be achieved. He highlighted three strategic benefits that might arise: it might "cultivate the company's reputation" specifically in order "help in future recruitment". Third, it might "help to reduce resistance to any future expansion the company might need to make". He clearly sees the donation in instrumental terms.

Margaret Heggs

Margaret's comment is closest to the pristine capitalist position. Her comment suggests that she believes that the social responsibilities of Biggo do not extend beyond the social benefits it already provides through employment and the provision of "excellent products". The purpose of Biggo is not to engage in costly social responsibility measures such as community donations, even if they can be shown to have a positive strategic benefit. That is not the purpose of a business. In accepting that the company had "no further contractual or ethical duties to the local government nor to the local community", she was demonstrating a pristine capitalist perspective.

(c)   **Social responsibility and short and long-term shareholder interest perspectives**

Definition

"Social responsibility" refers to the belief that companies such as Biggo must act in the general public interest as well as in the specific interest of their shareholders. This can apply to the company's strategy and the way in which the company is governed, but Albert is referring to the specific social footprint that the company has locally. It can also apply to the environmental footprint that a company has (i.e. the effect of company activities on resource consumption or the effect that emissions from operations have). It is possible to interpret this phrase narrowly, as Margaret has done, or more widely, as Albert has.

Short and long-term perspectives

Tutorial note: *This question recognises that the attitude that a company may take towards a particular stakeholder claim can vary when a time perspective is introduced.*

A short-term perspective is likely to consider a time period of days, months or perhaps up to a given financial year in terms of an action affecting short-term performance. A longer-term perspective, typically looking to years rather than months ahead, is likely to consider the legitimacy of a claim in terms of its effect on long-term shareholder value.

In the short term, Biggo may see the claim from Albert, on behalf of the community, as a cost because a "sizeable" contribution would have an effect on the profit for the year and hence the return to the shareholders. The case mentions that profits are likely to be low in the current year and so all costs should be carefully scrutinized for value for money and reduced or eliminated if possible. As Biggo is a public listed company, a short-term reduced profit can erode shareholder value because of reduced dividends and a potential reduction in share price.

In the longer term, Biggo can be seen to be cultivating two potentially key stakeholders (Albert and the local community) and hence may create longer term value in terms of the advantages identified by Robert (e.g. local employees and lower resistance to future factory enlargements). The case mentions the resistance from the local community and, given that the company will have to "live with" the community for many years to come, it may be in Biggo's long-term strategic interest to do what it reasonably can to reduce any friction with this key stakeholder. There may, therefore, be a strategic case for making the contribution as requested.

Answer 28 HAPPY AND HEALTHY

(a)   How an insider-dominated business differs from a public listed company

A family or insider-dominated business is one in which the controlling shareholding is held by a small number of dominant individuals. In many cases, these individuals will also work for the business making them owner-managers. When the insiders belong to a nuclear or extended family it is common to refer to the business as a family firm. In a listed company, the shares are dispersed between many shareholders, the shares are publicly traded and managers are unlikely to be substantial shareholders themselves (although they may own shares as a part of their reward packages).

Governance issues

The agency issues are quite different in the two types of business. There are usually lower agency costs associated with insider-dominated businesses owing to there being fewer agency trust issues. Less monitoring is usually necessary because the owners are often also the managers. Principals (majority shareholders) are able to directly impose own values and principles (business or ethical) directly on the business without the mediating effect of a board. Ken and Steffi have been the majority owners of "Healthy and happy" for its entire 40 years and as long as they trust each other, director monitoring costs should be very low. This is complicated by the new knowledge that there are trustworthiness questions over Ivan.

Short and long-term decision-making issues and the pursuit of motives other than short-term profits. A smaller base of shareholders is more likely to be flexible over when profits are realised and so the expectations of the rates and timings of returns are likely to be longer. This gives management more strategic flexibility especially if, as is the case at "Happy and healthy", the purpose of the business is simply to leave it in a good state to pass on to Ivan when Ken and Steffi retire. Ken and Steffi are motivated by factors other than the pursuit of short-term profit (e.g. promotion of healthy food, good service to customers, etc).

"Gene pool" and succession issues are common issues in family businesses. It is common for a business to be started off by a committed and talented entrepreneur but then to hand it on to progeny who are less equipped or less willing to develop the business as the founder did. When the insiders are unwilling or unable to buy in outside management talent then this issue is highlighted. There are clearly doubts over Ivan's commitment to the business if he has started up a competing business with his wife and this may mean an unfortunate outcome for "Happy and healthy".

"Feuds" and conflict resolution can be major governance issues in an insider-dominated business. Whereas a larger bureaucratic business is capable of "professionalising" conflict (including staff departures and disciplinary actions) this is less likely to be the case in insider-dominated businesses. Family relationships can suffer and this can intensify stress and ultimately lead to the deterioration of family relationships as well as business performance. Ivan's actions are likely to be relevant here as his transfer of inventory to Barong Company is likely to place a severe strain on the Potter family relationships.

Tutorial note: *The requirement to "explore" allows for a range of relevant responses.*

(b)   Accountants as professionals

Society accords professional status to those that both possess a high level of technical knowledge in a given area of expertise (accounting, engineering, law, dentistry, medicine) on the understanding that the expertise is used in the public interest. The body of knowledge is gained through passing examinations and gaining practical expertise over time. Acting in the public interest means that the professional always seeks to uphold the interests of society and the best interests of clients (subject to legal and ethical compliance).

Fundamental principles (responsibilities) of professionalism

Society has reasonable expectations of all professionals. The major professional responsibilities of any professional are as follows:

Integrity: The highest levels of probity in all personal and professional dealings. Professionals should be straightforward and honest in all relationships. This has clear implications for Mr Shreeves in his dealings with Ken and Steffi.

Objectivity: Professionals should not allow bias, conflicts of interest or undue influence to cloud their judgements or professional decisions. In this case, Mr Shreeves should not allow his friendship with the Potters to affect his judgement as an auditor.

Professional competence and due care: Professionals have a duty to ensure that their skills and competences are continually being updated and developed to enable them to serve clients and the public interest. This includes continuing to study and scrutinise ethical guidance from Mr Shreeves's own professional accounting body and also IFAC.

Confidentiality: Professionals should, within normal legal constraints, respect the confidentiality of any information gained as a result of professional activity or entrusted to them by a client.

Professional behaviour: Professionals should comply fully with all relevant laws and regulations and, at the same time, avoid anything that might discredit the profession or bring it into disrepute.

(c)   Professional and ethical dilemma facing Mr Shreeves

The normal behaviour for the auditor, regardless of the options available in this situation, would be to initially seek representations from Ivan to establish whether there is an explanation that has so far been overlooked or not known about. Following that, there are two options in Mr Shreeves's dilemma: to tell or not tell Ken and Steffi about Ivan's behaviour. In discussing these options, a number of issues are relevant.

Issues

Mr Shreeves is clearly in a difficult situation but he must be aware of his duty as a professional accountant which includes, in his role as auditor, a duty to the public interest. He has a duty of due care and diligence to society and government as well as the shareholders of a company being audited. Being complicit in Ivan's activity is clearly not an option as this would be incompatible with his duties to the shareholders and to society in his role as auditor. Furthermore, he has realised a disclosure of such transactions is required and it would be unprofessional not to discuss this with his clients.

He feels he owes a debt to the Potter family as a long-standing family friend and this has the potential to cloud his judgement as the company's auditor. The effect of Ken and Steffi finding out about Ivan's theft could be "devastating" and this is bound to weigh heavily on

Mr Shreeves's mind. In getting too close to the family, Mr Shreeves has compromised his duty as auditor as he is probably less objective than he should be. He should probably have chosen between being a family friend or being the auditor some years ago and that would have made his resolution of the dilemma somewhat easier.

Ivan has been unprofessional and has acted fraudulently in his dealings with "Happy and healthy". In such a situation, the auditor does not have latitude in how he deals with such a discovery. It is a very serious breach of trust by Ivan, regardless of whether he is the Potters' son or not, and it would be inexcusable to withhold this information from the owner-managers of the business.

Advice

Given that the auditor has a duty to the public interest and the company shareholders, he should inform the majority shareholders (Ken and Steffi) what he has found during the audit. To do anything other than this would be to act unprofessionally and irresponsibly towards the majority shareholders of the company. Family relationships or friendships must never be allowed to interfere with an auditor's professional duty and independence. This approach need not be in the form of a blunt confrontation, however, and it would not be unprofessional to speak with Ivan before he spoke to his parents in order to convey to him the potential seriousness of his actions.

Answer 29 HOGG PRODUCTS

(a)   **Purposes of codes of ethics**

- To convey the ethical values of the company to interested audiences including employees, customers, communities and shareholders.

- To control unethical practice within the organisation by placing limits on behaviour and prescribing behaviour in given situations.

- To be a stimulant to improved ethical behaviour in the organisation by insisting on full compliance with the code.

Tutorial note: *Other purposes, if relevant, would gain marks.*

Contents of a corporate code of ethics

The typical contents of a corporate code of ethics are as follows:

Values of the company: This might include notes on the strategic purpose of the organisation and any underlying beliefs, values, assumptions or principles. Values may be expressed in terms of social and environmental perspectives, and expressions of intent regarding compliance with best practice, etc.

Shareholders and suppliers of finance: In particular, how the company views the importance of sources of finances, how it intends to communicate with them and any indications of how they will be treated in terms of transparency, truthfulness and honesty.

Employees: Policies towards employees, which might include equal opportunities policies, training and development, recruitment, retention and removal of staff. In the case of HPC, the policy on child labour will be covered by this part of the code of ethics.

Customers: How the company intends to treat its customers, typically in terms of policy of customer satisfaction, product mix, product quality, product information and complaints procedure.

Supply chain/suppliers: This is becoming an increasingly important part of ethical behaviour as stakeholders scrutinise where and how companies source their products (e.g. farming practice, GM foods, fair trade issues, etc). Ethical policy on supply chain might include undertakings to buy from certain approved suppliers only, to buy only above a certain level of quality, to engage constructively with suppliers (e.g. for product development purposes) or not to buy from suppliers who do not meet with their own ethical standards.

Community and wider society: This section concerns the manner in which the company aims to relate to a range of stakeholders with whom it does not have a direct economic relationship (e.g. neighbours, opinion formers, pressure groups, etc). It might include undertakings on consultation, "listening", seeking consent, partnership arrangements (e.g. in community relationships with local schools) and similar.

Tutorial note: *Up to six points to be identified and described but similar valid general contents would be acceptable.*

(b) **Code of ethics and strategic positioning**

Strategic positioning is about the way that a whole company is placed in its environment as opposed to the operational level, which considers the individual parts of the organisation.

Ethical reputation and practice can be a key part of environmental "fit", along with other strategic issues such as generic strategy, quality and product range.

The "fit" enables the company to more fully meet the expectations, needs and demands of its relevant stakeholders – in this case, European customers.

The "quality" of the strategic "fit" is one of the major determinants of business performance and so is vital to the success of the business.

HPC has carefully manoeuvred itself to have the strategic position of being the highest ethical performer locally and has won orders on that basis.

It sees its strategic position as being the ethical "benchmark" in its industry locally and protects this position against its parent company seeking to impose a new code of ethics.

The ethical principles are highly internalised in Mr Hogg and in the company generally, which is essential for effective strategic implementation.

(c) **Mr Hogg's belief that employing child labour is "always ethically wrong"**

Deontological perspective

In the case scenario, Mr Hogg is demonstrating a deontological position on child labour by saying that it is "always" wrong. He is adopting an absolutist rather than a relativist or situational stance in arguing that there are no situations in which child labour might be ethically acceptable. The deontological view is that an act is right or wrong in itself and does not depend on any other considerations (e.g. economic necessity or the extent of the child's willingness to work).

If child labour is wrong in one situation, it follows that it is wrong in all situations because of the Kantian principle of generalisability (in the categorical imperative). Because child labour is wrong and potentially exploitative in some situations, the deontological position says that it must be assumed to be wrong in all situations.

The fact that it may cause favourable outcomes in some situations does not make it ethically right, because the deontological position is not situational and the quality of the outcome is not taken into account.

Teleological perspective

According to the teleological perspective, an act is right or wrong depending on the favourableness of the outcome. It is sometimes called the consequentialist perspective because the consequences of the action are considered more important than the act itself.

In the teleological perspective, ethics is situational and not absolute. Therefore child labour is morally justified if the outcome is favourable.

The economic support of a child's family by provision of wages for family support might be considered to be a favourable outcome that justifies child labour. There is an ethical trade-off between the importance of the family income from child labour and the need to avoid exploitation and interfere with the child's education. Education is clearly important but family financial support might be a more favourable outcome, at least in the short term, and if so, this would justify the child working rather than being in school.

For HPC, child labour is likely to be cheaper than adult labour but will alienate European buyers and be in breach of its code of ethics. Child labour may be ethically acceptable if the negative consequences can be addressed and overcome.

Tutorial note: *Other equally relevant points made in evaluating Mr Hogg's opinion would be valid. Teleology is often described in terms of utilitarianism and egoism. Although this distinction is not relevant to the question, candidates would not be penalised for introducing the distinction if the other points raised are relevant.*

Answer 30 MRS YTTRIA & MR MORDUE

(a)   **Explain "the public interest"**

Public interest concerns the overall welfare of society as well as the sectional interest of the shareholders in a particular company. It is generally assumed, for example, that all professional actions, whether by medical, legal or accounting professionals, should be for the greater good rather than for sectional interest.

Accounting has a large potential impact and so the public interest "test" is important. Mrs Yttria made specific reference to audit and assurance. In auditing and assurance, for example, the working of capital markets – and hence the value of tax revenues, pensions and investment – rests on accountants' behaviour. In management accounting and financial management, the stability of business organisations – and hence the security of jobs and the supply of important products – also depends on the professional behaviour of accountants.

(b)   **Ethical threats**

In its code of professional ethics, the International Federation of Accountants (IFAC) identified five types of ethical threat. These are (quoted verbatim):

(1)   Self-interest threats, which may occur as a result of the financial or other interests of a professional accountant or of an immediate family member;

(2)   Self-review threats, which may occur when a previous judgement needs to be re-evaluated by the professional accountant responsible for that judgement;

(3)   Advocacy threats, which may occur when a professional accountant promotes a position or opinion to the point that subsequent objectivity may be compromised;

(4)   Familiarity threats, which may occur when, because of a close relationship, a professional accountant becomes too sympathetic to the interests of others; and

(5)   Intimidation threats, which may occur when a professional accountant may be deterred from acting objectively by threats, actual or perceived.

There are obvious familiarity threats in supplying multiple services to the same client in that the firm will possibly be less likely to be rigorous in the audit and may tend to give the client the benefit of the doubt in marginal cases to avoid upsetting them and risk losing the other services.

The potential lack of impartiality may give rise to advocacy threats in that while acting as a "referee" in audit and assurance work, the firm may be lobbying for the client on other areas of work. The high degree of dependence that the firm has on the client opens it up to the threat of intimidation.

The more dependent the firm becomes on the client for its revenues and profits, the more tempting it may become for the client to seek favourable audit judgements from the firm with the implied threat that the firm could lose other business if it was too harsh.

A self-interest threat therefore arises as senior members of the accounting firm give precedence to the protection of their own financial position over the wider public interest of having an auditor partially captured by a client.

(c)   **Accounting profession and deep green (or deep ecologist) position**

Mr Nahum's remarks are similar to some of the positions espoused by deep green theorists, tending as they are, towards the anti-capitalist and the anti-corporatist political left.

Biased and value laden – the belief that accounting (and other professions) work within an unstated set of contestable values. The deep green position argues that accounting is captured by the minority interests of capitalism and acts as the "servant" of capital.

Environmental degradation is a key charge made by deep greens against business in general and, by implication, against accountants. Accountants serve the interests of business (rather than the environment) and hence accountants are complicit in the creation of environmental damage by their unquestioning adherence (in the opinion of the deep greens) to a set of rules that supports capital.

Poverty and "animal rights" are themes raised by deep greens as items that should be on accounting's agenda. One view among some deep greens is that humans have no more moral rights than animals and that activities perpetuating animal unfairness or human poverty should be challenged by accounting as a profession.

Inter and intra-generational "social injustices" are often cited as problems with the "unfettered" capitalist business model which, the deep greens argue, accounting supports and is therefore complicit in. Some business activities result in wealth disparities in this generation (intra-generational) and deprive future generations of resources (inter-generational injustice).

Tutorial note: *Other approaches to this answer would gain marks, if valid.*

Answer 31 MBABO COMPANY

(a)   **Integrity**

The ISEBA code of ethics explains integrity as follows:

The principle of integrity imposes an obligation on all professional accountants to be straightforward and honest in professional and business relationships. Integrity also implies fair dealing and truthfulness.

Integrity is therefore a steadfast adherence to strict ethical standards despite any other pressures to act otherwise. Integrity describes the personal ethical position of the highest standards of professionalism and probity. It is an underlying and underpinning principle of corporate governance and it is required that all those representing shareholder interests in agency relationships both possess and exercise absolute integrity at all times.

In terms of professional relationships, integrity is important for the following reasons:

It provides assurance to colleagues of good intentions and truthfulness. It goes beyond any codes of professional behaviour and describes a set of character traits that mean a person of integrity can be trusted. For auditors such as Potto Sinter, integrity means not only observing the highest standards of professional behaviour but also maintaining the appearance of integrity to his own staff and also to the client.

It reduces time and energy spent in monitoring when integrity and openness can be assumed (the opposite of an audit situation where the professional scepticism should be exercised). Costs will be incurred by Miller Dundas if colleagues feel that Potto Sinter is untrustworthy.

It cultivates good working relationships in professional situations. It encourages a culture of mutual support that can have a beneficial effect on organisational effectiveness. John Wang's professional relationship with Potto is very important to Miller Dundas. It is important, therefore, that Potto has personal integrity.

(b)   **Criticise Potto Sinter's ethical and professional behaviour**

The first criticism of Potto's behaviour in the case is that it gives rise to the appearance of unprofessionalism and possibly of corruption. $100,000 is a substantial amount but notwithstanding the amount, the allocation of company funds on what appears to be a home improvement on a director's house should be robustly challenged. It is possible that Potto is acting without integrity in this matter.

Potto's failure to act on the information strongly suggests that he has failed in his duty to other shareholders of Mbabo and to tax and other state authorities. The audit is for the benefit of several parties including shareholders and government/tax authorities and it is therefore vital that the information signed off is fairly presented ("true and fair" in the UK). Being fairly presented is normally evidenced by following all accounting standards. Other shareholders might be very intrigued to know why one director, even though a shareholder himself, has used company funds for his own private purposes.

The comment on the clearance document appears to be evidence that Potto accepted a weak explanation from Mr Mbabo or was prepared not to put any pressure on Mr Mbabo for other reasons (perhaps for reasons of an ethical threat such as familiarity, intimidation or self-interest threat or similar). Potto gave the appearance of a lack of objectivity in his actions, possibly as a result of the threats to independence. Auditors should be objective at all times.

Potto failed to satisfy the queries of, and to work well alongside, other important members of the audit team. Being able to be a leader of, and a member of, a team of people is an important part of professional behaviour and Potto's summary dismissal of Lisa's question after the sign-off was unprofessional and unhelpful.

As a senior member of the firm, Potto set a poor example to junior colleagues, such as Lisa, in his behaviour. Not only did he show evidence of poor audit practice but he also failed to satisfy Lisa's entirely justified curiosity over the matter.

Potto is complicit in a probable breach of IAS 24 on related party transactions. There is a disclosure requirement of all related party transactions regardless of value, and concealment of this is both unprofessional and technically irregular. Lack of disclosure should have led to a qualified opinion, a disagreement, on the audit report.

Tutorial note: *Reference to IAS 24 on related party transactions could be made as could reference to a disagreement leading to a qualified opinion on the audit report. Although appropriate credit would be given for these it is possible to get full marks on this part without referring to either of them.*

(c)   **John Wang's ethical dilemma**

John Wang may attempt to resolve his ethical dilemma in the following two ways. The two alternatives are:

- To confront Potto directly to see if the matter can be resolved in a professional manner between themselves. If Potto does not respond to this, John should take the matter higher up the organisation. John would be complying with the professional behavioural standards set out in the ACCA code of ethics and elsewhere, and, indirectly, insisting that Potto does the same.

- To take no further action and "let it drop". He would decide that the information provided by Lisa should not go any further and that any knowledge he had gained from her and her achievement log should be kept confidential.

The evaluation should make reference to the following four issues that may be used to argue in either direction:

- All professional accountants are required to comply in detail with the highest professional and ethical standards. In addition to the ACCA and other professional codes of ethics, most audit decisions are underpinned by regulation and, in some cases, legislation. There are also issues relating to quality control within Miller Dundas that need to be adhered to as best professional practice.

■ John Wang's leadership position in his role as training manager, partner and professional accountant. His decision would be an important signal to Lisa over the acceptability of Potto's behaviour in a professional situation and the importance placed on the complaints of junior staff such as herself. Assuming that John recognised the non-compliance issue, this would also be a form of professional negligence on his part to ignore it.

■ His confronting Potto would probably compromise their friendship and future professional relationship. It may also have an impact on John's future career at Miller Dundas. These factors may conflict, in John's mind, with his duty of objectivity. It is important to develop harmonious relationships in professional situations as far as possible as they can be of benefit to both people involved and to the organisation itself but never at the expense of professional objectivity. Whistle-blowers, whether internal or external, rarely have a stress free experience and John could possibly expect a certain amount of personal stress if he were to report Potto.

■ There is an issue over how determined Lisa Xu is to take the matter further. To confront Potto would mitigate any risk that Lisa might take it further and compromise both Potto and John. Lisa could, for example, approach the managing partner or even an outside body and implicate John as well as Potto: Potto for the unprofessional behaviour and John Wang for knowing about it but doing nothing.

Although there are two theoretical alternatives in this dilemma, John's required course of action is clear. He should confront Potto with the allegation and then pursue whatever course of action may ensue to satisfactorily resolve the situation.

Tutorial note: *The "pros and cons" of each option can be used in evaluating either option depending on how you approach the question. Considering consultation with a third party, such as a professional body, would obtain marks.*

Answer 32 JOJO AUDITORS

(a) **Conflict of interest**

A conflict of interest occurs when a person's freedom of choice or action is constrained by a countervailing interest, which means that the most objectively correct course of action cannot be taken. The discretion to act correctly is fettered by the need to protect a related but contradictory interest.

In the case of Jojo Auditors, Jack Hu experienced a conflict of interest between carrying out the agreed policy of dismissing all students assessed as "poor" (such as Polly Shah) and his familiarity with the Shah family and his making a personal gain from the family in the form of free holidays.

Jack acted against the best interests of the firm including his fellow partners. In his role as managing partner, he owes it to the other partners, and to the employees and clients of the firm, to act responsibly and always in the best interests of the firm. His conflict of interest prevented this from happening.

In acting as he did, Jack compromised the other committee members and made them compromise their own professional values. Both the training manager and the representative from human resources are engaged in order to maximise their benefit to Jojo and as managing partner, Jack "bullied" them into accepting his view. This decision undermined the training manager and thus circumvented the normal chain of command in matters of student assessment.

He knowingly allowed a technically weak student to be retained thereby potentially compromising the quality and integrity of the audits she would work on. He owes a professional duty to the shareholders of the companies that Jojo audits. Audits should be conducted diligently, and technical accuracy should underpin the application of auditing standards and in following procedures and protocols. A technical weakness (such as Polly's) would potentially weaken the effectiveness of the audit and hence be a failure of a duty of care to the client's shareholders.

In acting as he did, Jack gave the appearance of unfairness and a lack of objectivity. The appearance of integrity and probity is important in leading organisations and even were it not true, he allowed his integrity and objectivity to be seen as questionable. Once discovered, confidence in the assessment process at Jojo would have been lost and this could have the effect of damaging its reputation as a provider of training contracts, and therefore in the services provided by the firm.

(b) **Ethical safeguards**

- Jack could undergo some instruction or continuous professional development (CPD) on the fundamental principles of professionalism and the need to avoid conflicts of interest. As a professional accountant, he is bound in any case by the codes of ethics and/or rulebook of his professional body and the IFAC code. Most of these specifically warn against such conflicts, including the acceptance of gifts unless the value is trivial and inconsequential, and his professional body may provide such a course of instruction.

- Enforce a requirement to declare any conflicts of interest at the beginning of each meeting to consider student assessments. This could be made a "standing item" on the agenda so that it had to be considered before each time that assessments were considered. The declaration of conflicts of interests could also be made a part of the recruitment process for new partners where appropriate.

- Rotate the partner who chairs the assessment committee. This would mean that the chance of Mr Hu being the partner considering Polly Shah's case would be reduced (in the case of Jojo) to one in five. Other partners without the conflict of interest would, in any given meeting, be more likely to be chairing.

- Involve an additional partner in the review of student assessments, more able to confront Mr Hu than the training manager or HR manager, neither of whom are at partner level. Another partner would have the organisational "weight" to confront Mr Hu in a way that the training manager or HR manager evidently did not.

- The outcomes of the assessments could be validated by an external party (akin to the role that a non-executive director might play if Jojo were a public company). A retired partner could discharge such a role, for example, or a human resources consultant. The final decision on each student would not be made known until each had been "signed off" by the external party.

- Keep an internal HR file formally recording the list of students by assessment category. This would make the decision to retain Polly, in spite of her "poor" assessment, much more visible to relevant business managers. This would apply greater consistency because it would be more transparent that Polly was retained even though her assessment was rated as "poor".

Tutorial note: *Credit would be given for any reasonable safeguard that addresses the problem.*

(c) **Performance measurement criteria**

The criteria used to measure the performance of directors and/or partners (in a partnership) vary according to the situation. Some criteria will be much more important than others, and highly context-specific criteria may apply in some organisations. In general terms, however, there are four typical criteria that are helpful:

(1) The level of independence of the person (i.e. being free from external vested interests) and commitment to the public interest. This is especially important in accounting practices where serving the public interest is an important component of professional service.

(2) Preparedness and fitness to practise including maintaining the relevance of skills and undertaking relevant continuing professional development. For the partners and Jojo, this would involve maintaining knowledge of current audit and reporting standards, for example.

(3) Practice, including levels of participation in their allocated roles and their competence in those roles. Linked to this is the contribution made to the formulation and implementation of the organisational strategy.

(4) Contribution to committee work and administrative duties as appropriate. Jack's effectiveness in his role as member of the committee that evaluates student progress would fall within this area.

Difficulties of individual performance measurement at Jojo

As a privately-owned business, there is no external pressure for such a procedure. This is because, as an unincorporated business, there are no listing rules enforced by a stock exchange and no external shareholder pressures to be applied. There is no agency gap created by a separation of ownership and management.

There is unlikely to be an independent non-executive director (NED) structure in place to support and carry out the performance measurement. Because of the difficulties raised by full-time senior management appraising each other, NEDs take a role in this in listed companies. Without this element of external independent scrutiny, it would be very difficult to maintain independence and fairness in a performance measurement system.

The informality of relationships in a smaller partnership may make objective assessment impossible, especially if, as in a smaller practice, longstanding personal friendships may be a strong component of the culture. As the five partners are personal friends with each other, it would be very difficult for them to conduct objective performance appraisals on each other.

There is likely to be resistance from some partners, at least from Jack Hu, who, if appraised, would be likely to receive a poor assessment on some criteria. As the managing partner (the equivalent of a chief executive in a partnership), it would be difficult to arrive at a fair measurement process for Mr Hu without the involvement of external parties such as NEDs.

Answer 33 INTEGRATED REPORTING

(a) **Integrated thinking**

As defined within the Integrated Reporting Framework, Integrated Thinking is the active consideration by an organisation of the relationships between its various operating and functional units and the capitals that the organisation uses or affects.

Integrated Thinking leads to integrated decision making and actions embedded within the organisation that consider the creation of value over the short, medium and long term. It is the application of the collective mind of those charged with governance and the ability of management to monitor, manage and communicate (internally and externally) the full complexity of the value-creation process and how this contributes to the success of the organisation over time.

Integrated Thinking is the precursor to successful Integrated Reporting – the concise communication (internal and external) about how an organisation's strategy, governance, performance and prospects, in the context of its external environment, lead to the creation of value in the short, medium and long term.

Integrated Reporting demonstrates the linkages between an organisation's strategy, governance and financial performance and the social, environmental and economic context within which it operates. By reinforcing these connections, Integrated Reporting can help the business to take more sustainable decisions and enable investors and other stakeholders to understand how an organisation is really performing.

Entities must go beyond conventional corporate and social responsibility programmes and instead place sustainability at the heart of business strategies and operations to unlock the full commercial potential and sustainability benefits. New innovative ideas that deliver commercial, environmental and social benefit should be the key driver.

(b)   **Guiding principles**

Strategic focus and future orientation: The report should provide insight into the organisation's strategy and how it relates to the organisation's ability to create value over time and its use and effect on the identified capitals.

Connectivity of information: The report should demonstrate connectivity between the factors that affect the organisation's ability to create value over time.

Stakeholder relationships: The report should provide insight into the nature and quality of the organisation's relationships with its key stakeholders.

Materiality: The report should disclose information about items which significantly affect the organisation's ability to create value over time.

Conciseness: The report should be focused and avoid superfluous information that would not be relevant to stakeholders.

Reliability and completeness: The report should reflect all material items (both positive and negative) affecting the organisation and be free from material error.

Consistency and comparability: Information contained in an integrated report should be consistent over time and presented in a way which can be compared to other organisations.

(c)   **Integrated Report content**

The specific information in an integrated report will, necessarily, vary from one organisation to another because each organisation creates value in its own unique way. However, addressing the questions relating to the Content Elements, which apply to **all** organisations, helps ensure a suitable level of comparability between organisations.

The eight Content Elements are fundamentally linked to each and are not mutually exclusive:

Organisational overview and external environment: What does it do and under what circumstances does it operate?

Governance structure: How does this support the organisation's ability to create value in the short, medium and long term?

Business model: What is it?

Risks and opportunities: What specific risks and opportunities affect the organisation's ability to create value over the short, medium and long term, and how are they dealt with?

Strategy and resource allocation: Where does the organisation want to go and how does it plan to get there?

Performance: To what extent have strategic objectives been achieved during the period and what have been the effects on the capitals?

Outlook: What challenges and uncertainties are likely to be encountered in pursuing the organisation's strategy? What are the potential implications for its business model and future performance?

Basis of presentation: How are the matters to be included in the Integrated Report determined and quantified or evaluated?

Sufficient detail should be given within the Integrated Report to enable the above questions to be comprehensively answered. The detail does not need to be presented in any specific order or section of the report, as long as the Guiding Principles are applied.

(d)   Capital

Integrated reporting more clearly demonstrates an organisation's use of and dependence on different resources and relationships or "capitals". It is important that the governance framework and processes take account of and utilise the relationships between each capital that is a stock of value that can be built up, transformed or run down over time in the production of goods or services. The availability, quality and affordability of capitals can affect the long-term viability and sustainability of an organisation's business model and its ability to create value over time. The capitals must be maintained in an appropriate mix or balance and planned for the future, if they are to continue to help organisations create value now and in the future.

Capitals are defined as follows in the Integrated Framework:

Financial: The pool of funds that is available to an organisation for use in the production of goods or provision of services or obtained through financing.

Manufactured: Manufactured physical objects which are distinct from natural physical objects. Examples include buildings, equipment, and infrastructure.

Intellectual l: Organisational, knowledge-based intangibles.

Human: People's competencies, capabilities and experience, and their motivations to innovate.

Social and Relationship: The institutions and the relationship within and between communities, groups of stakeholders and other networks, and the ability to share information to enhance individual and collective well-being.

Natural: All renewable and non-renewable environmental resources and processes that provide goods or services that support the past, current or future prosperity of an organisation.

Answer 34 HYDRASPORTS

(a) **Performance indicators – social/environmental responsibility**

Member satisfaction

- Number of people on membership waiting lists (if any).
- Number of referrals/recommendations to club membership by existing members.
- Proportion of renewed memberships.
- Actual members: 100% capacity membership (sub-analysed between categories such as "peak", "off-peak" and pensioners).

Membership dissatisfaction

- Proportion of members requesting refunds per month/quarter.
- Proportion of memberships "lapsing" (i.e. not renewed).

Staff

- Average number of staff employed per month.
- Number of starters/leavers per month.
- Staff turnover/average duration of employment.
- Number of training courses for lifeguards and other staff per annum.
- Average hourly (weekly) wage: average national hourly (weekly) wage (or national minimum).

Predictability

- Number of late openings (say more than 5, 15 and 30 minutes after advertised opening times).

- Number of days closed per month/year of each facility (i.e. pool, crèche, sauna, gym) and centre.

Safety

- Incidents reports documenting the date, time and nature of each incident, the extent of damage and/or personal injury, and action taken.

- Number of accident free days.

Other society

- Local community involvement (e.g. facilities offered to schools and clubs at discount rates during "off-peak" times).

- Range of facilities offered specifically to pensioners, mothers and babies, disabled patrons, etc.

- Participation in the wider community (e.g. providing facilities to support sponsored charity events).

Environment

- Number of instances of non-compliance with legislation/regulations (e.g. on chemical spills).

- Energy efficiency (e.g. in maintaining pool at a given temperature throughout the year).

- Incentives for environmental friendliness such as discouraging use of cars/promoting use of bicycles (e.g. by providing secure lock-ups for cycles and restricted car parking facilities).

Evidence

Tutorial note: *As there is a wide range of measures of operational performance that could be suggested, there is a wide range of possible sources of assurance evidence. As the same evidence may contribute to providing assurance on more than one measure they are not tabulated here, to avoid duplication. However, candidates could justifiably adopt a tabular layout here.*

- Membership registers clearly distinguishing between new and renewed members, also showing lapsed memberships.

- Pool/gym timetables – showing sessions set aside for "over 60s", "ladies only", schools, clubs, special events, etc.

- Staff training courses and costs.

- Staff timesheets – showing arrival/departure times and adherence to staff rotas.

- Documents supporting additions to/deletions from payroll standing data (e.g. new joiner/leaver notifications).

- Engineer's inspection reports – confirming gym equipment, etc is in satisfactory working order. Also, engineer and safety check manuals and the maintenance program.

- Levels of expenditure on repairs and maintenance.

- Energy saving equipment/measures (e.g. insulated pool covering).

- Safety drill reports (e.g. alarm tests, pool evacuations).

- Accident report register – showing date, nature of incident, personal injury sustained (if any), action taken (e.g. emergency services called in).

- Any penalties/fines imposed by the local authorities and the reasons for them.

- Copies of reports of local authority investigations.

- The frequency and nature of insurance claims (e.g. to settle claims of injury to members and/or staff).

(b) **Identification and examples of**

Tutorial note: *The International <IR> Framework identifies six forms of capital to be addressed in integrated reporting.*

Financial capital

Hydrasports has financial capital in the form of money received:

- from memberships;
- from the bank loan for the construction of the new hydrotherapy pool; and
- in return for equity when the organisation was initially formed.

Manufactured capital

Hydrasports has manufactured capital in the forms of the following:

- Head office building;
- Building for each centre;
- Swimming pools;
- Exercise equipment;
- Sauna facilities;
- Hydrotherapy pool;
- Sound equipment used in fitness studios.

Intellectual capital

- Hydrasports has limited intellectual capital but will have at least one form of intellectual capital if the patent is acquired for the for design features of hydrotherapy pool.

- Expertise in design of new pool by owner.

Human capital

Examples of human capital include:

- Knowledge and experience of fitness instructors (all are licensed).
- Knowledge and expertise of owners/shareholders (each has over 10 years of experience in fitness instruction).

Social and relationship capital

Hydrasports has both positive and weak social and relationship capital.

The company should aim to improve the areas of weak social and relationship capital. In the past year, the organisation has had a chemical spill and closed all of its sauna facilities until further notice. Members have also been disappointed that staff members are not present to open doors at scheduled opening times. Child care facilities are struggling to meet regulations and may be removed from facilities.

Hydrasports is trying to improve social and relationship capital by building the hydrotherapy pool for retired members with more leisure time. It also offers various types of membership plans for members (including pensioners) and provides their employees with free use of facilities.

When insurance premiums were increased, Hydrasports adjusted the insurance coverage on their equipment rather than passing on the cost of the increased expense to its employees and the public. The company should also work to reopen the sauna facilities in all centres and take efforts to ensure that safety is a priority in the saunas.

Hydrasports needs to realise that the high turnover rate among employees may be costly to the organisation as time and money is having to be spent employing and training new employees. The company should aim to improve its employee retention rate.

Natural capital

The hot thermal springs located on the site of the centre (which will be used in the hydrotherapy pool) is an example of natural capital for Hydrasports. When opening new centres in the future, Hydrasports should consider properties that may have such forms of natural capital.

Answer 35 JGP CHEMICALS

(a)   **"Sustainability" in the context of financial reporting**

Sustainability is the ability of the business to continue to exist and conduct operations with *no effects on the environment that cannot be offset or made good in some other way*. The best working definition is that given by Gro Harlem Brundtland, the former Norwegian prime minister, in the Brundtland Report (1987) as activity that, "meets the needs of the present without compromising the ability of future generations to meet their own needs". Importantly, it refers to both the inputs and outputs of any organisational process.

- *Inputs (resources) must only be consumed at a rate* at which they can be reproduced, offset or in some other way not irreplaceably depleted.

- *Outputs (e.g. waste and products) must not pollute* the environment at a rate greater than can be cleared or offset.

Recycling is one way to reduce the net effect of products on the environment. The business activities must take into consideration the carbon emissions, other pollution to water, air and local environment, and should use strategies to neutralise their effects by engaging in environmental practices that will replenish the used resources and eliminate harmful effects of pollution. A number of reporting frameworks have been developed to help in accounting for sustainability including:

- the notion of triple-bottom-line accounting;
- the Global Reporting Initiative (GRI); and
- the International Integrated Reporting Framework.

All of these attempt to measure the social and environmental effects of a business in addition to its normal accounting.

Criticism of the finance director's understanding of sustainability

The finance director has completely *misunderstood the meaning of the term sustainable*. He has *assumed that it refers only to the sustainability of the business as a going concern* and not of the business's place in the environment. Clearly, if a business has lasted 50 years then the business model adopted is able to be sustained over time and a healthy balance sheet enabling future business to take place ensures this. But this has *no bearing at all on whether the business's environmental footprint is sustainable* which is what is meant by sustainability in the context of environmental reporting. In the context of integrated reporting, sustainability is regarded as the organisation's ability to create value over time for its financial stakeholders.

Stages in an environmental audit and issues in developing them

The first stage is agreeing and establishing the metrics involved and deciding on what environmental measures will be included in the audit. This selection is important because *it will determine what will be measured against, how costly the audit will be and how likely it is that the company will be criticised for "window dressing" or "greenwashing".* JGP needs to decide, for example, whether to include supply chain metrics as Professor Appo suggested, which would be a much more challenging audit. Given that the *board's preference is to be as "thorough as possible", it seems likely that JGP will include a wide range of measures* and set relatively ambitious targets against those measures.

The second stage is *measuring actual performance against the metrics* set in the first stage. The means of measurement will *usually depend on the metric being measured.* Although many items will be capable of numerical and/or financial measurement (e.g. energy consumption or waste production), others, such as public perception of employee environmental awareness, will be less so. Given the board's stated aim of providing a robust audit and its need to demonstrate compliance, this stage is clearly of great importance. If JGP wants to demonstrate compliance, then measures must be established so that compliance against target can be clearly shown. This is likely to favour quantitative measures.

The third stage is *reporting the levels of compliance or variances.* The issue here is *how to report the information and how widely to distribute the report.* The board's stated aim is to *provide as much information as possible "in the interests of transparency".* This would tend to signal the publication of a public document (rather than just a report for the board) although there will be issues on how to produce the report and at what level to structure it. The information demands of local communities and investors may well differ in their appetite for detail and the items being disclosed. Given that it was the desire to issue an environmental report that underpinned the proposed environmental audit, it is likely that JGP will opt for a high level of disclosure to offset the concerns of the local community and the growing number of concerned investors.

(c) **"Environmental risk"**

An environmental risk is an unrealised loss or liability arising from the effects on an organisation from the natural environment or the actions of that organisation on the natural environment. Risk can therefore arise from natural phenomena affecting the business (e.g. the effects of climate change, adverse weather, resource depletion and threats to water or energy supplies). Similarly, liabilities can result from emissions, pollution, waste or product liability.

Strategic risks

These arise from the overall strategic positioning of the company in its environment. Some strategic positions give rise to greater risk exposures than others. Because strategic issues typically affect the whole of an organisation and not just one or more of its parts, strategic risks can potentially involve very high stakes – they can have very high hazards and high returns. Because of this, they are managed at board level in an organisation and form a key part of strategic management. Examples of strategic risks include those affecting products, markets, reputation, supply chain issues and other factors that can affect strategic positioning. In the case of JGP, reputation risk in particular is likely to be one of the most far-reaching risks, and hence one of the most strategic.

Operational risks

Operational risks refer to potential losses arising from the normal business operations. Accordingly, they affect the day-to-day running of operations and business systems in contrast to strategic risks that arise from the organisation's strategic positioning. Operational risks are managed at risk management level (not necessarily board level) and can be managed and mitigated by internal control systems. Examples include those risks that, although important and serious, affect one part of the organisation and not the whole (e.g. machinery breakdown, loss of some types of data, injuries at work and building/estates problems).

In the specific case of JGP, environmental risks are strategic for the following reasons.

Environmental performance *affects the way in which the company is viewed by some of its key stakeholders*. The case mentions the local community (that supplies employees and other inputs) and investors. The threat of the withdrawal of support by the local community is clearly a *threat capable of affecting the strategic positioning* of JGP as its ability to attract a key resource input (labour) would be threatened. In addition, the case mentions that a "growing group of investors" is concerned with environmental behaviour and so this could also have *potential market consequences*.

As a *chemical company, Professor Appo said that JGP has a "structural environmental risk"* which means that its membership of the chemical industry makes it have a higher level of environmental risk than members of other industries. This is because of the *unique nature of chemicals processing* which can, as JGP found, have a major impact on one or more stakeholders and threaten a key resource (labour supply). Environmental risk arises from the potential losses from such things as emissions and hazardous leaks, pollution and some resource consumption issues. CEO Keith Miasma referred to this risk in his statement about the threat to JGP's overall reputation. As a major source of potential reputation risk, environmental risk is usually a strategic risk for a chemical company such as JGP.

Answer 36 R & M

(a) **Stakeholders**

(i) *Definition and identification*

A stakeholder can be defined as any person or group that can affect or be affected by an entity. In this case, stakeholders are those that can affect or be affected by the building of the Giant Dam Project. Stakeholding is thus bi-directional. Stakeholders can be those (voluntarily or involuntarily) affected by the activities of an organisation or the stakeholder may be seeking to influence the organisation in some way.

All stakeholding is characterised by the making of "claims" on an organisation. Put simply, stakeholders "want something" although in some cases, the "want" may not be known by the stakeholder (such as future generations). It is the task of management to decide on the strengths of each stakeholder's claim in formulating strategy and in making decisions. In most situations it is likely that some stakeholder claims will be privileged over others.

R&M's external stakeholders include:

- The client (the government of the East Asian country).
- Stop-the-dam pressure group.
- First Nation (the indigenous people group).
- The banks that will be financing R&M's initial working capital.
- Shareholders.

Tutorial note: *The best approach is to identify ALL the external stakeholders and then select the FOUR that best meets the requirement of part (ii).*

(ii)   Stakeholder claims

Four external stakeholders in the case and their claims are as follows.

The client (i.e. the government of the East Asian country) – wants the project completed to budget and on time. It may also be concerned to minimise negative publicity in respect of the construction of the dam and the possible negative environmental consequences.

Stop-the-dam – the vocal and well organised pressure group want the project stopped completely, seemingly and slightly paradoxically, for environmental and social footprint reasons.

First Nation – the indigenous people group currently resident on the land behind the dam that would be flooded after its construction want the project stopped so they can continue to live on and farm the land.

The banks (identified as a single group) – seem happy to lend to the project and will want it to proceed so they make a return on their loans commensurate with the risk of the loan. They do not want to be publicly identified as being associated with the Giant Dam Project.

Shareholders – have the right to have their investment in the company managed in such a way as to maximise the value of their shareholding. The shareholders seek projects providing positive NPVs within the normal constraints of sound risk management.

Tutorial note: *Only four stakeholders needed to be identified. Marks would be given for up to four relevant stakeholders only.*

(b)   Framework for assessing risk

Risk is assessed by considering each identified risk in terms of two variables:

- its hazard (or consequences or impact); and,
- its probability of happening (or being realised or "crystallising").

The most material risks are those identified as having high impact/hazard and the highest probability of happening. Risks with low hazard and low probability will have low priority. Between these two extremes are situations where judgement is required on how to manage the risk.

In practice, it is difficult to measure both variables with any degree of certainty and so it is often sufficient to consider each in terms of relative crude metrics such as "high/medium/low" or even "high/low". The framework can be represented as a "map" of two intersecting continuums with each variable being plotted along a continuum.

Consequences (impact or hazard)

	Low	High
Low		
High		

(Likelihood/probability on vertical axis: Low to High)

Tutorial note: *Other relevant risk assessment frameworks would be valid.*

(c) **Assessment of three risks**

Risk 1 - Stop-the-dam

Disruption and resistance by Stop-the-dam. Stop-the-dam seems very determined to delay and disrupt progress as much as possible. The impact of its activity can be seen on two levels. It is likely that the tunnelling and other "human" disruption will cause a short-term delay but the more significant impact is that of exposing the lenders. In terms of probability, the case says that it "would definitely be attempting to resist the Giant Dam Project when it started" but the probability of exposing the lenders is a much lower probability event if the syndicate membership is not disclosed.

Assessment: Impact/hazard = low. Probability/likelihood = high.

Risk 2 – First Nation

The risk to progress offered by First Nation can probably be considered to be low impact/hazard but high probability. The case says that it "would be unlikely to disrupt the building of the dam", meaning low impact/hazard, but that "it was highly likely that they would protest", meaning a high level of probability that the risk event would occur.

Assessment: Impact/hazard = low. Probability = high.

Risk 3 – Banks

There are financing risks as banks seem to be hesitant when it comes to lending to R&M for the project. Such a risk event, if realised, would have a high potential for disruption to progress as it may leave R&M with working capital financing difficulties. The impact would be high because the bank may refuse to grant or extend loans if exposed (subject to existing contractual terms). It is difficult to estimate the probability. Perhaps there will be a range of attitudes by the lending banks with some more reticent than others (perhaps making it a "medium" probability event).

Assessment: Impact/hazard = medium to high (depending on the reaction of the bank). Probability = low to medium (depending on how easy it would be to discover the lender).

(d)   **Chairman's statement at AGM**

Thank you for coming to the annual general meeting of Rowlands & Mendeleev. I would like to make a statement in response to the concerns that a number of our investors have made in respect to our appointment as the principal contractor for the prestigious and internationally important Giant Dam Project. We are very pleased and honoured to have won the contract but as several have observed, this does leave us in a position of having a number of issues and risks to manage.

As a project with obvious environmental implications, the board and I wish to reassure investors that we are aware of these implications and have taken them into account in our overall assessment of risks associated with the project.

(i)   A definition of "sustainable development"

One investor asked if we could explain the sustainability issues and I begin with addressing that issue. According to the well-established Brundtland definition, sustainable development is development that meets the needs of the present without compromising the ability of future generations to meet their own needs.

This definition has implications for energy, land use, natural resources and waste emissions. In a sustainable development, all these should be consumed or produced at the same rate they can be renewed or absorbed so as to prevent leaving future generations with an unwanted legacy of today's economic activity.

We believe that our involvement in the Giant Dam Project has implications for environmental sustainability and it is to these matters that I now turn.

Tutorial note: *Other relevant definitions of sustainability would be equally acceptable.*

(ii)   Environmental and sustainability implications of the Giant Dam Project

In our preparation for the bid to act as principal contractor for the Giant Dam Project, we established that there were two prominent negative implications of the project but these are, in our view, more than offset by two major environmental positives.

The environmental arguments against the Giant Dam Project both concern the flooding of the valley behind the dam. Regrettably, it seems that there will be some loss of important habitats. This, in turn, may mean the removal of balanced environmental conditions for certain animal and plant species. In addition, the flooding of the valley will result in the loss of productive farmland. This will mean reduced capacity for the host country to grow food and thus support citizens such as the members of First Nation.

From our point of view, as the board of R&M, however, we would remind shareholders and other observers that the decisions involving the size and positioning of the Giant Dam were taken by the client, the government. It is R&M's job, having won the contract as principal contractor, to now carry out the plans, regardless of our own views.

Happily, however, there are two very powerful environmental arguments in favour of the Giant Dam Project. It will create a large source of clean energy for economic development that will be sustainable, as it will create no carbon emissions nor will it consume any non-renewable resources as it does so (compared to, for example, fossil fuels).

At a time when people are becoming very concerned about greenhouse gases produced from conventional power generation, the Giant Dam Project will contribute to the East Asian country's internationally agreed carbon reduction targets. This, in turn, will contribute to the reduction of greenhouse gases in the environment.

It is clear that the construction of the Giant Dam Project is an environmental conundrum with strong arguments on both sides. The deciding factor may be the opinion that we each have of the desirability of economic growth in the East Asian country (which the energy from the dam is intended to support).

It seems that Stop-the-dam values the preservation of the original environment more than the economic growth that the energy from the dam would support. The client does not agree with this assessment and we are happy to be involved with a project that will create such a useful source of renewable and non-polluting energy.

(iii)   *Importance of confidentiality in the financing of the project and the normal duty of transparency.*

I have been asked to include a statement in my remarks on the balance between our duty to be transparent whenever possible and the need for discretion and confidentiality in some situations. In the case of our initial working capital needs for the Giant Dam Project, the importance of confidentiality in financing is due to the potential for adverse publicity that may arise for the lender. It is important that R&M have the project adequately financed, especially in the early stages before the interim payments from the client become fully effective.

In general, of course, we at R&M attempt to observe the highest standards of corporate governance and this involves adopting a default position of transparency rather than concealment wherever possible. We recognise that transparency is important to underpin investor confidence and to provide investors with the information they need to make fund allocation decisions.

Although it is normal to disclose the amount of debt we carry at any given point (in the statement of financial position) it is rarely normal practice to disclose the exact sources of those loans. In the case of the financing of initial working capital for the Giant Dam Project, I am sure you will realise that in this unique situation, disclosure of the lender's identity could threaten the progress of the project. For this reason we must resist any attempts to release this into the public domain. We are aware of one pressure group that is actively seeking to discover this information in order to disrupt the project's progress and we shall be taking all internal measures necessary to ensure they do not obtain the information.

Thank you for listening.

(e)   Control and sub-contractors

Specifically in regard to the maintenance of internal controls when working with sub-contractors, the prominent difficulties are likely to be in the following areas:

- ■   Configuring and co-ordinating the many activities of sub-contractors so as to keep progress on track. This may involve taking the different cultures of sub-contractor organisations into account.

- ■   Loss of direct control over activities as tasks are performed by people outside R&M's direct employment and hence its management structure.

- ■   Monitoring the quality of work produced by the sub-contractors. Monitoring costs will be incurred and any quality problems will be potentially costly.

■ Budget "creep" and cost control. Keeping control of budgets can be a problem in any large civil engineering project (such the construction of the new Wembley Stadium in the UK) and problems are likely to be made worse when the principal contractor does not have direct control over all activities.

■ Time limit over-runs. Many projects (again, such as the new Wembley Stadium, but others also) over-run significantly on time.

Tutorial note: *Only four difficulties need to be described.*

Answer 37 SWAN HILL

(a)   **Tucker's framework**

Is the decision:

Profitable? For SHC, the answer to this question is yes. Profits would potentially be substantially increased by the loss of all its competitors and the emergence of SHC, in the short to medium term at least, as a near monopolist.

Legal? The secrecy option poses no legal problems as it is a part of normal competitive behaviour in industries. In some jurisdictions, legislation forbids monopolies existing in some industries but there is no indication from the case that this restriction applies to Swan Hill Company.

Fair? The fairness of the secrecy option is a moral judgment. It is probably fair when judged from the perspective of SHC's shareholders but the question is the extent to which it is fair to the employees and shareholders of SHC's competitors.

Right? Again, this is a matter of ethical perspective. Is it right to pursue the subjugation of competitors and the domination of an industry regardless of the consequences to competitors? The secrecy option may be of the most benefit to the local community of Swan Hill that the company has traditionally valued.

Sustainable or environmentally sound? The case says that the sink method emits at a lower rate per unit of output than the existing process but this has little to do with the secrecy option as the rates of emissions would apply if SHC licensed the process. This is also an argument for the licensing option; however, as environmental emissions would be lower if other competitors switched to the sink method as well. There may be environmental implications in decommissioning the old plant to make way for the new sink method investment.

(b)   **Strategic and operational risks**

Strategic risks

These arise from the overall strategic positioning of the company in its environment. Some strategic positions give rise to greater risk exposures than others.

Because strategic issues typically affect the whole of an organisation and not just one or more of its parts, strategic risks can potentially concern very high stakes – they can have very high hazards and high returns. Because of this, they are managed at board level in an organisation and form a key part of strategic management.

Operational risks

Operational risks refer to potential losses arising from the normal business operations. Accordingly, they affect the day-to-day running of operations and business systems in contrast to strategic risks that arise from the organisation's strategic positioning.

Operational risks are managed at risk management level (not necessarily board level) and can be managed and mitigated by internal control systems.

Secrecy option

The secrecy option would be a strategic risk for the following reasons:

- It would radically change the environment that SHC is in by reducing competition. This would radically change SHC's strategic fit with its competitive environment. In particular, it would change its "five forces" positioning which would change its risk profile.

- It would involve the largest investment programme in the company's history with new debt substantially changing the company's financial structure and making it more vulnerable to short term liquidity problems and monetary pressure (interest rates).

- It would change the way that stakeholders view SHC, for better or worse. It is a "crisis issue", certain to polarise opinion either way.

- It will change the economics of the industry thereby radically affecting future cost, revenue and profit forecasts.

- There may be retaliatory behaviour by SHC's close competitor on 25% of the market.

Tutorial note: *Similar reasons if relevant and well-argued would attract marks.*

(c)   CEO statements

(i)   For the secrecy option

Important developments at SHC

This is an exciting time for the management and shareholders of Swan Hill Company. The research and development staff at SHC have made a ground-breaking discovery (called the "sink method") that will enable your company to produce its major product at lower cost, in higher volumes and at a much higher quality than our competitors will be able to using, as they do, the existing production technology. The sink process also produces at a lower rate of environmental emissions which, as I am sure shareholders will agree, is a very welcome development.

When considering the options following the discovery, your board decided that we should press ahead with the investment needed to transform the production facilities without offering the use of the technology to competitors under a licensing arrangement. This means that once the new sink production comes on stream, SHC shareholders can, your board believes, look forward to a significant strengthening of our competitive position.

The business case for this option is overwhelming. By pushing ahead with the investment needed to implement the sink method, the possibility exists to gain a substantial competitive advantage over all SHC's competitors.

It will place SHC in a near monopolist position in the short term and in a dominant position long term. This will, in turn, give the company pricing power in the industry and the likelihood of superior profits for many years to come.

We would expect SHC to experience substantial "overnight" growth and the returns from this will reward shareholders' loyalty and significantly increase the value of the company. Existing shareholders can reasonably expect a significant increase in the value of their holdings over the very short term and also over the longer term.

Ethical implications of the secrecy option

In addition to the overwhelming business case, however, there is a strong ethical case for the secrecy option.

SHC recognises that it is the moral purpose of SHC to make profits in order to reward those who have risked their own money to support it over many years. Although some companies pursue costly programmes intended to serve multiple stakeholder interests, SHC recognises that it is required to comply with the demands of its legal owners, its shareholders, and not to dilute those demands with other concerns that will reduce shareholder returns. This is an important part of the agency relationship: the SHC board will always serve the best economic interests of its shareholders: its legal owners.

The SHC board believes that any action taken that renders shareholder returns suboptimal is a threat to shareholder value and an abuse of the agency position. Your board will always seek to maximise shareholder wealth; hence our decision to pursue the secrecy option in this case.

The secrecy option offers the possibility of optimal shareholder value and because shareholders invest in SHC to maximise returns, that is the only ethical action for the board to pursue. Happily, this option will also protect the employees' welfare in SHC's hometown of Swan Hill and demonstrate its commitment to the locality. This, in turn, will help to manage two of the key value-adding resources in the company, its employees and its reputation. This will help in local recruitment and staff retention in future years.

(ii)   For the licensing option

Important developments at SHC

Your board was recently faced with a very difficult business and ethical decision. After the discovery by SHC scientists of the ground-breaking sink production method, we had a choice of keeping the new production technology secret or sharing the breakthrough under a licensing arrangement with our competitors. After a lengthy discussion, your board decided that we should pursue the licensing option and I would like to explain our reasons for this on both business and ethical grounds.

In terms of the business case for licensing, I would like shareholders to understand that although the secrecy option may have offered SHC the possibility of an unassailable competitive advantage, in reality, it would have incurred a number of risks. Because of the speed with which we would have needed to have acted, it would have necessitated a large increase in our borrowing, bringing about a substantial change in our financial structure. This would, in turn, increase liquidity pressures and make us more vulnerable to rising interest rates.

A second risk with the secrecy option would involve the security of the sink technology "secret". If the sink process was leaked or discovered by competitors and subsequently copied, our lack of a legally binding patent would mean we would have no legal way to stop them proceeding with their own version of the sink process.

As well as avoiding the risks, however, the licensing option offers a number of specific business advantages. The royalties from the licences granted to competitors are expected to be very large indeed. These will be used over the coming years to extend our existing competitive advantage in the future.

Finally, the "improvement sharing" clause in the licensing contract will ensure that the sink process will be improved and perfected with several manufacturers using the technology at the same time. SHC's sink production may, in consequence, improve at a faster rate than would have been the case were we to have pursued the secrecy option.

Ethical implications of the licensing option

In addition to the business case, there is also a powerful ethical case for the decision we have taken. As a good, responsible corporate citizen, Swan Hill Company acknowledges its many stakeholders and recognises the impacts that a business decision has on others.

Your board recognises that in addition to external stakeholders having influence over our operations, our decisions can also affect others. In this case, we have carefully considered the likelihood that keeping the new technology a secret from our competitors would radically reshape the industry.

The superior environmental performance of the sink process over existing methods will also mean that when fully adopted, the environmental emissions of the entire industry will be reduced. SHC is very proud of this contribution to this reduction in overall environmental impact.

There seems little doubt that the secrecy option would have had far-reaching and unfortunate effects on our industry and our competitors. The licensing option will allow competitors, and their employees and shareholders, to survive. It is a compassionate act on our part and shows mercy to the other competitors in the industry. It recognises the number of impacts that a business decision has and would be the fairest (and most just) option given the number of people affected.

(d)   Corporate annual reports

(i)   Mandatory and voluntary disclosures

Mandatory disclosures are components of the annual report or integrated report that are mandated by law, regulation or accounting standard.

Examples include (in most jurisdictions) income statement (profit or loss), statement of financial position, cash flow statement, statement of changes in equity, operating segmental information, auditors' report, corporate governance disclosure such as remuneration report and some items in the directors' report (e.g. summary of operating position). In the UK, the business review is compulsory.

Voluntary disclosures are components of the annual report or integrated report that are not mandated in law or regulation but disclosed nevertheless. They are primarily narrative rather than numerical in nature.

Examples include risk information, operating review, social and environmental information, the chief executive's review and key performance indicators.

(ii)   *Accountability to equity investors*

Voluntary disclosures are an effective way of redressing the information asymmetry that exists between management and investors and other stakeholders. In adding to mandatory content, voluntary disclosures give a fuller picture of the state of the company and insights into its operations and strategy. For example:

■   More information helps investors decide whether the company matches their risk, strategic and ethical criteria, and expectations.

■   Makes the annual or integrated report more forward looking (predictive) whereas the majority of the numerical content is backward facing on what has been.

■   Helps transparency in communicating more fully thereby better meeting the agency accountability to investors, particularly shareholders.

■   Helps transparency in communication to other stakeholders such as employees, business partners, local communities, regulators and policy makers

■   There is a considerable amount of qualitative information that cannot be conveyed using statutory numbers (such as strategy, ethical content, social reporting, etc).

■   Voluntary disclosure gives a more rounded and more complete view of the company, its activities, strategies, purposes and values.

■   Voluntary disclosure enables the company to address specific shareholder concerns as they arise (such as responding to negative publicity).

Tutorial note: *Other valid points would equally be recognised.*

Answer 38 GLOBAL-BANK

(a)   *(i)*   *Three Kohlberg levels*

At the pre-conventional level of moral reasoning, morality is conceived of in terms of rewards, punishments and instrumental motivations. Those demonstrating intolerance of regulations in preference for self-serving motives are typical pre-conventionalists.

At the conventional level, morality is understood in terms of compliance with either or both of peer pressure/social expectations or regulations, laws and guidelines. A high degree of compliance is assumed to be a highly moral position.

At the post-conventional level, morality is understood in terms of conformance with "higher" or "universal" ethical principles. Post-conventional assumptions often challenge existing regulatory regimes and social norms and so post-conventional behaviour is often costly in personal terms.

Level 1: Pre-conventional level Stage/Plane 1: Punishment-obedience orientation Stage/Plane 2: Instrumental relativist orientation
Level 2: Conventional level Stage/Plane 3: Good boy-nice girl orientation Stage/Plane 4: Law and order orientation
Level 3: Post-conventional level Stage/Plane 5: Social contract orientation Stage/Plane 6: Universal ethical principle orientation

(ii)   The level that Jack Mineta operated at

The evidence from the case suggests that Mr Mineta operated at the pre=conventional level.

Although he seemed less concerned with punishment, his actions were strongly driven by the incentives of financial rewards suggesting a rewards orientation consistent with pre-conventional thinking.

He seemed prepared to ignore internal control systems ("I'm in this job for what I can get for myself – big risks bring big returns and big bonuses for me").

The internal control systems at Global-bank placed clear limits on traders' behaviour in terms of limits and exposure to the highest risk derivative instruments. Mr Mineta was unconcerned about compliance with controls and prevailing rules would have suggested conventional thinking. Had he complied with the internal control constraints, he would not have lost the large amount of money. Nor would he have made the large prior profits but these were manifestly not sustainable.

Miss Hubu's comment that he "didn't believe in right and wrong" excludes any suggestion that his ignoring of rules was driven by post-conventional assumptions.

(iii)   Stage most appropriate for a professional bank employee

The most appropriate level of moral development for Mr Mineta in his work is stage 4 within the conventional level (level 2). This level stresses compliance with laws and regulations rather than the 3rd stage which is about compliance with norms to gain social acceptance.

Stage 4 is concerned with legal and regulatory compliance and the moral right is that which is the most compliant with prevailing regulatory systems.

Tutorial note: *It is possible to argue for other stages. Credit would be given for this only when robustly defended with evidence. Unsupported assertions gain no marks.*

(b)   Typical causes of internal control failure and the performance of Global-bank

There are several possible causes of internal control failure. The UK Turnbull report gives examples of causes of failure but this list is not exhaustive.

- Poor judgement in decision-making. Internal control failures can sometimes arise from individual decisions being made based on inadequate information provision or by inexperienced staff.

- Human error can cause failures although a well-designed internal control environment can help control this to a certain extent.

- Control processes being deliberately circumvented by employees and others. It is very difficult to completely prevent deliberate circumvention, especially if an employee has a particular reason (in his opinion) to do so, such as the belief that higher bonuses will be earned.

- Management overriding controls, presumably in the belief that the controls put in place are inconvenient or inappropriate and should not apply to them.

- The occurrence of unforeseeable circumstances is the final cause referred to in the Turnbull Report. Control systems are designed to cope with a given range of variables and when an event happens out of that range, the system may be unable to cope.

Tutorial note: *Other, equivalent explanations or valid references to other governance codes would gain marks. The above points can also be expressed in different ways.*

In assessing the performance of Global-bank, there is evidence of a widespread failure of internal control systems and a weak internal control environment. It is possible to highlight five specific failures.

- Poor judgement by Mr Mineta as he breached trading rules (exceeding his trading limit and trading in unauthorised instruments).

- Poor judgement and management over-rides by Mr Evora and an inability or unwillingness to enforce trading rules at the Philos office.

- Mr Evora's withholding of compliance information. He seems to view the Philos office as his own personal fiefdom in which head office directives on trading rules and internal controls do not apply.

- Failure of the head office system to insist on full compliance by acting on failure by Mr Evora to return the required compliance information.

- Mrs Keefer/head office's attitude does not inspire confidence that the incident could not recur. She has failed to enforce controls throughout the company including at its remote offices. Her denial that the board had any responsibility for the loss would only apply if they had ensured that all internal controls had applied throughout the company including at the Philos office. This was not the case.

(c) **Agency relationship in the case**

Any agency relationship involves two parties: a principal and an agent. The agent is accountable to the principal. The relationship arises from the separation of management and ownership in public companies (and in other situations in society).

In the case scenario, the principal is the Shalala Pension Fund. Its purpose is to manage a fund of many different shares and investments with the explicit aim of maximising the fund's value for the benefit of its members' pension values. Accordingly, it is unable and unwilling to take part in directly controlling the organisation itself and indeed, this would be outside the area of expertise of the fund's management. Shalala therefore entrusts the agents – the directors of Global-bank – with the task of acting in its interests and it holds the directors (agents) to account for their performance.

The agent in the scenario is Mrs Keefer and the board of Global-bank. As CEO, Mrs Keefer is entrusted with running the company and ensuring strategies and controls are in place to achieve the objectives set by the principal. She is, therefore, accountable to the principal for all her actions and she has an unambiguous fiduciary duty to act in the sole interests of the principal. Because the principal (in this case the Shalala Pension Fund) invests for maximum capital growth, this should be Mrs Keefer's primary concern.

Anything that means that capital growth is less than it otherwise might be is a failure of her agency responsibility (such as failing to enforce internal controls resulting in Mr Mineta's aberrant behaviour).

(d) **Narrow and wide stakeholders**

According to the technical article in Student Accountant in February 2008 narrow stakeholders are those that are the most affected by the organisation's policies and will usually include shareholders, management, employees, suppliers, and customers that are dependent on the organisation's output.

Wider stakeholders are those less affected and may typically include government, less-dependent customers, the wider community (as opposed to local communities) and other peripheral groups."

The three narrow stakeholders identified in the case are investors, employees and the directors.

Investors

Investors such as the Shalala Pension Fund have experienced a real reduction in the value of their Global-bank holding and the publicity associated with the loss means that the share price will suffer in the short to medium term. These investors are being asked to re-finance the capital base of Global-bank to make good the losses, via the rights issue.

The investors would look for some reassurance that their further investment would not be squandered before committing. If the rights issue goes ahead and Shalala chooses not to increase its investment, Shalala's 12% holding could be diluted, thereby reducing its influence over the company. In the worst case scenario, should the re-financing fail, Shalala would be unlikely to recover much value from its holding if Global-bank was consequently forced into administration.

Employees

Employees such as Miss Hubu and Mr Evora are likely to experience some concerns about their job security in the aftermath of the loss with those at the Philos office perhaps being the most likely to be affected. Mr Evora may be the subject of disciplinary action for his repeated failures of internal control compliance.

Directors

Directors such as Mrs Keefer are likely to experience a much higher level of investor scrutiny for some time to come and Mrs Keefer herself may not survive in her post. The apparent failure of the Global-bank board in its agency responsibilities is likely to increase the amount of intervention by investors and this will be an inconvenience for the board until such time as investor confidence is fully restored.

Benefits such as bonuses may be subject to revisions at general meetings and other directors, seen as complicit in Mr Mineta's losses, may not survive their next retirement by rotation election.

Tutorial note: *Some parts of the assessment may be assumed to apply to more than one stakeholder. For example, individual employees listed as separate stakeholders would only attract marks for one stakeholder group in total.*

(e)   **Letter to Mrs Keefer**

Shalala Pension Fund
Spanner Street
Big City
8 June

Global-bank
16 St Thomas's Doubt
London
WC2T 8XX

Dear Mrs Keefer

Internal control issues within Global-bank

I have been asked by the trustees of the Shalala Pension Fund to convey our expectations of you in respect of your roles and responsibilities in internal controls. We very much regret the circumstances that have made this reminder necessary. In line with the COSO recommendations, the trustees of the Shalala Pension Fund expect you to adopt four major responsibilities in respect of overseeing internal controls in Global-bank.

At the outset, the trustees of the Shalala Pension Fund would like to express their disappointment that you should suggest, as you did at the recent EGM, that the loss incurred by Mr Mineta was "genuinely unforeseeable". From our reading of the situation, you are highly complicit in the loss through your failure in respect of the company's internal controls.

Ultimately, it is the chief executive of any organisation who must assume final responsibility for all internal controls. It is you as CEO who must assume "ownership" of the systems and this ownership must be a part of the manner in which you lead the company. In particular, this means that you must set the tone from the top in both establishing and enforcing the control environment.

We understand that a number of failures to return compliance information from Philos were not acted on and this is a clear failure on head office's part to enforce the internal control environment throughout the company. The control environment is enforced through having internal control compliance embedded within the culture of the company and it was, in our view, clearly your responsibility to facilitate this. From what we can gather, the culture in the Philos office was more driven by Mr Evora's personality than by your imposition of norms from head office and this was clearly one of the causes of Mr Mineta's behaviour.

This setting of the tone should express itself in terms of the way that managers are treated and the way that the tone is cascaded down through the company including to individual branch offices such as Philos and other subsidiary companies if relevant.

It seems self-evident, in hindsight, that the Philos office felt they could act in breach of the relevant internal controls with impunity and this most certainly should not have been allowed.

Finally, as major shareholders in Global-bank, the Shalala trustees expect you to pay particular attention to those areas most vulnerable or open to damaging breaches. The financial products being traded at Philos clearly fit into this in our view as the company has demonstrated its vulnerability to losses on derivatives trading when inadequately controlled.

In addition, I have been asked in particular to draw your attention to the failure of the company to operate an effective internal audit function. We understand that the audit committee has been compromised by a shortage of members to the point that its reporting was criticised by the external auditors.

The Shalala Pension Fund considers the internal audit function to be an imperative part of the governance structure and we are disappointed that you have seemingly failed to give it the priority it clearly deserves. We trust that recent events have reinforced this importance to yourself and other members of the Global-bank board.

I would emphasise again the seriousness with which the trustees of the Shalala Pension Fund view your management failures in this unhappy episode and we look forward to hearing your considered responses to the points made.

Yours sincerely

M Haber

On behalf of Shalala Pension Fund

Tutorial note: *The term "extraordinary" general meeting was removed from company law in England and Wales by the Companies Act 2006. Now, any meeting of the shareholders other than the AGM is simply a "general meeting". However, the term is still used widely used around the world and the word "extraordinary" and has been retained in the P1 Syllabus and Study Guide for September 2015–June 2016 examinations*

Answer 39 SEA SHIPS COMPANY

(a)   **Seven-step (AAA) model**

Step 1: What are the facts of the case?

The facts are that the Mary Jane, one of the company's ships, has sunk and that one contributory cause of the disaster was that the ship had not received the necessary modifications for operating in the rougher seas between Eastport and Northport. Had the recommended structural changes been made, the Mary Jane would not have sunk.

Step 2: What are the ethical issues in the case?

The ethical issues are whether to disclose the information publicly, thereby providing bereaved families with a better explanation of why their loved ones died (and potentially opening the company up to greater liability), or to conceal the information, thereby limiting the value of any punitive damages and protecting shareholder value, at least in the short term.

Step 3: What are the norms, principles and values relevant to the case?

The company is bound by the norms and expectations of its stock exchange and it has voluntarily claimed to have "the highest standards of corporate ethics", particularly valuing its reputation for "outstanding customer care". This means that it owes an implicit and explicit duty of care to both its customers and its shareholders.

As a company that seemingly values its reputation as a well-governed organisation, it is also bound by the underlying principles of corporate governance that include integrity, probity and transparency. Health and safety issues are also very important in all shipping operations and Sea Ships should ensure that all its ferries are compliant with the highest health and safety standards.

Step 4: What are the alternative courses of action?

Alternative 1 is to disclose the information about the advice on structural work to the Mary Jane to the media, the government and the bereaved families. Alternative 2 is to seek to suppress the information within the company and hope that there is no leak.

Step 5: What course of action is most consistent with the norms, values and principles identified in Step 3?

The information is material to a number of parties' better understanding of why the Mary Jane sank. The bereaved families, maritime accident investigators, the government, the ship's insurers and other shipping companies would all benefit from having the information. Disclosure would seem to be the most appropriate course of action notwithstanding the potentially unfortunate consequences for Sea Ships Company of this information leaking out. However, disclosure may result in greater penalties which will be harmful to shareholder value.

Step 6: What are the consequences of each possible course of action?

If the company makes the disclosure, there is a risk that the punitive damages (not yet agreed by the court) would be higher. The case says that "the size of [the punitive damages] would ... reflect the scale of Sea Ships' negligence in contributing to the disaster". A large enough fine would threaten future cash flows and hence future shareholder value. It would also threaten employees' jobs and the ability of the company to continue to provide the existing level of service to customers. Disclosure would potentially invalidate any insurance policy they had to deal with such a disaster, further harming shareholder value.

If the company were to suppress the information, then each person in possession of the knowledge would not only have to examine his own responsibilities in the matter but each would also have potentially damaging information if they were to leave Sea Ships or become disillusioned with it. The consultant who recommended the upgrade will also be a potentially major risk in the leaking of the information.

Step 7: What is the decision?

Alternative 1 is that the company should make a full and detailed disclosure, probably with an acceptance of full responsibility for the failure to make the necessary amendments to the ship. This would be a very costly choice but would be consistent with the company's claimed ethical values and also with the important core values of corporate governance (integrity, transparency, etc).

Alternative 2 is to suppress the information and take all necessary measures to ensure that it is not revealed. This would be a very risky option as the cost to the company and to the directors personally, if the information was ever to emerge, would be very serious. It would also be against the letter and spirit of the core values of corporate governance. It would be unlikely to protect shareholder value in the longer term, is the least ethical of the options and so should be avoided.

Tutorial note: *It is possible to argue for suppression of the report in the short term protection of shareholder value. Marks can be obtained for logic of reasoning process if coherently argued but alignment with the stated values of the company does not allow for suppression as a final decision.*

(b) **Internal control failures**

The company ignored important advice about necessary structural changes needed to the Mary Jane to make her seaworthy for the Northport route. If there was an internal procedure for processing advice, presumably as a part of an economic evaluation of transferring the Mary Jane to the Northport route, then it was clearly ineffective. The document identified a major risk, but had been suppressed within the company and not brought to the attention of any party who could have authorised this to go ahead.

At head office, an "oversight in the company's legal department" resulted in the full value of the Mary Jane's liabilities not being insured. Presumably a human error, this created uninsured liabilities for Sea Ships after the Mary Jane sank. All insurance policies should be reviewed annually and major changes in cover or changes of terms be recommended to the board so that issues like this do not arise. All insurance policies should be reviewed annually and major changes in cover or changes of terms be recommended to the board so that issues like this do not arise.

On the Mary Jane herself, lax internal controls produced four internal control problems. There should be a "safety first" culture on board all ships in which safety considerations outweigh all commercial issues such as meeting schedules.

(1)   A system put in place to ensure that each department head signalled readiness for sea departure was abandoned. This is an example of a "reporting by exception" system being wrongly assumed to be appropriate. Internal control reporting systems are there because they are important and the fact that they may be inconvenient should not be a reason for abandoning them.

(2)   There was a "mistake" in loading vehicles onto the car deck. A sound internal control system would have ensured that such a mistake could not have happened, possibly using physical "fit" issues of loading ramps, appropriate signage, staff training, or similar mechanisms to ensure compliance. The result of the "mistake" was that it created time pressure to leave the port and this contributed to the oversight of the rear doors not being secured and, possibly, the excess speed after leaving port.

(3)   The confusion over responsibility for ensuring that the rear doors were closed – a key safety procedure for any ferry. It is baffling that two people were, seemingly simultaneously, responsible for this and is a problem created by the poor design of internal reporting systems. According to the case, both had assumed that the other person was checking the doors.

(4)   The Mary Jane was going too fast and exceeding the maritime rules about speed in that section of sea. This created swell and caused turbulence at the back of the ship. This, in turn, caused water to enter the ship that would not have been the case at lower speed. This was a failure to observe regulatory speed restrictions on the part of senior ship officers.

(c)   **Contribution that NEDs might make**

The board of Sea Ships appears to be in need of help on a number of issues, some of which may be addressed by the use of non-executive directors.

Mrs Chan's conclusions noted that the board lacked independent scrutiny. One of the most important purposes of any nonexecutive appointment is to bring an outside perspective (sometimes acting as a "corporate conscience") on what can at times be an insular executive culture. In the case of Sea Ships, a number of important internal control issues went unchallenged and a strong non-executive presence could have helped that.

Also mentioned by Mrs Chan was the fact that the board lacked nautical and technical expertise. This is a disturbing finding as some detailed knowledge of a company's products or operations is very important in guiding discussions about those parts of the business. The non-executive appointment of serving or retired senior ferry operating personnel from other companies would rectify this and bring the requisite level of expertise.

The UK's Corporate Governance Code and other statutory and advisory codes of corporate governance, specify that every listed company should have an audit committee made up entirely of non-executive directors. The functions of the committee include reviewing "the company's internal control and risk management systems' and monitoring and reviewing 'the effectiveness of the company's internal audit function". Both of these are deficient at Sea Ships and so an effective audit committee would be a major contribution. We are not told if the company currently has one but we can assume that if it has, it is ineffective.

There are legal compliance issues at Sea Ships, including a failure to enforce the observation of maritime speed limits among its senior ships' officers. One of the advantages of any independent non-executive presence is the enforcement of regulatory and legal rules on company boards with the knowledge that all directors, including non-executives, can be held legally accountable for non-compliance.

(d)   **Memo**

(i)   *Importance of information on operational internal controls and risks*

From: Wim Bock (CEO)
To: All Sea Ships senior officers
Date: xx/yy/zzzz

Re: Information on internal control and risks following the loss of the Mary Jane

Colleagues,

I know you all share with me and the other directors our heartfelt sorrow at the sinking of the Mary Jane with so many lives being lost. Our deepest sympathies go out to the families and friends of all those involved. In the light of the tragic loss, the board felt it vital to write to you all at this time to remind you all of a number of crucial aspects of internal control and risk.

First, I wanted to make clear to you all why the flow of information upwards to the board on matters of internal control and risk is so important. We feel that one contributory factor in the loss of the Mary Jane was a lack of information flow on relevant issues hence my writing to you about this at this time.

In the first instance, the information provided enables the board to monitor the performance of the company on the crucial issues in question. This includes compliance, performance against targets and the effectiveness of existing controls. We, the board, need to know, for example, if there are issues with internal controls on board our ships, in ports or in any other area of ships' operations. By being made aware of the key risks and internal control issues at the operational level, we can work with you to address them in the most appropriate way.

We also need to be aware of the business impact of operational controls and risks to enable us at board level to make informed business decisions at the strategic level. If we are receiving incomplete, defective or partial information then we will not be in full possession of the necessary facts to allocate resources in the most effective and efficient way possible.

You will be aware that at board level we have the responsibility to provide information about risks and internal controls to external audiences. Best practice reporting means that we have to provide information to shareholders and others, about our systems, controls, targets, levels of compliance and improvement measures and we need quality information to enable us to do this. This brings me to the second purpose of this memo.

(ii)   Qualitative characteristics of information needed

Secondly, I want to write to you about the most helpful ways in which to convey this crucial information to us. The information we receive on risks and internal controls should be high quality information. This means that it enables the full information content to be conveyed to the board in a manner that is clear and has nothing in it that would make any part of it difficult to understand. In particular I would ask that you consider that your communications should be reliable, relevant and understandable. They should also be complete.

By reliable I refer to the trustworthiness of the information: the assumption that it is "hard" information, that it is correct, that it is impartial, unbiased and accurate. In the event that you must convey bad news such as some of the issues raised by the loss of the Mary Jane, we expect you to do so with as much truthfulness and clarity as if you were conveying good news.

By relevant I mean not only that due reports should be complete and delivered promptly, but also that anything that you feel should be brought to the board's attention, such as maritime safety issues, emergent risks, issues with ports, etc. should be brought to our attention while there is still time for us to do something about it. In the case of the Mary Jane there were technical issues with the fit of the ship with her berth at Eastport that were important and we should be made aware of such problems as soon as possible.

Not all directors of Sea Ships possess the technical and nautical knowledge of senior operating personnel on board the ferries. It is therefore particularly important that information you convey to us is understandable. This means that it should contain a minimum of technical terms that have obvious meaning to you on board ships, but may not be understandable to a non-marine specialist. All communication should therefore be as plain as possible within the constraints of reliability and completeness. This brings me to my final point.

By complete, I mean that all information that we need to know and which you have access to, should be included. Particularly with relevance to on-board accidents or risks, you must convey all relevant information to us regardless of the inconvenience that it may cause to one or more colleagues.

As we have learned at the highest cost to those involved in the loss of the Mary Jane and to ourselves commercially, the flow of information on controls and risks is of vital importance to us. Timely receipt of, and appropriate response to, high quality information is not only important to the safe operation of the ships but also to the company itself.

Thank you very much for your understanding and full co-operation on behalf of Sea Ships.

Wim Bock
Chief executive

Answer 40 COASTAL OIL

(a)   **Corporate code of ethics**

General purposes

A corporate code of ethics (sometimes contrasted with a professional code) has five general purposes.

(1)   Communicating the organisation's values into a succinct and sometimes memorable form. This might involve defining the strategic purposes of the organisation and how this might affect ethical attitudes and policies.

(2)   Identifying the key stakeholders and promoting stakeholder rights and responsibilities. This may involve deciding on the legitimacy of the claims of certain stakeholders and how the company will behave towards them.

(3)   Conveying these values to stakeholders. It is important for internal and external stakeholders to understand the ethical positions of a company so they know what to expect in a given situation and to know how the company will behave. This is especially important with powerful stakeholders, perhaps including customers, suppliers and employees.

(4)   Influencing and controlling individuals' behaviour, especially internal stakeholders such as management and employees. The values conveyed by the code are intended to provide for an agreed outcome whenever a given situation arises and to underpin a way of conducting organisational life in accordance with those values.

(5)   An important part of an organisation's strategic positioning. In the same way that an organisation's reputation as an employer, supplier, etc. can be a part of strategic positioning, so can its ethical reputation in society. Its code of ethics is a prominent way of articulating and underpinning that.

Evaluation of Coastal Oil's performance

The company appears to have failed its own code of ethics in terms of its pledges on full compliance with regulation in all jurisdictions: safety and care of employees, transparency and communication with stakeholders, social contribution and environmental responsibility.

Coastal Oil stated its aim to achieve full compliance with regulation in all jurisdictions. The contract with Well Services was clearly contestable in terms of who was liable, partly due to the complexity of the documentation. There is no evidence from the case that the company was criminally negligent but health and safety or environmental controls, relevant to companies operating in Effland waters, may have been breached.

In terms of the safety and care of employees, the company also did not perform well against its own standards. The deaths of eight employees on the Effland Coastal Oil Rig resulted from health and safety failures because of a number of internal control failures. If Coastal Oil saw the protection of employees as an ethical issue, it might have adopted, or ensured that its JV partners adopted, the "highest standards" of performance in ensuring their safety.

The company gave the appearance of a lack of transparency and communication failure. Because of the internal arguments between Coastal Oil and Well Services, it took seven days to make a public statement about the event. Clearly, there would be many stakeholders eager to hear Coastal Oil's view on what had happened, including the families of those killed and injured, and the delay caused by the internal arguments was a breach of its own code of ethics on this issue.

In terms of social contribution, the oil spill had a number of negative social consequences. The oil spill caused a number of problems to the communities along the Effland coast. Business was damaged during the important tourist season meaning that communities were less supported, in terms of income, over those important months.

The valve failure caused an oil leak on the sea floor which took several months to stop. This is an environmental failure and, given that Coastal Oil stated that environmental responsibility was a key heading in its code of ethics, stakeholders will be reasonably entitled to conclude that it has failed against its own ethical standards. Given that the company operates in such an environmentally sensitive industry, it would clearly require a high level of commitment to internal controls to maintain this, whether directly by Coastal Oil employees or through the partners in the JV such as Well Services.

(b) **Disclosure and environmental risk management**

Difference between voluntary and mandatory disclosure

Company reporting, usually in annual reports, interim reports or on websites and now in integrated reports (when issued), contains both mandatory and voluntary disclosures. Mandatory disclosures are those statements that are compulsory under relevant company laws or stock market listing rules. In most jurisdictions, mandatory items are the main financial statements such as income statement, statement of financial position and statement of cash flows. Listing rules in many jurisdictions, such as in the UK, also mandate some corporate governance disclosures such as directors' shareholdings and emoluments, and details of directors' contracts.

Voluntary disclosures are not required by any mandate but are provided, usually in narrative rather than quantitative form. There is a belief that some information of interest or relevance to shareholders or other stakeholders cannot be conveyed numerically and so additional information is needed. The chairman's statement, chief executive's review, social and environmental disclosure, intellectual capital reporting and risk reporting are all examples of voluntary disclosure in most jurisdictions.

Tutorial note: *Mandatory and voluntary disclosures vary slightly between jurisdictions.*

Why additional voluntary disclosure would be material to shareholders

Voluntary disclosure is of interest to shareholders because it provides information that cannot be easily conveyed in statutory statements or in numerical form. In the case of environmental risk reporting at Coastal Oil, it is likely that shareholders will welcome the environmental risk measures put in place after the accident as reported in the annual report for the following reasons:

(1)   The fact that there has been a recent and expensive environmental accident means that environmental risk is clearly material to shareholder value and is likely to remain so while the company continues to extract and process oil. This is a "structural" risk resulting from the company's core activity. This makes environmental disclosure potentially highly material and capable of affecting the value of the company. The extent of potential exposure (total impacts), and hence the potential losses, would be a key piece of information needed, and also the previous environmental accident statistics.

(2)   It will allow the shareholders to understand the extent and nature of the risk which clearly wasn't fully known before the accident. By knowing this, shareholders can assess whether the risk profile of the business matches their own attitudes to or appetite for risk. In a portfolio of shares, some investors will want to blend certain risks and returns, and knowing about a company's risks is important in making these judgements.

(3)   The additional environmental risk information will allow the shareholders to judge how the risk might affect company value and hence the potential volatility and attractiveness of the share. The case says that the disclosure would contain "value relevant" information meaning that the risks described will be capable of affecting returns, costs or both. The materiality of environmental risk reporting is potentially quite high: shareholders were unaware of the poor internal controls on the Effland Coastal Oil Rig and, had they been more aware, may have discounted the share price accordingly.

(4)   Risk reporting can explain the new risk controls put in place. After a confidence-threatening event such as the valve rupture and oil spill on the Effland Coastal Oil Rig, the explanation of these measures could be vital in restoring investor confidence. In particular, they should reassure shareholders that the accident should not re-occur, or that if it were to re-occur, further controls would be in place to offset the worst of the damage. It is likely that more detailed and granulated environmental reporting would be valued by shareholders, especially those specialist institutional shareholders made cautious by the Effland accident.

(c)   Statement for the special committee

(i)   Internal control failures

In keeping with Coastal Oil's stated commitment in its code of ethics to transparency, I have been authorised by my board to provide a full and frank statement on the internal control failures that led to the accident on the Effland Coastal Oil Rig. I will be happy to explain any particular point in more detail if required, but if you will allow me I will outline where I believe our internal controls were below standard.

I should inform the committee that the ownership and management of the oil rig was complicated by the fact that Coastal Oil was part of a joint venture in which, despite being the major partner, we did not have complete control. This means that other partners had responsibilities, including control of some operations crucial to the safety of staff and the oil supply.

The complexities of ownership may have led to the first of the failures which was a lack of clarity on individual and collective legal responsibilities. Accordingly, liability for the valve failure was ambiguous even though it was another company, Well Services, who directly caused the problem. We work very closely with joint venture partners on projects such as the Effland Coastal Oil Rig and rely on each other's controls. In this case, the situation was made worse for Coastal Oil by a lack of clarity on these agreements and this is salutary for future projects.

It is my understanding that the engineers belonging to Well Services failed in regard to two operational controls. The valve that was the site of the pipeline's rupture was not tested in accordance with their normal procedures. Also, a connecting part was deployed at a depth beyond that at which it was designed to operate (i.e. beyond its safety tolerance). I was troubled by the suggestion that cost may have been a partial explanation for this. In both of these cases, a failure of operational controls contributed to the failure of the valve.

I sadly have no reason to doubt reports suggesting that the culture on the rig was less rigorous than it should have been. It is important that stringent controls are operated throughout Coastal Oil and it is especially important at the sites of operation where hazardous work takes place. There are issues with the reporting of exceptions to the land-side and hence the management style of a rig's individual manager becomes the defining issue on whether a certain internal control problem is reported to us. On reflection, this could have been more robust and it relied more on objective measures and less on human judgement.

Finally, we had no effective contingency plan in place for sealing the well-head or stopping the flow of oil from the well after the valve ruptured. This was the cause of the leakage of oil into the sea over several months. Contingency plans or system backups may have helped in this regard but we were unable to respond with the speed necessary and this resulted in such environmental and economic damage.

(ii)   Subjective and objective risk assessment

I would like to respond directly to Senator Jones's remark in the media that I as the company's CEO "should have known this was going to happen". Whilst I understand the senator's anger at the events that have so badly affected his constituency, I owe it to Coastal Oil's shareholders to respond to him for the purposes of clarity.

Risk assessment is an important but complicated process and involves establishing both the probability of a particular risk event happening and also the impact or hazard that would arise if it was realised. A key point is that some of these calculations can be made with some degree of objectivity whilst others rely more on subjective assessment. There is an important distinction, then, between objective and subjective assessments. A risk can be objectively assessed if we can "scientifically" measure the probability of a given outcome or predict, with some certainty, the impact. I can predict with some confidence, for example, based on past data, the number of working days likely to be lost in a given year through absenteeism of employees. I can predict with much less certainty, the probability that the stock market will rise or fall on a given day. In such a situation, I must use more subjective judgement.

Similarly with regard to impact, I might be able to assess the impact of my loss should my car get stolen but I could much less accurately predict the number of people hurt or injured in an accident. Again, I would use a more subjective figure for assessing that risk. The probability of having my car stolen would increase if I were to leave it unlocked and this underlines the importance of controls to help reduce the probabilities of adverse events happening.

Arguing against Senator Jones's view

This brings me to Senator Jones's remark that I "should have known" the accident was going to occur. I'm afraid that his remark does not recognise the complexities of risk management and risk assessment. I have outlined the reasons for uncertainty in both assessing the probabilities and impacts of risk events.

Accidents do occur in many industries including in the petrochemicals industry. Given that Coastal Oil operates hundreds of similar deep sea rigs in waters all over the world, I could not, with any degree of certainty, predict the probability of a fatal accident on a given oil rig and much less could I have known about the probability of an accident on the Effland Coastal Oil Rig. Similarly, there is no information that I could have received that could have predicted the scale of death or injury in the event of a given incident.

I concede that there were a number of internal control failures on the rig in question, but would point out to the senator that I was unaware of those failures because of the nature of the information systems linking rigs to our land-side operations. It is the responsibility of each rig's management to enforce safety controls on that rig and no such information would have reached me except by exception. He may be justified in criticising these, and I have explained already that I view these information failures as an internal control issue that we must resolve.

(iii)   "Health and safety" risk

The board of Coastal Oil was deeply saddened to hear of the loss of life on the Effland Coastal Oil Rig. As a petrochemical company involved in each stage of the extraction, processing and distribution of oil products, we are naturally very aware of the health and safety risks that we face. These are risks to individuals, employees or others, arising from any failure in our operations giving rise to compromised human welfare.

Health and safety risk, and particularly the probability of a given health and safety risk materialising, is generally increased by three factors.

(1)   The lack of a health and safety policy. In some industries, including petrochemicals, large parts of this policy are underpinned by legislation, depending on jurisdiction, but it is also in the interests of a business to ensure that robust policies are in place covering all aspects of health and safety and indeed this was the case on the oil platform in question.

(2)   The lack of emergency procedures or a failure to deal with hazards that arise. Once identified, a new hazard or impact must be addressed with a policy or a way of dealing with it. Ineffective operational controls, such as was the case on the Effland Coastal Oil Deep Rig, contribute to this failure.

(3)   A poor health and safety culture can undermine an otherwise good policy if management and staff are lax towards health and safety, or believe it to be unimportant. There is some evidence that this was sadly the case on the rig.

(iv)   Why ALARP principle cannot guarantee to prevent further failures

I understand and share the committee's desire to ensure that an accident of this type does not happen again. However, risk management is partly a trade-off between the cost of control and level of perceived risk. We operate to a principle known as ALARP or that risks should be "as low as reasonably practicable". There is an inverse relationship between a risk and the acceptability of that risk or, in other words, a risk is more acceptable when it is low and less acceptable when it is high. Accordingly, risks assessed as "high" in terms of probability and/or impact, must have credible and affordable strategies put in place for their management. The extent and cost of that risk strategy is a matter of judgement and you will appreciate that as the chief executive of Coastal Oil, I owe it to our shareholders and customers to control costs. This means that risks cannot be completely eliminated, much as I might wish that they could.

Accordingly, then, each risk is managed so as to be as low as is reasonably practicable because we can never say that a risk has a zero value. It would be financially and operationally impracticable to completely eliminate health and safety risks, and so we must live with the ever-present possibility that they can happen. This does not mean we would ever become complacent, of course, but merely that I should be honest in saying that the probability of occurrence cannot be zero. Because of this, we maintain a number of controls that should reduce the probability of the risks materialising, such as by having a policy in place and enforcing it. We also have protections in place, such as the compulsory wearing of safety equipment, to reduce the impact of an event should it occur.

Thank you for listening to this statement. I am now happy to take questions.

Answer 41 HAYHO

(a)   Risk appetite

Risk appetite describes the willingness of an entity to become exposed to an unrealised loss (risk). It is usually understood to mean the position taken with regard to two notional preferences: risk aversion and risk seeking. Both preferences are associated with different levels of returns: those that are risk-seeking favour higher risks and higher returns with the converse being true for the risk averse.

Risk-averse entities will tend to be cautious about accepting risk, preferring to avoid risk, to share it or to reduce it. In exchange, they are willing to accept a lower level of return. Those with an appetite for risk will tend to accept and seek out risk, recognising risk to be associated with higher net returns.

Investment selection

The Jayland option has a higher political risk, a threat to the integrity of the company (by paying the bribe) and an element of reputation risk. There is also a risk arising from the lack of business culture in Jayland and a possibility that it will be more difficult to maintain normal operations there than in Pealand. Offset against these risks is the potential return of $2 billion over 10 years, which is twice that of the Pealand option.

The Pealand option has negligible political risk but a slightly higher risk that internal controls will be difficult to implement. It has a much lower likelihood of reputation risk and there is no risk connected with bribery. The return is half that of the Jayland option (for an approximately equal investment value).

The two options offer two different risk and return profiles: the Jayland option offers a higher return but a higher risk profile and the Pealand option offers a lower return but also a lower risk profile. If the company has a higher risk appetite it is more likely to choose Jayland and if it has a lower risk appetite it is likely to select the Pealand option.

(b)   **AAA seven-step model**

(1)   What are the facts of the case?

The facts of the case are that there are two investment options and each has a different ethical and risk profile although the AAA model is mainly concerned with the ethical aspects. The ability to operate the necessary internal controls for Hayho manufacturing also differs between the two options. Only one option can be pursued and both are capable of making an acceptable level of return.

(2)   What are the ethical issues?

The ethical issues are over the potential complicity of Hayho in supporting a corrupt regime in Jayland, in paying what appears to be a bribe to Mr Popo under the Jayland option and in operating under less stringent regulatory conditions in Jayland compared to Pealand. Another issue to consider is that it is alleged the president of Jayland maintains order by abusing the rights of the people. The company is very sensitive to allegations of human rights abuses after criticisms of Hayho were made in Arrland recently and it is reluctant to expose itself to similar criticisms again.

A further ethical issue is whether there is a corporate social obligation for companies to invest in developing or transitional economies to help stimulate these economies. However, these disadvantages have to be weighed against the likelihood of making twice the return for shareholders in Jayland against the option of operating sustainably in a more stable Pealand. In Pealand, there may be ethical issues concerning taking over an existing workforce and changing working terms and conditions, perhaps in terms of changed expectations, contractual issues and redundancies.

(3)   What are the norms and principles that apply?

The norms and principles that apply in this situation are that business investment decisions should be taken on a sound commercial basis with risk, return and ethical considerations fully taken into account.

The case says that the company seeks to "always uphold the highest standards of integrity, human rights and environmental protection whilst at the same time "responsibly" supporting developing countries by providing jobs and opportunities to enable greater social and economic development".

This would tend to favour decisions that do not involve bribery (against integrity), human rights abuses (perhaps through supporting corrupt governments), but at the same time seeking, where possible, to use investments to support local economic development (perhaps by investing in developing countries, all other things being equal).

(4)   What are the alternatives?

The first alternative is to invest in Jayland, where a "new-build" factory would enable Hayho to implant its culture and systems but where there is a poorly developed education system, a potentially unstable political environment and an absence of internal control and corporate governance regulations.

The other alternative is the Pealand option, to take over an existing plant and an inherited workforce in a more highly regulated business environment.

(5)   Which option is most consistent with norms and principles?

Both options have strengths and weaknesses, depending upon how the different factors are evaluated. The Jayland option would meet the criteria for financial acceptability and would be favourable through supporting economic growth and by providing net additional employment in a developing country.

The option most consistent with stated norms and principles is the Pealand option. This option has the benefit of inheriting a trained and competent workforce and avoids the reputation risk of providing credibility for the Popo regime and of being exposed, perhaps by a whistle-blower, for paying the "royalty" (which is effectively a bribe to Mr Popo). The Jayland option would provide a greater financial return and provide net additional employment in a developing country. But it also would violate the principle of sound risk management because investing in an unstable and potentially hostile political environment could expose Hayho to unacceptable levels of long-term operational, financial and reputational risk.

(6)   What are the consequences of each option?

In Jayland, as opposed to Pealand, a completely new factory would be built providing new additional employment, although there could be an issue with sourcing the appropriate staff, given the poor levels of education and training. The Jayland option would provide a higher potential return to shareholders, but at a greater risk. It would make implementing the internal controls potentially easier but would risk reputation-damaging allegations of supporting Mr Popo's regime. Were the "royalty" to be made public, it would have severe consequences for the trustworthiness of the Hayho board, having given the reassurances it did after the Arrland incident.

The Pealand option would make a smaller return and involve lower risk, but could introduce potential problems with implementing the necessary internal controls. This option would be more ethically acceptable. Hayho would be severely criticised for supporting a corrupt regime if it invested in Jayland. But if it invested in Pealand, no bribery would be necessary and it could publicise the fact that it chose to invest in Pealand over Jayland because it is seeking to honour its commitments made after the previous Arrland incident.

(7)   What is the decision?

The decision most aligned to the company's stated norms and principles is the Pealand option. Other powerful countervailing factors would also have an influence, however, as risk and internal control considerations would also be taken into account.

Tutorial note: *Credit would be given for arguing for Jayland if shown to be based on reasoning from step 6.*

(c)   Internal control systems

The general purpose of internal control is to achieve the orderly conduct of business by facilitating effective and efficient operation of an organisation's activities. In doing this, it must be able to respond appropriately to relevant risks and to configure activities to be able to achieve the organisation's strategic objectives. This includes safeguarding the assets of the organisation from external and internal threats and to ensure that all actual and potential liabilities and sources of loss are identified and controlled. The protection of value is important in underpinning confidence in internal controls and in providing the capacity for future value adding.

Internal controls are essential in ensuring the robustness, quality and timeliness of both internal and external financial reporting. The provision of this information is important in managing internal systems (e.g. budgetary controls) and in maintaining and cultivating confidence among shareholders and capital markets. This involves maintaining accurate records and processes capable of generating and processing the relevant information.

Internal control is necessary to ensure compliance with any external laws, standards or regulations that apply. These could arise from companies' legislation, listing rules or, in some industries, regulations imposed by sector-specific regulators.

Jayland challenges

Jayland was very under developed until relatively recently and the national culture is, according to Emily Baa, unfamiliar with modern business practice and behaviour. Achieving effective and efficient operation of the business would be an early priority for the Hayho investment and this limitation would necessitate substantial initial training and cultural-familiarisation. If these cultural values (e.g. time-keeping, work commitment, honesty of workers, etc) cannot be taken for granted in a national culture then it represents a major obstacle in achieving normal plant operation.

Emily reported an unknown security situation in the region with regard to the safeguarding of assets. Being able to ensure that non-current assets owned by Hayho are secure and being used for the intended purpose is an essential element of internal control. The value of Hayho belongs to its shareholders and it would be irresponsible of the board (as agents) to invest in assets in Jayland unless reasonable assurances could be given that they will be safe from sabotage, damage, theft, deterioration or inefficient utilisation.

Emily also raised a point about the level of necessary skills in the local labour pool. She mentioned the state of quality control and accounting skills and both of these are necessary for a sound system of internal control.

Appropriate quality control staff are necessary to ensure that the product complies with the stringent international product standards that apply to Hayho's products. Where technical skills such as these are difficult to obtain in local labour markets, unskilled people may need to undergo training, or expatriates may need to be persuaded to move to the Jayland facility.

Guaranteeing that outputs from the Jayland plant were fully compliant with all applicable standards would be an important early priority for customers and investors and so this issue is likely to be of great importance.

Accounting skills are necessary for guaranteeing accurate and complete accounting records and for reliable financial information. Gathering required data and reporting to management at head office is required (e.g. on metrics such as variance against agreed targets). For a new investment such as those being considered by the Hayho board, the provision of accurate and timely information is essential in controlling activities under either of the options.

(d)   **Briefing notes**

Subject: Board meeting briefing notes prepared for Helen Duomo.
Prepared by: Emily Baa
Date: Wednesday 20 June 2015.

Accountability of the Hayho board

The two letters received raise important issues of accountability, and specifically, the issue of to whom the board of Hayho is accountable. In reflecting on how to deal with this and how to frame our response, it may be helpful to consider the accountability situation we face as a board.

Accountability is a key relationship between two or more parties. It implies that one party is accountable to, or answerable to, another. This means that the accountable entity can reasonably be called upon to explain its actions and policies.

This means that the accountable party can be held to account and may be required to actually give an account. This has the potential to influence the behaviour of the accountable party, in this case Hayho, because of the knowledge that they will have to answer for it when they give that account.

Whilst it is clear that the board is accountable to the shareholders as stewards of their investment, it may be the case, nevertheless, that the board may need to account to Watching Business (WB) because of its influence among politicians and in wider society, as outlined below.

Influence of Watching Business

The Mendelow framework is a way of mapping stakeholders with regard to the two variables of interest and power. The combination of these is a measure of any given stakeholder's likely influence over an entity such as Hayho. The framework is dynamic in that stakeholders move around the map as their power and interest rise and fall with events. WB has a moderate degree of power and a variable degree of interest. Because its interest (in Hayho) has recently increased, its overall influence has risen. Our response to WB must be responsive to this.

WB's power derives from its ability to conduct research and mobilise opinion, including among policymakers and trade organisations, against businesses like Hayho. We do not need to agree with its agenda to appreciate its power. Its power is expressed as influence when its interest is also increased.

It was news of our possible investment in Jayland that increased WB's interest in Hayho. This, combined with its evident power, increases its net influence over Hayho. This makes WB difficult to ignore in our decision over whether to invest in Jayland or Pealand.

Agency and demands from WB

The board of Hayho exists in an agency relationship with its shareholders, who collectively own the company and have the legal and moral right to determine objectives. As agents of our shareholders and appointed by them, we have a fiduciary duty to seek to manage the company's resources for their overall economic benefit. In the case of Hayho, as with most business organisations, this involves maximising returns consistent with our complying with relevant laws, regulations and norms. Quark Investments, as one of our major shareholders, has every right to remind us of this duty and we should take its reminder very seriously.

Whilst being well-meaning, the lobby group WB is against one of the investment options we have at this time. It claims that an investment in Jayland would be damaging to human rights in that country. Without commenting on the accuracy or validity of that claim, we should remind colleagues why we might think carefully about the investment, as it would bring us into conflict with WB. The matters to note are:

- WB is respected and its views are trusted by many people. In terms of reputation, it has highlighted our problems in Arrland and, as a result of that, has been monitoring our activities. We may need to consider public opinion before going ahead with a potential Jayland investment as we need the general support of society to operate.

- WB has influence among politicians and policymakers both in this country and abroad. We risk the censure of influential people and increase the pressure for increased regulation if we disregard or act against the lobby group's demands. Our reputation in international markets is one of our strategic assets and it may compromise our commitment, given the Arrland incident, if we were not to uphold the highest standards of integrity, human rights and environmental protection from now on.

- WB is very adept at mobilising public opinion through the media. This means that it can stimulate interest in conditions in Jayland and we would be likely to be heavily scrutinised on an ongoing basis were this investment to be made. This could attract public anger and risk disruptions (e.g. boycotts of our products).

Because of these issues, it would seem prudent to consider these issues as a part of our investment appraisal between the Jayland and Pealand options.

End of briefing notes.

Answer 42 P&J

(a)   Social footprint

The term "footprint" is used to refer to the impact or effect that an entity (e.g. a commercial organisation) can have on a given set of concerns or stakeholder interests. A "social footprint" is the impact on people, society and the well-being of communities.

Effects can be positive (e.g. providing jobs and community benefits) or negative (e.g. when a plant closure increases unemployment or when people become sick from emissions from a plant or the use of a product). Professor Kroll's findings have both positive and negative impacts on society and communities in the case of P&J.

Potential implications

The discovery by Professor Kroll will lead, whether by a tightening of controls or by a reduction in P&J's activities, to lower exposures to X32 in Aytown and Betown; hence, over time, there will be less X32-related disease. There will, in consequence, be fewer people suffering, and, accordingly, less misery for the affected families and friends of sufferers. A lower mortality from X32-related disease will benefit communities and families as well as those individuals directly affected. However, as they are continuing to manufacture the product, if Professor Kroll's findings prove correct, larger numbers of people using the product will ultimately be affected worldwide.

The forecast loss of jobs in the various stages of the P&J supply chain, even in the best case scenario, would be likely to involve fewer jobs and lower employment levels at P&J plants and its suppliers. The worst case scenario, in which the company itself would be lost, would involve the loss of the 45,000 P&J jobs plus many more among suppliers and in the communities supported by the P&J plants (e.g. in local businesses in Aytown and Betown).

The loss of, or serious damage to, communities in which the operations are located includes the economic and social benefits in the developing countries and a very high level of social loss in Aytown and Betown (in Emmland), where both towns are highly dependent on a single employer. It is likely that Aytown, effectively a "company town" with 45% of the jobs at P&J, will be very badly affected and the good causes in Betown (e.g. the nursery and adult education classes) will no longer be able to be supported. The loss of a major employer from a town can lead to a loss of community cohesion, net outward migration and a loss of, or deterioration in, community facilities.

There will be a loss of economic value for shareholders and a reduction in the standards of living for those depending upon the company's value for income or capital growth. This might result in a reduction in pension benefits or endowment values, where P&J shares are a part of the value of such funds. Individuals holding P&J shares may lose a substantial proportion of their personal wealth.

Tutorial note: *Other relevant effects such as loss of taxes to fund states services, increases in state funding to support unemployed/sick workers, would earn marks.*

(b)   Risk diversification

Diversification of risk means adjusting the balance of activities so that the company is less exposed to the risky activities and has a wider range of activities over which to spread risk and return. Risks can be diversified by discontinuing risky activities or reducing exposure by, for example, disposing of assets or selling shares associated with the risk exposure.

Diversify the X32 legal risk

In the case of P&J, the case highlights a number of issues that make P&J particularly vulnerable and which would place constraints on its ability to diversify the X32 legal risk.

A key risk is that the company's portfolio of activities is heavily skewed towards X32 with 60% of its business in X32 when Kroll's findings were published. This is a very unbalanced portfolio and makes the company structurally vulnerable to any health threat that X32 poses. It means that a majority of its assets and expertise will be dedicated to a single material and anything that might be a risk relating to sales of that material would be a risk to the whole company.

The case says that the plant cannot be adapted to produce other materials. A mine, for example, cannot suddenly be "adapted" to produce a safer alternative. The case also says that processing plants are dedicated exclusively to X32 and cannot be modified to process other materials. This means that they either continue to process X32 or they must be completely refitted to work on alternative materials.

As a result of that, P&J is unlikely to be able to dispose of X32 assets profitably now that Kroll's findings are known about and the reasons for the health concerns have been identified. The reaction of society to X32 was highlighted by Hannah Yin as a key factor in determining the likelihood of the risk and this might make it difficult to sell the assets on to others.

Finally, the obvious way to diversify the risk is to expand the remaining 40% of the portfolio to become more prominent. However, the company has little by way of retained earnings and is already highly geared with little prospect of further borrowing. This is likely to limit its options for developing new products as a means of diversification. Share issues would be a possible way of re-financing, but with such a high exposure to X32 losses, this would be problematic.

Tutorial note: Credit would be given for attempting to interpret the data in the case numerically if relevant points are made.

(c)   **Hannah Yin's behaviour**

There are five fundamental principles that apply to all professionals including professional accountants. They are integrity, objectivity, professional competence and due care, confidentiality and professional behaviour. In this case, the fundamental principles that Hannah Yin has breached are integrity, objectivity and professional behaviour.

Integrity

Hannah betrayed the trust of shareholders, making a disclosure in her name precisely because she knew she would be believed. This shows a lack of integrity and is also very unprofessional behaviour.

Her status as a professional and her performance over recent years had built up a stock of trust in her. It was her responsibility to maintain and cultivate this trust and to continue to give shareholders good reason to trust her as a professional accountant. To make biased and partial disclosures precisely because she was trusted is cynical and a betrayal of her duty as a company director and as a professional.

As a professional with integrity, Hannah should have the highest levels of probity in all personal and professional dealings. Professionals should be straightforward and honest in all relationships, and never take part in anything that might undermine, or appear to undermine, the trust which society has placed in them.

Objectivity

Hannah accepted inducements to comply with Mr Ho's wishes. A significant increase in share options made her disproportionately concerned with the short-term maintenance of the company share price, and this helped to cloud her judgement and reduced her objectivity as a professional. She may have reasoned that it would have been against her own economic self-interest to disclose the worst case scenario because it would reduce the value of her share options in the short term.

Hannah should not have allowed bias, conflicts of interest or undue influence to cloud her judgements on professional decisions. This means, for example, that she must not allow the possibility of particular personal gains to over-ride the imperative to always uphold the public interest and represent the best interests of shareholders.

Professional behaviour

Hannah knowingly and intentionally misled shareholders by only reporting the most optimistic risk forecasts. This is a clear breach of the integrity and professional behaviour required of a person in her position. The principles of transparency and fairness require companies to be truthful and complete in their disclosures to shareholders, especially when price-sensitive information (e.g. the health risks of X32) is involved. Professionals such as Hannah should comply fully with all relevant laws and regulations, whilst at the same time avoiding anything that might discredit the profession or bring it into disrepute. This involves complying with the spirit as well as the letter of whichever regulations apply.

(d) **Trouble at P&J – draft article by A.N. Journalist**

These must be difficult times to be a director at P&J, Emmland's largest producer of X32. What does a board do when it is faced with having caused a large number of terrible health problems for employees and users of X32, whilst at the same time having no strategic alternative but to carry on and try to manage what are sure to be enormous long-term liabilities?

Strategic and operational risks

The company is facing a highly strategic risk since the publication of Professor Kroll's findings (ref Academic Journal ABC dated xx/xx/xxxx). Whereas operational threats are those affecting a part of a company, perhaps a risk to a raw material or the loss of a product market, a strategic risk is one that has the possibility, if realised, to affect the company as a whole and its future strategic success. We have seen similar risks before to important industries where, for example, entire industries have disappeared from some developed countries because of changes in international labour market costs and political changes. These are examples of strategic risks materialising, and the effects can be disastrous for those affected.

Impact on P&J

P&J shareholders will appreciate knowing that Kroll's report has the effect of being a strategic risk for P&J for at least three reasons. To begin with, his findings potentially affect the whole company rather than just parts of it; such is the extent of P&J's exposure to this commodity through vertical integration. Presumably this strategy had previously been thought a good idea, with the company directly owning all three stages in the supply chain, from mining, to processing, to the manufacturing operations in Emmland. All stages are threatened by Kroll's findings. Plus, if product sales eventually slow down and stop, its sources of cash flow will also disappear.

Second, this is bound to affect P&J's strategic positioning and the way that it is viewed by investors, suppliers, employees and a range of other stakeholders. It has a weaker offering to potential skilled employees than before Kroll's findings were published, it will be harder to raise capital and also to sell its products. Its reputation as a sound company will be reduced as a result, and these things matter in a highly developed country such as Emmland.

Third, and perhaps most importantly, this could eventually be a threat to the company itself. This depends upon how large the liabilities eventually become and how well the company handles the issue in the coming years, but this is a real possibility if the worst-case projections turn out to be accurate. Its heavy reliance on X32 over many years has left it with a 60% dependence on X32, which was fine when the material was in high demand, but it leaves the company very vulnerable when and if that market falls away.

Given these risks facing P&J, this is not a company that will be attractive to investors for the foreseeable future.

Where was the Board?

Readers will also be alarmed to hear of the decision by CEO Laszlo Ho to impose a limited tightening of X32 process controls that only involved doing so where the company was visible to the Emmland public, a compromise he called "Plan B". The board's responsibilities for internal control are detailed in the COSO guidance on this subject and are very clear. Mr Ho's, and the P&J board's, responsibilities for effective internal controls include, in this case, control over X32 fibres in the working environments of each stage in the whole X32 supply chain.

The board's responsibilities include establishing a control environment capable of supporting the internal control arrangements necessary. This includes a suitable "tone from the top" and a high level commitment to effective controls. It also involves conducting risk assessments to establish which risks need to be controlled by the internal control processes (health risks, perhaps?). The introduction of relevant control activities is especially important when a hazardous material like X32 is being considered. This, of course, applies to all of the company's employees and not just those based in Emmland.

It is also the board's responsibility to provide information and maintain relevant communications with those affected by the control measures, and to ensure that important measures are fully implemented and understood.

In addition, the COSO guidelines specify that all controls should be monitored for the degree of compliance and for their effectiveness. This should be a continuous, ongoing process, capable of immediately highlighting any weaknesses or breaches in the implemented controls.

Tutorial note: *Other models can be employed rather than COSO.*

Mr Ho's "Plan B"

In the case of P&J, Mr Ho has taken a deliberate and premeditated decision to ignore the health needs of some of the company's employees on the basis of cost. X32 has been clearly shown to be a health risk and Mr Ho is knowingly allowing employees to be exposed to the material in the course of their normal jobs. The people in the mines and processing facilities will still be exposed to X32, and will presumably continue to get ill and die in the full knowledge of the company management. This is a failure of the fiduciary duty that the P&J board owes to its employees.

Mr Ho is implementing an upgrade to internal control, not on the basis of need but on the basis of how visible the changes will be to investors, most of whom will be based in the developed world. So residents of Aytown and Betown can look forward to a tightening of controls to limit their X32 exposure whilst those in countries with no health and safety legislation cannot. This could be seen as a cynical move to manage the company's image in Emmland. They are taking advantage of the relative weakness of their developing countries' host governments and being selective in whom they extend the necessary X32 process controls to.

Recent events have raised a number of very serious issues for P&J. It is difficult to know what the future will hold for the company, with such a substantial external threat and with management so determined to act unethically in managing that threat. I do not predict an easy time ahead for P&J shareholders.

End of article

JUNE 2013

Answer 1 HOPPO COMPANY

(a)   **Related and correlated risks**

Related risks are risks that vary because of the presence of another risk or where two risks have a common cause. This means when one risk increases, it has an effect on another risk and it is said that the two are related.

Risk correlation is a particular example of related risk. Risks are positively correlated if the two risks are positively related in that one will fall with the reduction of the other, and increase with the rise of the other. They would be negatively correlated if one rose as the other fell.

Correlation between legal risk and reputation risk

At Hoppo, legal risk and reputation risk are likely to be positively correlated because it is likely that as legal risk rises, then, for the reasons explored below, so will reputation risk. Were the legal risk to recede, then risk of reputational damage would also recede. In the case of legal and reputation risks at Hoppo, legal risk is the independent variable and reputation risk is the dependent variable. This is because the reputation risk incurred will largely depend on the legal risk.

The legal risk in this case is the possibility that, if Red's outsourced manufacturing contract is cancelled, Red will pursue a legal case against Hoppo. Because so many jobs (about 1,000) and a lot of future earnings for Red are at stake, Red may vigorously pursue the case and seek to gain damages for the loss of a valuable contract and employee termination costs. It is not certain that Red would take this option, though, and so the probability of this occurring is not known.

The reputation risk is the loss to Hoppo if issues were to be raised in the public consciousness that might cast the company in a negative light. It is hard to know in advance how a legal challenge would be reported but Hoppo could be accused, justly or unjustly, of several things. Legal cases sometimes raise issues in the public consciousness that the company would have otherwise not had exposed. Some of these may be perfectly legitimate in business terms but may offend one or more stakeholders.

In the case of Hoppo, they may be accused of incompetence in drawing up the outsourcing contract with Red. The fact that the legal agreement is considered by some to be ambiguous suggests incompetence and this may erode Hoppo's reputation for competence. The loss of about 1,000 jobs at Red, arising from the loss of the Hoppo contract, is likely to be widely reported, particularly in Teeland. Although jobs are likely to be created in Yuland if the new facility is built there, some may interpret this re-location as a breach of good faith with Red and demonstrating a lack of business integrity on Hoppo's part. The effect of any loss of reputation for Hoppo could be serious.

Hoppo may also be portrayed as an unreliable business partner and this may affect future outsource opportunities, especially where the other company is in another jurisdiction and legal complications may consequently arise. In addition, any loss of reputation is probably quite important for Hoppo, as the case makes clear that both customers and some key employees interact with the company partly based on its favourable social and environmental reputation. In that case, an eroded reputation may affect product sales and also recruitment.

(b)   **Environmental report**

In most jurisdictions, the production of environmental information is voluntary in that it is not required by any accounting standard or legal statute. In some cases, environmental information is included in the regular annual report and in other cases, "stand alone" environmental and/or sustainability reports are published, usually annually. Although these are usually published as hard copy documents, they are also made available on company websites.

In each case, however, the purpose of an environmental report is to report on some of the details of the company's environmental impact or "footprint". Because some of this information is technical in nature, systems need to be put in place to generate and internally assure the data, similar to those systems necessary for generating accurate financial data.

The contents of an environmental report typically include information on the company's direct environmental impact (through its own manufacturing and distribution) and also its indirect impacts (through its forward and backward supply chains). It involves recording, measuring, analysing and reporting on the environmental effects, usually in respect of two aspects: consumption (of energy and other resources) and production. This latter aspect involves the measurement and reporting of the environmental effects of products and also any other emissions (e.g. by-products and pollutants).

Advantages for Hoppo and its shareholders

An environmental report can be considered to have the following advantages:

■   Providing information to investors on the sources and ways of mitigating environmental risk, and of those risks correlated with environmental risk. The events at Red have the potential to damage Hoppo's reputation and potentially turn some customers away from buying Hoppo products because of the implication that Hoppo has poor environmental controls in its supply chain.

■   Enables Hoppo to demonstrate its responsiveness to major issues such as the leakage of TY13 at Red. Likewise, it would be a suitable place to inform shareholders on the "state of the art" environmental performance of its new factory in Yuland. Some customers are known to buy from Hoppo partly because of its environmental reputation, and some employees, similarly, are attracted for the same reason. These factors make this responsiveness potentially very important.

■   The regular production of an environmental report would necessitate the establishment of measurement systems able to generate the information for the report. This would mean that the company would have greater knowledge of, and control over, its resource consumption, environmental efficiency and emissions. This knowledge could then, in turn, save costs and improve internal controls in the company.

■   In the case of a new-build facility in Yuland, systems for gathering this data can be "designed-in" to ensure that information is meaningful, accurate and timely. These measures may help convince investors that Hoppo is a sound long-term and sustainable source of shareholder value.

■   Environmental reporting strengthens the accountability to the shareholders and encourages better environmental performance as a result. Once a company reports on a policy, a measure or a target (for example), it provides something against which it can be later held to account.

For shareholders, the publication of environmental information means that the company can be required to respond to queries on underperformance against agreed standards. This could serve, over time, to make the board more answerable to shareholders and reduce the agency gap.

(c)   Strategic internal controls

Internal controls can be at the strategic or operational level. At the strategic level, controls are aimed at ensuring that the organisation "does the right things"; at the operational level, controls are aimed at ensuring that the organisation "does things right". The overall objective of internal control is to ensure the orderly conduct of business and this requires effective controls from the top to the bottom of the organisation.

Those controls that operate at the strategic level are capable of influencing activities over a longer period. This concerns issues capable of affecting the strategic positioning of the organisation.

In the case of Hoppo, the shortage of the supply of TY13 is capable of affecting its output and hence its ability to meet its strategic objectives in terms of the TY13-containing products.

Internal controls in the Yuland factory

Internal controls apply to all processes and procedures within an organisation. For controls in an internal value chain for a manufacturer, effective internal controls are necessary to ensure the efficient adding of value to inputs and the minimisation of waste. In the case of working with TY13, however, the case describes several specific reasons that need to be taken into account. Red, having worked with TY13 for many years, has developed some competence in this, but evidently not entirely so, as evidenced by the leakage of TY13 from its plant in Teeland.

There are several issues that make internal controls over TY13 so important.

- ■   High cost and the fact that small inefficiencies can disproportionately affect final product costs and hence profitability. As a highly specialised material, TY13 is used in small quantities but any inaccuracies in application, or losses in the process, can affect the economics of the production process. This may affect the profitability of production in extreme cases.

- ■   TY13 is highly toxic and so should be controlled internally (to prevent exposure to employees) and externally, to prevent leakage such as happened at Red. This is likely to be controlled by regulation in Essland but the situation is unclear in Yuland. It is likely that stringent controls will be needed to minimise the chances of leakage or loss and this is not only an economic issue (protecting value) but also a social and environmental issue.

- ■   General supply problems. TY13 is a rare material as highlighted by the report. This means that relationships with suppliers may become strategically important. The case indicates that Red had cultivated strong relationships with suppliers and a challenge for Hoppo would be to build up similar relationships, so that supply would be safeguarded if world shortages occur.

■ Because supply quality varies, the testing of TY13 at the "factory gate" can be important in ensuring that the delivered material is fit for purpose. Because the performance of the finished product depends heavily on obtaining the required grade of TY13, control over this test is likely to be very important. Hoppo would need to have stringent material tests if this variability of supply quality is not to undermine the quality of its finished goods.

(d) **Press release**

Hoppo Company press release dated xx/xx/xxxx

Responding to the recent issues raised in the media by Bob Hope and others

Hoppo is pleased to respond to allegations made in the media about the events surrounding recent discussions concerning its outsourcing activities. In seeking to protect Hoppo's business and ethical reputation, it is true that we are considering the future of our links with one of our outsourcing partners. Hoppo was very disappointed to learn of the poor employee conditions at Red and also the leakage of TY13 into a local river. The company is considering options for the future to prevent such events from happening again. This includes the option of taking manufacturing under direct control.

We take this opportunity to inform the public and our shareholders about the importance we place upon the highest levels of integrity and transparency, and why we believe these to be of the utmost importance in corporate governance. We also wish to explain the circumstances around the demand for an irregular payment from an individual in Ootown and why Hoppo considers it wrong to consider paying this in pursuit of its business objectives.

Integrity at Hoppo

For the avoidance of doubt, Hoppo accepts and agrees with the International Federation of Accountants' (IFAC) definition of integrity as that which "imposes an obligation… to be straightforward and honest in professional and business relationships. Integrity also implies fair dealing and truthfulness".

Hoppo believes that integrity is steadfast adherence to strict ethical standards despite any other pressures to act otherwise. Integrity describes an ethical position of the highest standards of professionalism and probity. It is an underlying and underpinning principle of corporate governance and requires anybody representing shareholders to possess and exercise absolute integrity at all times. Hoppo unreservedly and unambiguously accepts this and the duty it places on the board of directors.

Transparency and Hoppo

Hoppo regrets the perception that it lacked transparency in considering issues concerning its investment in Yuland. The company also wishes to re-emphasise its belief in the importance of transparency in matters of corporate governance. To Hoppo, transparency means providing open and clear disclosure of relevant information to shareholders and other stakeholders. Hoppo believes that it should not conceal information when it may materially affect others. It means open discussions and a default position of information provision rather than concealment. This means that when there is no good and legitimate reason to conceal discussions or other information, it should be disclosed as a matter of course. This has been, and remains, Hoppo's position.

The issue of the "personal gift" (bribe)

Hoppo would like to publicly explain, to reassure our stakeholders and again for the avoidance of any doubt, why it believes that paying a bribe to the mayor of Ootown is wrong. This is despite the fact that, all other things being equal, Ootown was and remains an attractive location for the construction of the new factory. The board accepts that this is a serious issue relating directly to the integrity of the board and so a direct and detailed response is merited. As a company that believes in the highest standards of conduct in all business matters, Hoppo always seeks to apply best practice and, accordingly, believes it is never appropriate to consider paying bribes, whatever the circumstances.

There is a strong business case for rejecting this demand. It is very important that Hoppo is trusted by its shareholders and others. It is equally important that employees find Hoppo a good and ethical company to work for, and to invest their working lives with. In both cases, any suggestion of a lack of probity would be potentially very damaging and this may harm Hoppo's goodwill and the quality of the relationship with its employees. Even though, all other things being equal, we believe that Ootown may be a very good option for the new factory, being exposed for paying a bribe would do long-term damage to the business.

More importantly, though, there is an overwhelming ethical case to reject the option to pay the bribe and to investigate the feasibility of using Ootown without doing this, or choosing Aatown.

Tutorial note: *This is the deontological perspective.*

From one perspective, Hoppo believes that principles and duties are important in business. Businesses and individuals have an ethical duty to act with integrity and the highest standards of professionalism at all times. We believe that the world would be a poorer place and that business would be very badly affected if bribery became an acceptable and a normal part of business life. If everybody practised bribery in making business transactions, then this would undermine trust in business and make international business investments, like that in Yuland, almost impossible. Because it would, if generalised, have a negative set of outcomes, Hoppo believes it is unethical in principle. If it is wrong in general, then it cannot be right in specific cases.

Tutorial note: *This is the consequentialist perspective.*

Hoppo also believes that paying the bribe is wrong in terms of achieving the outcomes that the company seeks. Were the company to pay the mayor of Ootown in order to facilitate the planning permission needed, two very unfortunate consequences might arise. First, Hoppo might gain a very unhelpful reputation in the region as a company that can be bribed, and this, in turn, would increase the possibility of repeat occurrences. Second, even if the payment were not discovered, it would mean that the threat of public disclosure would make Hoppo vulnerable to other demands from the mayor of Ootown.

We hope that this statement has addressed the concerns of all of our stakeholders.

Answer 2 BLUP CO

(a) **Internal audit**

Internal audit is an independent appraisal function established within an organisation to examine and evaluate its activities as a service to that organisation. The objective of internal audit is to assist those charged with governance and management of the organisation in the effective discharge of their responsibilities. To this end, internal audit furnishes them with analyses, appraisals, recommendations, advice and information concerning the activities reviewed. The main functions of concern to internal audit are reviews of internal controls, risk management, compliance and value for money.

Tutorial note: *Evidence of understanding of internal audit could be presented elsewhere in an answer to earn credit.*

Internal audit in regulated industries

Internal audit is generally considered to be more important in highly regulated industries (utilities, such as water or energy, and pharmaceuticals, defence equipment, etc) because there is a need, not only to deliver an internal service to aid organisational efficiency, but also to ensure compliance with externally-imposed requirements. These may involve a range of technical product compliance issues, product safety issues, hygiene issues, production facility issues or other, similar regulations. They may be legal in nature or may be enforced by an industry regulator at "arm's length" from government.

Where requirements are imposed by external regulation, the company must usually provide compliance information to that external regulator. This involves the establishment of *systems for collecting and analysing* that data, and also producing *reports to demonstrate the levels of compliance*. Because compliance information may not always report "good news", it is important that the auditor is independent of those being audited and, for this reason, a formal internal audit function is usually more necessary in such circumstances.

In regulated industries, the *assurance of compliance is a strategic asset* and is somewhat more important than (merely) a desirable outcome. Compliance failure may mean that the company loses its licence to operate, or it may be subjected to punitive fines. In either case, it could be unable to continue to conduct normal business and so internal audit's role is a key part of the company's strategic success.

(b) **Audit committee**

Criticisms of audit committee

There are three ways in which Blup's audit committee fails against best practice criteria.

(1) The committee is not sufficiently independent of the executive board, with its entire membership being retired executives. Some jurisdictions place a time limit (after retirement) before a former executive member can take up a non-executive director (NED) position. This is because of the likely lack of independence and objectivity that such a person would have.

(2) Because the audit committee is required to monitor and review the company's accounts and internal controls, it is often required that at least one member has recent, relevant financial experience (in Singapore, this requirement is more stringent). In Blup, all three members are water engineers. Although clearly an important area to understand in the case of Blup, this does not appear to provide the level of financial literacy that the committee needs to perform its roles.

(3) The audit committee has allowed, and possibly encouraged, the appointment and retention of an external auditor who appears to lack independence. The fact that the head of the external audit practice was a member of the chairman's extended family could give the appearance of a lack of independence (even if not actually true) and is clearly a familiarity threat.

Shareholders rely on external auditors to provide a rigorous and independent scrutiny of the company. The audit committee is responsible for recommending external auditor appointments to the board and, in doing so, should ensure that there are no factors that might threaten their independence from the company being audited.

Overseeing internal audit

There are several reasons why internal audit is overseen by, and has a strong relationship with, the audit committee.

- To ensure that internal audit's remit matches the compliance needs of the company. The internal audit function's terms of reference are likely to be determined by strategic level objectives and the risks associated with them. The audit committee, being at the strategic level of the company, will frame these for implementation by the internal audit function.

- The audit committee will be able to ensure that the work of the internal audit function supports the achievement of the strategic objectives of the company. Whilst this applies to all functions of a business, the supervisory role that the audit committee has over the internal audit function means that this responsibility rests with the audit committee in the first instance.

- Oversight by the audit committee provides the necessary authority for the internal audit function to operate effectively. This means that no-one in the company can refuse to co-operate with the internal audit function and that members of that function, whilst not being necessarily senior members of staff themselves, carry the delegated authority of the audit committee in undertaking their important work.

- By reporting to the audit committee, internal auditors are structurally independent from those being audited. Because they and their work is sanctioned and authorised by the audit committee, the IA function should have no material links with other departments of similar hierarchical level which might compromise independence.

(c) Effective internal controls in assuring the integrity of financial reporting

The integrity of financial reporting is an essential underpinning of sound corporate governance. Shareholders and others rely on this information for their own decision-making and in influencing their perceptions of the value of the company. Many corporate governance codes, in recognising this link, require the publication of a report on the effectiveness of controls over financial reporting. All of these can be made subject to internal audit review to ensure ongoing compliance. In some jurisdictions, the internal controls over reporting are made compulsory through such instruments as financial reporting standards.

Effective internal controls (IC) are necessary for several reasons.

- They are more likely to create systems capable of generating accurate and reliable information. A lack of IC systems may allow for subjective and "best guess" figures to be fed into the reporting process, but a robust system of internal control, with specified ways of measuring and reporting, can minimise this. These systems also provide information systematically to include within financial reports.

■ To identify specific people and functions responsible for operating a particular control. A robust IC system will not expect reporting information to "just happen", but rather, a certain control and/or named person can be made accountable for the delivery of a specific input or set of inputs into the reporting process.

■ To make the process visible and amenable to scrutiny by either internal or external auditors. By having a clear allocation of controls over each stage of the reporting process, an auditor can analyse the quality of control and the information it has produced, at any stage. Or, in the case of an error, the auditor can easily trace back to find how and where the error was introduced.

Answer 3 BIGBANK

(a) Risk assessment

Risk assessment is the process of evaluating the importance of a risk by making an estimate of two variables: the probability of the risk event being realised and the impact that the risk would have if it were realised.

Probability refers to the likelihood of the risk materialising and is expressed either as a percentage or as a proportion of one (e.g. a 0·5 risk is considered to be 50% likely). The impact refers to the value of the loss if the risk event were to materialise.

The estimated values of these two variables can be plotted on a risk assessment "map", where the two axes are impact and probability. Then, different risk management strategies can be assigned depending upon the area of the map the risk is plotted in.

Risks assessed at low probability and low impact can be accepted or tolerated, those with high impact but low probability are often transferred or shared, risks with low impact but high probability are typically reduced and those with high impact and high probability are typically avoided. Risks that are known to be more likely to occur in the near future ("proximate" risks) may be assessed as higher probability and have more urgent strategies applied for managing them.

Tutorial note: *When an answer refers to a particular model, in this case the risk assessment/management model, a diagram can be included as an aid to explanations. However, very few marks would be earned for just a diagram.*

Continuous and ongoing

A primary reason why there needs to be a continuous and ongoing risk assessment is because of the strategic importance of many risks and because of the dynamic nature of those risks being assessed.

Some risks reduce over time and others increase, depending upon changes in the business environment that organisations exist in. Accordingly, it should not be seen as a "once and for all" activity. If there is a risk that companies who borrow money become less able to repay their loans than previously, this is a negative change in the business environment (thereby affecting liquidity risk). When business recovers and bank customers' ability to repay large loans improves, the liquidity risk for the banks is reduced.

It is also necessary to always have accurately assessed risks because of the need to adjust risk management strategies accordingly. The probabilities of risk occurring and the impacts involved can change over time as environmental changes take effect. In choosing, for example, between accepting or reducing a risk, how that risk is managed will be very important. In reducing their lending, the banks have apparently decided to reduce their exposure to liquidity risk. This strategy could change to an "accept" strategy when the economy recovers.

For BigBank, changes in the economic environment of Dubland mean that liquidity risks have increased. As business confidence rises and falls in Dubland, the probabilities and impacts of different risks will change. In this case, BigBank has decided that a reduction in lending is a suitable response to mitigate its financial risks, but this measure is likely to change as business confidence improves and, indeed, the finance minister has asked the banks to consider this.

(b) **Fiduciary duty**

A fiduciary duty is often an onerous duty of care and trust that one party owes to another, mainly defined in terms of a financial duty of care in a business context. It can be a legal duty or a moral duty (or both). In the case of a legal duty, it is legally required, for example, for a solicitor to act in the best interests of a client, or a nurse to act in the best interests of a patient. In other situations, the legal responsibilities are more blurred but an ethical duty may remain. Many would argue, for example, that people owe a fiduciary duty to certain ancient monuments or to the preservation of a unique landscape. The issue here is the fiduciary duty owed by Mr Ng, the chief executive of BigBank. In terms of his agency relationship with the BigBank shareholders, he is legally correct in his belief that he has a pre-eminent duty to the shareholders.

In support of his belief about his "only duty" being to shareholders (a pristine capitalist perspective) is the fact that as an agent of the shareholders, he is employed by them and legally and morally bound to act primarily in their economic best interests. It will often be the case that one strategy favours one constituency (e.g. the shareholders) whilst disadvantaging another, but this does not warrant him adopting a course of action that would increase the bank's risk exposure or reduce shareholders' returns. Such an action would be a de facto theft of company value and hence very unethical. If he were to weaken the bank's risk management in order to reduce the harmful effects on borrowers (and satisfy the finance minister's requirements), he would not be acting in the best interests of the shareholders, who have every right to expect him to protect their interests over all other claims upon the bank.

Arguments against his remark arise from the belief that he is being naïve and short-sighted by suggesting that his only duty is to the shareholders. There are both strategic and ethical reasons why, in this case, assuming a narrow and short-term focus on shareholder value is wrong. The finance minister mentioned the importance of banks in wider society and the fact that the lack of lending has had negative effects on the Dubland economy. Not only might this be unfair to other businesses and individuals unable to gain loan capital, but it might have a longer term effect on BigBank itself, and its shareholders, if the economy shrinks and there is less demand for lending when the economy recovers.

(c) **Financial risks**

Financial risks are those arising from a range of financial measures. The main impacts of financial risk are on either cash flow or cost of capital (or sometimes both). They are very important to a business because of the extent to which cash flows facilitate normal business operations. When cash flows are insufficient to meet cash needs, they can create difficulties including, ultimately, the failure of the business.

The most common financial risks are those arising from financial structure (gearing), interest rate risk, liquidity, credit, cash flow and currency risks. High gearing can be a source of financial risk, when, for example, monetary pressure in the economy increases interest payments and causes reduced cash flows from the income statement. This is similar to interest rate risk, which concerns the company's vulnerability to rising or falling interest rates (depending on whether the company relies on the interest rate from borrowings or from bank deposits). Liquidity risks concern the ability of the business to meet short-term financing challenges, credit risk is the risk of not being paid on time (or at all) and currency risks are risks arising from adverse movements in exchange rates that might devalue the value of cash held in a given currency, make imported goods more expensive or exported goods less competitive.

Embedding financial risk management

Risk management becomes most effective when it is embedded into the company. This means that it is not a "stand alone" activity but becomes normal behaviour. The value of managing and controlling the risk becomes widely accepted and made a part of many people's roles, as a part of their normal behaviour. In particular, embedding financial risk management can be achieved in BigBank by the use of several measures:

- Because financial risks are technical in nature (concerned with risks that might affect the company's cash flow), it may be necessary to inform and educate a wide range of employees to understand and recognise risk factors. This may also involve advising on the importance of financial risks by discussing the impacts they can have and hence the necessity of managing them. The extent of this education and information will depend upon the specific structure of the company and the levels of the business that are deemed to "need to know".

- Technical accounting and monitoring systems need to be implemented that measure and report (to management) on agreed targets, measures and compliance with those. These might involve regular reports against key targets (perhaps monthly) and "alerts" if one or more of the measures strays out of its specified range.

- Human resource systems can be designed to provide incentives for monitoring and alerting management about the risks. Rather than encouraging risk taking in BigBank, staff appraisals and the reward structures could be designed to reward behaviour more likely to control and mitigate the financial risks.

- Awareness of financial risks, and those things that can increase them, can be normalised as a part of BigBank's culture. This would mean that it became a normal thing to discuss, tell stories about, create rituals around, etc. In the same way that health and safety risks have become a part of the culture in many organisations, financial risks could be more firmly embedded by achieving this.

Answer 4 BOOM CO

(a) **Codes of corporate governance**

A code (of corporate governance) is a document that specifies certain standards, principles, norms of behaviour or specific instructions over matters of corporate governance. Some have evolved over time as different previous reports were written for different aspects of governance, which were then brought together in combined codes. Others have borrowed from existing codes, perhaps amended slightly to account for national differences.

Tutorial note: *The UK Corporate Governance Code is an example of a code that has developed over time and was once referred to as the UK Combined Code.*

Codes of corporate governance are issued by regulatory authorities (such as stock exchanges, governments or semi-autonomous government bodies) and are statements of general principles and detailed guidelines on many matters of corporate governance. They can be implemented either as listing rules (in principles-based jurisdictions) or in law (in rules-based jurisdictions). They typically cover all relevant aspects of corporate governance including the roles of the board, risk management, internal controls, executive remuneration and contracts, reporting issues and similar relevant themes. The purpose is to ensure that companies are well-run and in line with shareholders' interests.

Purposes of such codes

■ To guide and specify behaviour in matters of governance, internal control and risk management with the objective that by complying with the code, corporate governance will be improved and enhanced.

■ To encourage best practice and to improve management performance by preventing practice that might reduce value added or shareholder value.

■ To underpin investor confidence as high levels of compliance tend to be appreciated by shareholders and poor levels of compliance are sometimes punished. It enables boards to demonstrate the value they place upon the agency relationship and to more adequately discharge the agency responsibilities placed upon them.

■ To reduce fraud, waste or inefficiency. One of the main causes of the development of codes (e.g. in the UK and in the USA) was in response to high profile frauds, and it was hoped at the time that codes would address this.

■ In principles-based jurisdictions, the implementation of codes is thought to be a way of reducing the chances of governmental legislation being implemented. Governments are more likely to legislate where other regulatory failure is evident and so an effective code applied as listing rules should (many hope and believe) reduce the likelihood of having inflexible laws applied.

(b) **Components of reward package**

Sarah Umm told the remuneration committee that the rewards should be linked strongly with the company's strategy and that these strategic priorities were to "incentivise medium to long-term growth whilst retaining the existing executive board as long as possible".

The retention of the existing board will be aided by providing a basic salary that meets market rate with in-kind benefits commensurate with the role. This is to ensure that the director is satisfied, and believes himself to be fairly rewarded, regardless of performance in the role. Retention can be helped by the payment of one or more loyalty bonuses for staying more than an agreed time period. Again, these would be regardless of performance and intended solely to reward loyalty. These may not necessarily be monetary rewards. It may be, for example, that a director receives a car upgrade or additional days paid holiday after the agreed time period.

Incentivising medium to long-term performance will require the use of reward components such as performance bonuses and share options. Performance bonuses can be included for achieving certain targets in alignment with strategy. The dates on which these are paid can reflect the time-element of the incentives. Sarah Umm wants to incentivise medium to long-term performance, so this is likely to refer to years rather than months. In addition, the package could include share options which can be exercised after a number of years. These enable directors to benefit directly from increases in share value and because this is often a longer-term effect, share options may be designed to come into effect after, say, three years.

(c) **Roles of non-executive directors (NEDs)**

Four general roles of NEDs are: the strategy, scrutinising, risk and people roles.

In the strategy role, NEDs may challenge any aspect of strategy they see fit and offer advice or input to help to develop successful strategy.

The scrutinising or performance role is where the NEDs' independence is perhaps the most important. NEDs are required to hold executive colleagues to account for decisions taken and company performance. In this respect, they are required to represent the shareholders' interests against any vested interests or short-term executive pressures.

The risk role involves NEDs ensuring the company has an adequate system of internal controls and systems of risk management in place.

Finally, in the people role, NEDs oversee a range of responsibilities with regard to the management of the executive members of the board. This typically involves issues concerning appointments and remuneration, but might also involve contractual or disciplinary issues, and succession planning.

NEDs and performance-related elements

The main reason why NEDs are usually not allowed to receive share options or other performance-related elements as part of their reward packages (as Sam South asked) is because it could threaten their independence and hence their usefulness to the company's shareholders. Whereas executive directors may, for example, be incentivised to take excessive risks to maximise their own rewards, a non-executive, without the performance-related element, will have no such incentive and will be likely to take a more objective view of the strategy being discussed.

In order to be effective in their roles, NEDs need to be motivated in different ways to their executive colleagues and too much similarity can mean that the scrutiny role is weakened. If both executive and non-executive directors are similarly motivated, there will be less scrutiny of proposed strategies for wider impacts, risks, complications and stakeholder impacts, because there will be no-one incentivised to exercise effective scrutiny.

If they received a similar mix of rewards to executives, they would be motivated to act in similar ways and this might involve favouring short-term measures at variance with longer-term strategic perspectives. A concern over short-term share price movements, for example, might take the NEDs' focus away from longer-term strategic issues and make them more concerned with maximising market value in the short term.

Because non-executives comprise the remuneration committee, it would be inappropriate for them to decide on their own rewards. It would be an abuse of the responsibility and trust invested in them by shareholders were NEDs to reward themselves too much or incentivise themselves in an inappropriate way. Accordingly, it is usual for NEDs to be paid a fair rate based on external comparison figures (often a daily rate or similar), so that there is no question of it being seen as excessive. A NED's pay is usually a small fraction of that for executive colleagues.

DECEMBER 2013

Answer 1 HIAKA ENERGY COMPANY

(a) **Sustainability**

Concepts of sustainability

Save Our Wilderness (SOW) is referring to environmental sustainability. Resources should not be taken from the environment, or emissions made into the environment, at a rate greater than can be corrected, replenished or offset. The effects of the Hiaka pipeline on the environment should not exceed the ability to replace used resources or clean up spills or emissions as they occur.

The government of Exland refers to the sustainability of its economy and the economic sustainability of Hiaka Energy Company (HEC) which has a significant influence on the national economy. As Exland gets 90% of its oil from one single source (HEC) it is disproportionately dependent on the Hiaka pipeline. In the majority of countries, oil underpins economic growth and the wellbeing of citizens (e.g. jobs, health, education and other essential aspects of infrastructure). Without a regular and reliable source of oil from HEC, and assuming that Exland is unable to find other sources of oil at reasonable cost, the Exland economy would be badly damaged resulting in unfortunate social consequences.

Tensions between the two concepts of sustainability

Attempting to balance environmental conservation and economic development has always been a political consideration and applies wherever business activity takes place. A lot of business activity takes place at a net cost to the environment and so the sustainability of one (environment or economy) may be achieved only at a net cost to the other. Although many believe that a lot of business activity can be made more environmentally sustainable, the economic costs and burdens (e.g. accepting a lower rate of economic growth with its associated effects) may be unpopular.

The economies of both Hiakaisland and Exland are very dependent on the Hiaka pipeline. Thousands of jobs on Hiakaisland depend on it and the economy of Exland is underpinned by the oil. The business transaction with Exland is also an important source of foreign currency for the government of Wyland. These benefits all depend on the economic arguments outweighing the claims of SOW.

Reasons why many are unconvinced by the case for environmental sustainability include the issues of measurement and time perspective. Essentially, economic value can be measured whilst environmental value is more difficult to measure. Economic consequences can be seen over the short term whilst environmental consequences may not be visible for many years. Some socio-political structures are thought to militate against longer-term perspectives, for example the need to provide short-term shareholder returns (as HEC's shareholders have traditionally demanded) and the relatively short time-frame between government elections. In the case scenario, SOW would probably claim to have a longer-term perspective whilst the government of Exland and HEC will have shorter-term perspectives; Exland because its government needs to be re-elected every four years and HEC because it is a public company whose shares are traded on the Wyland stock exchange. The expectations for strong annual returns have, in the opinion of the market analyst, been unhelpful in allowing the company to work with longer-term perspectives.

The extraction of oil is ultimately unsustainable because it requires the exploitation of a non-renewable energy source – once it is gone, it is gone. The view of HEC's board that it should be "as sustainable as is economically possible" is unlikely to satisfy SOW and may be seen effectively as no commitment to environmental sustainability at all. Some countries have taken steps to reduce the net effects of business activity including investing in renewable energy (e.g. wind and water power) and both Wyland and Exland could reduce their dependence on oil by diversifying their energy sources to help to increase environmental sustainability. A lack of dependence on a single energy source (e.g. oil) can also make the country more economically robust, thereby helping its long-term economic sustainability.

(b)   **Assessment of the risks, suitable risk management strategies and subjective risk**

Risk 1 (risk of terrorist attack)

Probability is low, with a likelihood of an attack thought to be 10% at some point in the next 10 years. The effect of such an event would be very high, however, as it would involve severe spillage and complete supply disruption. Oil would not be delivered to the port at Hiakatown and this would cause a loss of supply to Exland.

The usual strategy to adopt for any risk assessed as low probability but high impact is to transfer or share the risk. An insurer may share the risk with HEC and, because of the strategic importance of the pipeline to the regional economy and to Exland, the Wyland government may contribute to this effort.

The company and the government of Wyland would also be advised to take necessary measures to reduce the probability through suitable security measures, for example increased monitoring of the pipeline (perhaps by electronic surveillance or similar). An insurer may well insist on such measures before accepting to insure.

Risk 2 (geological movement and/or earthquake)

This risk has an assessed 10-year probability of 5% which is relatively low. The impact that the event would have, though, would be potentially very high. As has happened elsewhere in the world, seismic activity can cause serious and often catastrophic failure of civil engineering installations. This can result in loss of life and, in the case of the Hiaka pipeline, "severe long-term supply disruption". This would be damaging to the Hiakaisland economy and also to the Exland economy.

The strategy for this is also to transfer or share. Given the relatively low probability (5% in 10 years equates to 0·5% probability in any given year), it should be possible to get an insurer to share the risk for a suitable premium.

Risk 3 (technical failure of a pipeline joint)

This is assessed as having a low probability of occurring. At the same time, the impact of such a failure, presumably because of the technical design of the joints in the pipeline, is quite low. There is the potential for a disruption to supply but only by a few hours and with no leakage of oil.

The strategy for this risk (being low probability and low impact) is to accept it. Given that the costs of reducing the risk (perhaps by replacing the joints with more robust ones) would exceed the value of the potential losses, there is no reasonable case for any other course of action. In addition, careful and ongoing maintenance of the pipeline may help to reduce this risk.

Risk 4 (animal or natural damage to the pipeline)

Because of its northern situation, it is likely that much of the pipeline will be exposed to extremes of weather and it is seemingly possible for large animals also to have some effects on the pipeline over time. The 10-year probability was calculated at 60% and the case mentions that one such event happened recently, demonstrating the vulnerability to this risk. Given the design and construction of the pipeline the impact of any of these risks occurring is low (given as "causing superficial damage to pipeline but no disruption to supply").

The strategy for a risk assessed as high probability but low impact is to reduce it as far as possible, for example, reinforcing the pipeline at its most vulnerable points to extreme weather and erecting defences to deter animals where they are most present.

Tutorial note: *Notice that although there are four risks this does not mean that each risk should be managed differently (TARA). The examiner often sets scenarios that "double up" (e.g. two players have the same Kohlberg level or stage).*

Subjective risk assessment

Subjective risk assessment is distinguished from objective risk assessment by how the figures for probability and impact are determined. If these figures can be determined accurately and with reference to some certainty, it will be more objective than when an estimate is based more on a "best guess" basis. Subjective assessments must be treated with more caution than estimates based on more objective data.

In the case of Gerry Jupp's estimates, the case does not say how his figures are arrived at, but it is likely, given that the pipeline is 10 years old, that it may be based partly on past performance and partly on a "best guess" about future events. The estimate of the probability of extreme weather events can be partly predicted based on past weather behaviour but estimation of the probability of terrorist events are likely to be much more subjective.

The outcome of this is that data generated objectively is likely to be more reliable and useful than data based on more subjective probability or impact determinations.

(c)   **Executive pay**

Labour market conditions

The price paid for any good or service (including labour) is related to the equilibrium point between supply and demand. An excess of supply or a reduction in demand will tend to suppress prices whilst a reduction in supply (say of a key skill in the labour market) or an increase in demand for those skills will tend to increase the market price.

In the case of the levels of rewards for chief executives, supply into that market is influenced by the number of suitable people offering themselves for employment and the levels of skills offered by those people. At the same time, organisations buying in the market will seek to match applicants (suppliers) with their own skills requirements. Because there are mismatches between supply and demand, the price rises and falls over time and between countries and regions, just like any other good or service being traded.

Because Hiakaisland is a remote location, it may be difficult to recruit to senior positions in the company. Given that highly qualified and suitably experienced people can potentially work anywhere, they may choose employment openings based partly on non-job related factors (e.g. quality of life issues, climate, levels of infrastructure development, quality of schools for children, etc). Hiakaisland must compete with other locations and HEC must compete with other employers to attract high quality people to work for it and may have to pay a market premium.

Arguments for a high level of reward to Mr Hoo

The company needs to have a highly skilled and capable person in charge of its operations and there is unlikely to be a supply of such labour locally prepared to work for a lower rate.

As the supplier of a key export and a major employer in Wyland, the regional economy of Hiakaisland depends on the company's success whilst the people of neighbouring Exland depend on it for 90% of their oil needs.

The costs of recruiting an underqualified or inadequately experienced CEO may be much higher than the reward package paid.

In highly skilled areas labour markets can be global. This results in a competitive situation for both applicants and employers, so that a global equilibrium price (level of reward) can seem high in some countries compared to local labour rates (as in Hiakaisland). If there is no suitable applicant prepared to work for a level of reward commensurate with local rates of pay, the company is compelled to pay the going "global" rate whether it wants to or not, possibly including a local market premium.

Arguments against a high level of reward to Mr Hoo

Where senior management is "parachuted in" at such a high level of reward compared to local rates, it can make the chief executive in question appear to be grasping and greedy. This, in turn, can be bad for cohesion and loyalty in the workplace. It may also affect the motivation of employees and their willingness to co-operate with management initiatives at times.

There is an argument that there should be a fixed multiple between the highest and lowest paid in any organisation. This enables the organisation to demonstrate its commitment to fairness, and to respect local sensibilities about rates of pay. By Mr Hoo accepting a fixed multiple, the company could strengthen its reputation locally and this might create a strategic advantage, especially where the local press and trade unions are concerned.

Because living costs are significantly lower on Hiakaisland than in some of the large cities on the Wyland mainland, the "real income" on Hiakaisland of a global equilibrium CEO salary is likely to be disproportionately high. In order to enjoy a comfortable life on Hiakaisland, Mr Hoo does not need a salary equivalent to those living in other, more expensive, places.

If rewards are not adjusted for local prices, this not only creates the unrest as reported in the case scenario, but also creates additional costs to the employer and hence poorer value for the shareholders.

The CEO's high salary, compared to local rates, may make it difficult for Mr Hoo to argue convincingly for cost restraint or in negotiating rewards with employees or trade unions. As his own rewards are disproportionately high by local labour standards, Mr Hoo may be seen as being hypocritical by those he negotiates with and this may affect their willingness to negotiate in good faith or to accept his demands.

The idea of a social contract is important in many organisations where all parties must believe themselves to have a "fair" deal. This can be difficult when one person is seen to have a larger "slice" compared to others and this, in turn, can affect cohesion and motivation.

(d) **Letter**

Hiaka Energy

Address line 1
Address line 2
Date

Minister of Industry
Address line 1
Address line 2

Dear Minister

Thank you for your recent letter on the subject of internal controls at Hiaka Energy Company (HEC) following the Gojo incident. You may be aware that I have just recently taken over as the chief executive officer (CEO) of HEC. In this letter I would like to explain the plans I have for introducing more stringent internal controls and how I believe that a formal internal audit function in the company should help to address issues like that which arose in Gojo in the future.

Internal controls

Turning first to the difficulties in the recent past, you will be aware of the rough and dramatic terrain over which the Hiaka pipeline has been constructed. At 1,000 km long, this was a very substantial civil engineering project and required a great deal of technical expertise in its construction. It passes through hundreds of kilometres of a remote area in which accessing the pipeline is difficult. This can mean that a visual monitoring of the pipeline and its surroundings, perhaps for threats like rock slides, can be difficult.

Despite this challenge, the company does implement maintenance encampments at strategic positions along the length of the pipeline. In taking over from the previous CEO, I have regrettably learned that conditions on these bases are not as comfortable for workers as I would like and as the workers deserve. One of the consequences is that work in these locations is not seen as attractive, morale is sometimes low and it is difficult to recruit people for this work. This can result in a lack of motivation and perhaps less attention to technical detail than is required in providing the highest levels of internal control.

Recent years have also witnessed some poor industrial relations between workers and management. You will be aware of the importance of a high level of trust in an organisation and I suspect these problems may have had an effect on the effectiveness of our internal controls. This is not to excuse a lack of attention to internal controls, but it may go some way to explain why things have deteriorated to the extent that they have.

In order to provide the levels of maintenance required along the length of the pipeline, HEC has relied for some time on foreign labour. A number of languages are spoken by these people, and it is sometimes difficult to convey detailed technical messages to people when they are uncertain in the language of Wyland. Clear and unambiguous information is necessary in the effective implementation of internal controls and this has not always been possible in the past because of these language barriers.

Internal audit function

In addressing these problems, however, I am pleased to convey to you that I have recently gained the support of the board to establish a full internal audit function at HEC reporting directly to the board of directors. I see a number of benefits from this once it is established and operating effectively. I hope this will reassure the Wyland government and our other stakeholders.

Internal audit functions, such as the one envisaged for HEC, have traditionally had four general roles:

(1)   To address and assure the quality and effectiveness of internal control systems
(2)   To assure risk management
(3)   To identify and appraise technical and legal compliance issues
(4)   To assess the value for money returned to our shareholders and others.

I personally see these roles as interconnected and believe that a great deal of benefit will result in the future.

With regard to the effectiveness of internal controls, HEC faces a unique challenge with the physical size and geographical spread of its operations. With such a complex operation and so many stakeholders in the successful delivery of energy from Hiakaisland, internal audit will provide an effective control over these operations.

The same applies to the risks which HEC faces. Our new risk manager, Gerry Jupp, has already begun the task of registering and assessing the risks, but internal audit will systematise this and ensure that these are subjected to a regular and thorough audit process. This will provide assurance that there are no omissions and that each risk is assessed and recorded as required by the internal audit procedures.

As an energy company working under Wyland law, HEC is subject to both national regulations and technical rules. Our new internal audit function will provide assurance that each requirement is taken into account and that the levels of compliance are monitored and corrected as necessary. This also applies to the contractual terms of our supply agreement with the government of Exland.

Finally, our new internal audit department will help the company to achieve value for money. This is not only important for the shareholders but we are aware that sound financial management is a key part of corporate governance and that we also want to achieve value for our customers and employees. Ensuring that procurements and other asset purchases are best value, for example, will help us to achieve this. Had such an effective internal audit function been in place at the time of its construction, the pipeline could have been constructed within budget and on time rather than being late and over budget as was actually the case.

I hope I have been able to address some of your concerns about HEC and that the company continues to enjoy good relations with the Wyland government.

With all best wishes

Yours sincerely

Gavin Hoo
Chief executive

Answer 2 SARBANES-OXLEY

(a) **Rules and principles based corporate governance**

Rules and principles are the two general approaches taken to the regulation of corporate governance practice. The US and Sarbanes-Oxley is the only major example of a rules-based approach, with most countries preferring to regulate governance behaviour through the observation of general principles.

Rules-based approach

In a rules-based approach the legal enforceability of the Act requires total compliance in all details. This places a substantial compliance cost on affected companies and creates a large number of compliance advice consultancies to help companies ensure compliance. It is the judiciary rather than investors which monitors and punishes transgression and this means that there is no theoretical distinction drawn between major or minor compliance failures. This is sometimes seen, therefore, to be clumsy or un-nuanced as a means of enforcement.

Principles-based approach

In a principles-based jurisdiction, listed companies are required by the stock exchange (rather than the law) to meet certain standards of compliance. These standards are usually expressed in a corporate governance code. Companies are required, by the stock exchange's listing rules, to comply in detail with all provisions in the code but may, if unable to do so, report to the shareholders the ways in which compliance is not fully achieved, the reasons for the lack of compliance and when the company expects to be back in full compliance. The shareholders may then assess the transgression and take appropriate action themselves. Such action can be in the form of direct complaints to management or investor relations, or reducing their holdings of those shares, thereby reducing company value. In other words, the market rather than the state enforces and regulates compliance and this is considered to be a more efficient enforcement mechanism.

Disadvantages of rules-based approaches

- Costs are incurred in ensuring and demonstrating compliance. It can be convincingly argued that a substantial proportion of this cost adds very little value to shareholders, especially in small companies, and resources are diverted to demonstrating minor areas of compliance which could be used more effectively elsewhere (such as in company operations). Because compliance on the "big" issues is accorded equal weight in law to compliance with "small" issues, costs are disproportionately incurred in demonstrating compliance in some non-critical areas.

- Compliance is seen to be an inflexible "box ticking" exercise and this can sometimes mean that companies lose perspective of what are the most important aspects of governance and what can sometimes be a less important provision to comply with. Disproportionate amounts of management time can be used in ensuring compliance in an area which may be less important to shareholders, but which is nevertheless an important "box" to have ticked.

■ Infringements and transgressions are punished by the state through its judiciary and not by those most directly affected by such transgressions: the shareholders. Those in favour of principles-based approaches argue that there is a greater economic efficiency in having governance monitored by those with the strongest stake in gains and losses (the shareholders), rather than the (in comparison) inefficient and undiscerning agents of the state. In many cases, agents of the state are unable to distinguish between major and minor infringements, merely noticing that a "box" is "unticked" and pursuing punishment as a result.

(b)   Agency

In the context of corporate governance, agency refers to the relationship between the principal and an agent. The principal appoints an agent to act on his behalf in order to maximise the outcome sought by the principal. In the case of a business organisation with a separation of ownership and control, this relationship comprises shareholders (principals) and directors (agents). As agents, directors' responsibilities should be primarily concerned with maximising the long-term returns to shareholders and providing timely, accurate and truthful information to shareholders in terms of reporting. The production of reports on internal controls is an important part of this reporting.

Benefits of "maintaining a system of internal control over financial reporting"

■ The system is important for ensuring that information can be accessed as necessary for management decision-making purposes, for reporting, or as part of an audit trail. Information needs to be reliable whenever it is used, either for internal management purposes or for shareholders, and a robust system to produce reporting information is necessary for that. This includes the benefit of the timely delivery of reports.

■ The case describes the importance of accurate "evidential matter" in the preparation of reports. This may be important in providing an audit trail and to demonstrate that the systems and reporting are compliant with GAAP or other relevant systems of accounting rules (such as IFRS). These make it more likely that the reports will be truthful and reliable, both of which are important information qualities for shareholders. The evidential matter is likely to be able to demonstrate that the contents of the external report have been arrived at by using outputs from measurement systems compliant with relevant standards and this will satisfy external auditors, and, in turn, shareholders.

■ The report on internal control (IC) is capable of providing assurance to investors that the company is being well run and that it has effective internal controls capable of supporting a strategy which can maximise the long-term returns needed. As agents of the shareholders' interests, directors must demonstrate they are responsible stewards of shareholder value. A report on the adequacy of internal controls in place in the company is a convincing way of achieving this.

■ Because code compliance is mandatory in a rules-based jurisdiction (Sarbanes-Oxley in the case scenario), the maintenance of an effective system of internal control allows management to clearly demonstrate its compliance with the effective laws governing corporate governance. Because there are legal and reputational penalties for any compliance failures (even small ones), the clear and unambiguous signalling of compliance is important to shareholders and the availability of legal sanctions for non-compliance provides greater deterrents and provides greater assurance about the effectiveness of internal controls to shareholders.

(c) **Small company exemption**

Smaller companies generally exist in less complicated environments than larger companies (i.e. with fewer potential risks and less dynamic risks) and are consequently less exposed than larger companies. The larger the entity, the greater its political visibility with a wider range of stakeholder claims on the organisation. There is less risk to society and to investors from individual smaller company losses. For example, a large company with inadequate internal controls (IC) (that does not report those inadequacies) may cause thousands of job losses, large losses to share portfolios and individual investors should it fail, there is likely to be less overall risk to society and to general investors if a small company misreports the adequacy of its internal controls.

Small companies usually do not have widely distributed share ownership, as in many cases the majority of the shareholders are also the managers (owner managed) with the remaining shareholders often connected to the managers (e.g. family members). This may mean that shareholders may not need or want the full levels of disclosure of such monitoring compared to larger companies with more distributed share ownership and a greater "distance" between ownership and management.

There are also likely to be disproportionate costs (compared to output volumes) of putting systems in place for gathering the necessary "evidential matter". Even when infrastructure is installed, management time is required to prepare evidence of compliance. The preparation and publication of required reports (e.g. s.404 under Sarbanes-Oxley) itself can also be disproportionately expensive for a small company because of the fixed costs of report preparation which apply regardless of the variable costs of volumes actually produced.

In addition, the fixed costs of the infrastructure systems which need to be put into place are disproportionately high for a small company. For a larger company which can allocate the overheads of this investment over a high number of outputs, such costs are manageable or even negligible. For a smaller company with fewer outputs, fixed cost allocation per unit may be seen as unfairly high, especially when cash flow is already very tight and the scope for investment in systems for compliance are very limited.

Finally, the costs of compliance could be a barrier to growth for smaller companies and a disincentive to entrepreneurship. Many believe that any regulation seen as unnecessarily bureaucratic or which does not enjoy the broad support of those affected by it can discourage value creation. This might mean, for example, that affected companies do not grow as quickly as they might, that they may make lower profits and thereby create fewer jobs.

Tutorial note: Notice that these are the prime arguments for the use of a principles-based approach.

Answer 3 HELP-WITH-LIFE

(a) **Nominations committee**

Nominations committees have five general roles, all of which are concerned with the recommendation of appointments to the board of directors.

- To establish the appropriate balance between executive and non-executive directors (NEDs). For example, the UK corporate governance code specifies that at least half of the whole board should be NEDs.

- To ensure that the board contains the requisite skills, knowledge and experience to effectively lead the company and provide leadership. Any identified gaps in these requirements should be filled by new appointments.

- To ensure the continuity of required skills, the retention of directors and succession planning.

- To determine the most desirable board size given the skill needs, cost constraints and strategies of the company.

- To consider issues of diversity and to ensure that the company's board is adequately representative of the society in which it operates.

Help With Life (HWL)

In appointing new directors to the board of HWL, the challenge is finding directors who share the values of the charity and who are also prepared to serve at a market discount. The pressure from Marian Ngogo is to find competent people who match both of these criteria and this is likely to be a substantial challenge.

At HWL, the nominations committee could help in several ways with this through:

- Using personal recommendations and business contacts of current or past executive and non-executive directors. In most industries, there is a network of people with similar interests and who are known to each other. These can be used and the recommendations of reliable people can be pursued as necessary.

- Using search companies and consultancies to find people likely to be willing to serve on the board. These may have databases of people serving on other charity boards or people who might be interested in working for a charity for a period of time in seeking to serve the wider public interest rather than just his own economic interests.

- Instructing the human resources function to advertise for suitable persons. This is likely to be the most common way of recruiting executives who may be required to have specific technical skills such as accounting or marketing.

(b) **Advantages of diversity**

Diversity policy aims to achieve a board which is demographically representative of the community in which it operates, such that no single demographic segment is over or under-represented. In the case of HWL, a diverse board of directors would provide several advantages.

- The board will be more representative of the community it is serving, including its donors and supporters. In doing so, HWL would increase its social legitimacy and enjoy a stronger social contract with its community and also with the service users. If the board were homogenous with a certain dominant demographic, it would be open to the charge of being aloof and with a weak connection to the local ethnic groups not represented on the board.

- HWL will be able to meet the local government requirements for diversity and thus to continue receiving that portion of its funding from the local government. As a large proportion of HWL's funding is coming from the local government (40%), HWL is effectively required to comply with the diversity requirements because it would be difficult to replace such funding in the short term.

- Allows the organisation to benefit from a wider pool of talent than would be the case with a less diverse board. Having a wide range of demographic segments represented should mean that a wider range of skills, abilities and competences are available. A demographically narrow board would exclude the talents possessed by those outside of the narrow representation and this would be against the board's best interests in seeking to be effective in its duties.

- Enables a wider range of views and opinions to be expressed. The dominant opinion of the majority and the phenomenon of "group think" can lead to the adoption of positions and policies which can often be shown to be inappropriate in the longer term. So some contrary and challenging voices, especially from those speaking from the perspective of a demographic minority, can be important contributions in policy discussions.

- Provides a greater understanding of the particular values and beliefs of the communities within HWL's catchment area. Given that HWL's work is most effective when the service providers share some of the values and beliefs of the clients, a board of directors able to understand as wide a range of beliefs as possible is a clear advantage.

Tutorial note: *As some countries are beginning to regulate for diversity on boards credit would be given if placed in a particular national context.*

(c)   **Corporate social responsibility (CSR)**

CSR is a term used to include a series of measures concerned with an organisation's stance towards ethical issues. These include the organisation's social and environmental behaviour, the responsibility of its products and investments, its policies (over and above compliance with regulation) towards employees, its treatment of suppliers and buyers, its transparency and integrity, how it deals with stakeholder concerns and issues of giving and community relations.

Behaviour in all of these areas is largely discretionary and it is possible to adopt a range of approaches from being very concerned about some or all of them, to having no such concern at all.

CSR can be expressed and undertaken in several ways. It has been the case for some time that companies have exercised a social concern for employees (over and above regulatory compliance) and communities, but in more recent times, the idea has emerged that CSR can be integrated into an organisation's strategy. To be strategic about CSR is to undertake CSR initiatives which can have meaning for the organisation as well as those to whom the initiatives are directed.

Ethical "filters" and scrutiny procedures may be installed to ensure that the company acts in accordance with a set of agreed principles, perhaps expressed in a code of ethics. The organisation's ethical reputation may be viewed as a strategic asset and a key part of its competitive positioning.

Comparison between HWL and commercial businesses

As a charity, HWL's central strategic purpose is to be socially beneficial in nature. The reason why any charity exists is to pursue a benevolent purpose. In the case of HWL, this is "to help individuals and families with social problems and related issues". It performs this service for no charge to the service users and seeks to maximise the quality of this service over other concerns of the organisation. A commercial business is likely to have a strategic purpose framed in terms of competitive or financial measures.

HWL measures its success in social outcome rather than in profits. The case scenario says that HWL's strategic (i.e. most important) aim is to deliver its charitable services ("to help its service users") whereas a commercial business is more likely to measure success in financial terms such as returns on investment, net or gross margins, etc.

HWL supports its charitable purpose through a number of operational measures. It asks those staff members working for it to espouse certain values and beliefs (consistent with those service users being helped) and also asks its directors to forgo income to work for it. HWL's attitude towards money was that it would rather spend what money it had on service provision than directors' pay. So asking people to accept a personal discount is perhaps made possible because those who help lead the charity (its directors) are more likely to share a belief in the value of what it does. Such an alignment of personal belief with company policy is rarely asked for in a business organisation and few would ask or expect directors to work for a level of remuneration below the market rate. Increasing personal incomes is often a strong concern of directors in commercial businesses, in contrast with the attitude asked for by Marian Ngogo at HWL.

Answer 4 LOBO COMPANY

(a) Directors

Leaving a board of directors

There are several ways in which a director can leave the service of a board.

- They can leave is by *retiring by rotation* meaning that upon the expiry of a predetermined fixed term (three years in Frank Bub's case), they do not offer themselves for re-election by shareholders or, having offered themselves for re-election, are not re-elected.

- A director can resign at any time with or without a financial pay-off depending on contract.

- They can be *dismissed for gross misconduct* such as theft, violence and fraud or similar. In some cases, this may take the form of a legal disqualification or disbarment.

- As with other employees of an organisation, directors can be *dismissed for incompetence*, weak performance or failing to meet targets or similar.

- In some cases, the director may *fall ill* or be otherwise unable to continue (including becoming incapacitated or dying).

- Finally, directors will leave the company if the company is *declared insolvent* or otherwise becomes unable to pay and thus retain the services of a director.

Frank Bub's case

In most cases, probably including Frank Bub's case, the easiest course of action is to allow the current contract to elapse. This is easiest for the company because the fault for the error is partly shared by the rest of the board due to its (the board's) lack of oversight of Frank Bub's activities, and the principle of joint responsibility.

In any company with strong governance, such decisions would never be made by a single individual. In Frank Bub's case, the contract elapses in nine months' time. The problem with, say, dismissing him, would be in showing how he failed as a director: it can often be problematic as performance is difficult to assess or evaluate with a small number of performance measures. Whilst he was responsible for the error in the specification, there is a joint liability as others should have signed off on this project too. It may be possible to pay him until his contract expires without having him in a position of responsibility ("gardening leave") or he may agree to perform another role in that time period.

Unless the board supports his re-election, he would be unable to offer himself for re-election by shareholders and so his period of tenure as a director would expire naturally. Assuming there is no expensive termination payment in force on his contact, it should be inexpensive for him to leave the service of the Lobo board.

Tutorial note: *Other ways to remove Frank Bub would earn credit if adequately justified.*

(b) **Technological risk**

Technological risk concerns the potential losses and damage incurred by the failure of any technology. People often associate technology with computers but it need not be so – it could also be engineering, designs, etc. The effects of technological risk depend on those activities that depend on the particular technology in question. In the case of lost data or a computer storage failure, recent work may be lost, or more seriously, a patient may suffer if a piece of medical technology fails during use. In some financial systems, technology failures can also have very high impacts if all financial data is lost, for example.

Technological failure at Lobo

The errors which led to the technology failure were serious and avoidable. Frank Bub had ordered a system which was unfit for purpose in that it was not correctly specified. This means that it was not capable of processing the number of tasks required of it and this caused the system to fail when placed under normal loading. Having a person in a senior position capable of this magnitude of error may reflect on the remainder of the board and also its appointments processes and this may ultimately affect shareholders' confidence in the board as a whole.

Frank Bub was seemingly allowed to make a large investment decision alone and with no purchasing procedure or controls in place to monitor and assess the quality of such a large asset purchase decision. For something as important as an operational control system, this is an organisational and systemic oversight which reflects badly on the purchasing procedures for the company as a whole. A project team might instead have been formed with technical specialists and product users meeting together to ensure that the system ordered was suitable for the intended purpose.

The system was not pilot tested before it was fully implemented. For such an important system as the one which controls the company's main operations, discussion of this project should have been a regular and standing item on the board meeting agendas in the period leading up to its implementation. Thus, shareholders are unlikely to see the blame as being attributable to just one person. Such a major decision should have been taken by the board and full implementation procedures agreed by the board. Therefore, even with the removal of Frank Bub, shareholders may not regain full confidence in the board.

(c) **Fundamental principles of professional ethics**

Professional behaviour

By over-riding the normal procedures for purchasing at Lobo Company, Frank Bube acted unprofessionally and failed to observe the fundamental principle of professional behaviour. Procedures in organisations are agreed and imposed for good reason, including, in the case of large capital purchases, ensuring that systems meet value for money criteria and possess adequate operational capabilities. It was by the circumvention of these procedures that the events described in the case occurred.

Professional competence and due care

By purchasing a system unable to cope with the demands placed upon it, and failing to correctly specify the system requirements, he also failed to observe the fundamental principle of professional competence and due care. In the same way that accountants are employed because they are trusted with certain areas of expertise, engineers are employed because they are trusted with such matters as technical system specifications.

Objectivity and sound judgement

By purchasing the system on the advice of a friend and failing to take further advice beyond that, he was lacking objectivity and sound judgement. Professionals should act without bias, conflicts of interest and undue influence in all decisions. When a decision involves a large capital investment such as that at Lobo Company, this criterion becomes especially important as it can affect the operational capability of the business and also, eventually, its strategic positioning.

Public interest

All professionals are required to act in the public interest. Because the status of a professional in society is accorded a special privilege, the requirement to act in the public interest at all times *is an expectation of society*. This applies to professional engineers as well as to professional accountants. An awareness of this would have meant that Frank Bub would have considered a wider range of factors before making the incorrect specification decision.

If Frank Bub was aware of this duty, he *would be aware that he owed a duty of professional care* to "clients, lenders, governments, employers, employees, investors, the business community and others who rely on the work" (from the IFAC definition of professionals).

Acting in the public interest also reminds Frank Bub that his status as a professional is supported by society in exchange for an understanding that he will explicitly *not act for any sectional interest* or in any way which lacks competence, objectivity or professional care. Because, in the case of his role at Lobo, he is acting on behalf of its shareholders, employees and others, their legitimate claims should be uppermost in his mind in his professional duties.

Tutorial note: *Notice how ACCA's Code of Professional Ethics and Conduct parallels similar codes for professionals in general.*

JUNE 2014

Answer 1 WORLD JUSTICE

(a) **Underlying principles of corporate governance**

Transparency

This is the important quality of governance which specifies that companies should disclose all material information to shareholders and others unless there is a valid and defensible reason to withhold it. It implies a default position of disclosure over the concealment of information.

Given the information provided in the case, Xaxa cannot be fairly criticised for a lack of transparency. There was no attempt to hide the reasons why Xaxa had remained in the baby food business, with the chief executive saying that it was a "profitable business opportunity" and that he "owed it to the shareholders to maximise their return". Likewise, when the Oublie Group put the questions to management, it received direct and seemingly honest replies to each one. There is no evidence from the case which suggests that Xaxa sought to be surreptitious or concealing in its behaviour or dealings with shareholders.

Judgement

Because corporate governance is based on decision-making, the ability to make sound and balanced judgements is an important underlying principle. In many cases, judgement is the ability to decide between two credible courses of action, and making finely-tuned calculations in so doing. The decision-maker's personal attitudes to risk, ethics and the timescale of likely returns are likely to be important factors in how a person judges a given decision.

It is clear from the case that the Xaxa board strongly discounted any ethical consideration in reaching its judgement in remaining in the baby food market in developing countries. By adopting a "stockholder" or pristine capitalist/expedient view on the importance of profits over and above the ethical and reputational issues, the board of Xaxa demonstrated something about its attitudes to ethics and risk. When the other two companies named in "Killer Companies" judged that it was safer to withdraw from the market, Xaxa reached the opposite conclusion and this says something significant about the board's judgement. Some will conclude, as MWC and the Oublie Group did, that the Xaxa board has demonstrated poor judgement and blatant opportunism on this issue.

Reputation

It is important that companies are seen by stakeholders as competent, ethical, fair to others and reputable. Company boards must enjoy the full confidence of several important stakeholders in order to enjoy full access to resource and product markets. A poor reputation can quickly affect a company's ability to, for example, attract high quality employees, sell its products or attract capital.

The fact that, of the three companies criticised in "Killer Companies", two withdrew straightaway, suggests that there were strong reputational issues to be considered. MWC is actively seeking to challenge Xaxa's reputation as an ethical company with its slogan ("Xaxa kills babies") and its calls for a boycott of other Xaxa products, supported by the information in the television programme. Similarly, the board's effective dismissal of the concerns of the Oublie Group suggests that the Xaxa board may struggle to maintain the full confidence of some shareholders, especially those 50 institutional shareholders in the Oublie Group.

It looks likely that Xaxa's reputation will have been damaged by the events over the baby food debate, and the board should perhaps consider measures which would partly restore its reputation if it wants to avoid longer term damage to its name. Legal risk could negatively affect the reputation of Xaxa if it were sued because of insufficient or inadequate preparation instructions on the product.

(b) **Purposes of a corporate code of ethics**

There are five broad purposes which a corporate (as distinguished from a professional) code of ethics can achieve:

(1) To *establish the organisation's core values* and to stimulate internal discussions about these values. These form part of the organisation's underlying environment (infrastructure) and help to promote behaviour in support of the organisation's mission.

(2) To *recognise and promote stakeholder responsibilities*. This may include identification of the important stakeholders, which stakeholders to privilege over others and the postures to adopt towards those stakeholders.

(3) Corporate codes of ethics are designed to *control behaviour and guide decision-making*. When drafted as a de facto policy document, employees and management can use the code to guide them whenever a given ethical situation arises. It can ensure a uniformity of approach to ethical issues and help to prevent unethical behaviour.

(4) The code can be an important element in the organisation's *strategic positioning*. Ethical reputation can be as important a component of a company's strategic positioning as much as its power over suppliers or buyers, or its ability to increase the switching costs of competitor products.

(5) As a public document, the code can help to *convey values and ethical standards* to stakeholders. This could mean, for example, that shareholders could scrutinise the code to see if the company's values accorded with their own. Alternatively, current or potential employees could use it to see if the company is one they would like to work for.

Xaxa Company reconsidering its participation in baby food markets

The first way in which having a code of ethics might cause Xaxa to reconsider its strategy is in *considering the stakeholders affected by its operations*. If the evidence offered by "Killer Companies" and the television programme is accurate, then a stakeholder analysis would highlight the negative effects that its baby food marketing was having. In the reply to the Oublie Group, the board remarked that it was unprepared to consider "other claims made against the company strategy" but were such an analysis to be conducted, the company would be fully aware of the effects of its business in the poorer countries. Also, as an "inward-looking" company (according to Hugh Oublie's belief), the Xaxa board may not be fully aware of the effects of its business in those countries.

Second, it would have the potential for Xaxa to consider its *strategic positioning* in respect to ethical issues. Given the reaction by MWC and other groups, the ethical reputation of Xaxa has probably deteriorated and a review of this would have the potential to improve its ethical positioning. Withdrawal from the baby food market in developing countries would remove the threat of MWC protests and of consumer boycotts of its other products.

Linked to this, the code would allow Xaxa to clearly demonstrate its commitment to certain ethical standards. This would enable external stakeholders to *hold Xaxa to account*, by comparing actual behaviour against disclosed intent, and help to challenge poor ethical behaviour. It would be very difficult, for example, to convey an ethical aspiration that shareholder value should be pursued regardless of other stakeholder impacts, and so some change in behaviour may be necessary to help with this.

Tutorial note: *Appropriate credit would be given for other relevant points.*

(c)   **Intervention in governance**

> *(i)   Investor intervention*

It is considered to be a serious matter when investors seek to intervene directly in the running of a company. This is because intervention, by definition, represents a partial failure of the agency relationship in which directors are entrusted, by shareholders, to run a company responsibly on their behalf.

There are several situations in which investors might attempt to intervene directly, either by challenging management at a general meeting or by writing directly to the chairman to challenge his or her position. *Concerns about company strategy* are the most common and perhaps most serious reasons for intervention. If the board is pursuing a strategic course of action which is not in keeping with the wishes of the shareholders, either in terms of its ability to make adequate returns or because of its risky or unethical nature, shareholders may object directly to the company. Second, a sustained period of *poor operational performance* or inadequate levels of return, given the amount of risk incurred, could bring about direct intervention.

Third, *weak non-executive directors* (NEDs), unable or unwilling to scrutinise the executive board, may be a reason for intervention. The NEDs are appointed specifically to represent the interests of shareholders and therefore they must be able to discharge their role effectively. Fourth, any particular or serious *internal control failures* which would restrict value adding or add significant waste to organisational systems. A failure to be able to operate safely and efficiently is a serious management failure and could cause some shareholders to seek to intervene in the company.

Fifth, any unexplained or sustained *compliance failure* can be serious enough to merit intervention. This could be a failure to comply with legal statutes, to comply with accounting standards, to meet filing deadlines, to keep tax affairs in order, etc. Finally, there may be *concerns over governance and ethics* at the company. Issues such as excessive remuneration or poor ethical performance would fall into this category.

> *(ii)   Intervention by Oublie Group*

At Xaxa, the case highlights two prominent reasons for intervention:

> (1)   There is evidence of weak *non-executive scrutiny*, certainly in the opinion of longstanding shareholder Hugh Oublie. Given that the non-executive component of the board is ineffective when it comes to strategic scrutiny, Hugh Oublie believes that the executive board is not being adequately held to account by the NEDs. A board which is "inward-looking" is unlikely to have an effective NED presence, for example. In addition, however, the risk advisory role of NEDs may help to ensure that the board considers the risks involved in its baby food marketing, especially its reputation risks and the risks to its resource and product markets. Given that they feel there is no effective NED representation on the board, the Oublie Group believes itself within its rights to confront the board about this issue.

(2) The concerns about governance and its *poor attitudes towards ethics*. The company's disregard for the consequences of its baby food sales in poorer countries suggests a questionable ethical stance, and this is certainly the case in the view of the Oublie Group of shareholders and other influential stakeholders such as MWC. Not only is poor ethical behaviour a potential source of reputation and other risks (such as customers boycotting Xaxa products), it may also contribute to an unfortunate repositioning of the company as a "bad" company. Such a reputation is unlikely to be what prominent shareholders seek from their investment and if management is intransigent, the case for direct intervention by the Oublie Group may be strong.

A third reason for intervention is the concern, expressed by Hugh Oublie, over the *strategy and strategic management at Xaxa*. Although profitable, it is likely that the Xaxa board is paying insufficient attention to the medium-term business risks which could arise as a result of the baby food controversy. The belief of the board that concern over the baby food marketing was a temporary concern might demonstrate a short-sightedness and a lack of insight on the nature of business risk. Boards of directors, as stewards of shareholder value, must always be aware of the potential effects of controversial business decisions on reputation and other factors which can give rise to business risks.

(d) Guidance on audit risk

(i) Stages in a risk audit

Thank you for commissioning this consultancy to advise Xaxa on risk auditing and related issues. In the first instance, we have drafted notes to assist in the stages of the risk audit. We have carried out a preliminary analysis of the company to serve as a basis for discussion and hope this will help in the board in being able to see the benefits of this service.

Risk audit is an important component of sound corporate governance and highlights the risks affecting a company and the measures taken to mitigate those risks. In most jurisdictions, there is no specific direction as to who should carry out this role and both internal and external auditors can be employed. We will return to the issue of internal and external audits later in these notes. We now turn to the stages in a risk audit.

The first stage in a risk audit is risk *identification*. It is especially important that all relevant risks are identified because it is only when risks are identified that subsequent stages of the audit can be conducted. The maintenance of a risk register is one way in which companies achieve this, with new risks being added and obsolete ones being deleted if they no longer apply. In the case of Xaxa, there are several obvious risks which will apply because of its size and the complexity of its business. Operating in many different countries will incur exchange rate risks, for example, and the issues which have arisen over the marketing of baby food may give rise to political risks, reputation risks, product market risks and resource market risks, if, for example, the company has difficulty in recruitment.

Once identified, each risk must then be assessed. This requires estimating the probability of each risk materialising and the impact of such a risk realisation. For some risks, these might be relatively straightforward to calculate but for others, more subjective estimates must be made. We have noted, for example, that the effect of the publicity generated by "Mothers Who Care" may have not only increased the risk of a consumer boycott but may have made the impact worse by the use of inflammatory and provocative slogans such as "Xaxa kills babies". Accurate risk assessments then enable the company to see which risks should receive the most management attention.

The *review of controls* is the third stage of the audit. Once a risk has been identified and assessed, this stage considers the effectiveness with which it is controlled or mitigated. Those risks with higher probabilities or higher impacts may, for example, require more effective mitigation strategies than those assessed as less so. If a control is found to be inadequate, this stage of the risk audit will highlight the need for strengthening the control. If a control is currently more than is necessary (perhaps costing a disproportionate amount given the probability or the impact), it can be reduced.

The final stage is to issue a *report* to management for future planning and decision-making. This report will highlight the key risks, those requiring the most immediate and urgent attention, and a comment on the quality of existing assessment procedures. Any assessment shortcomings or resource constraints will be clarified and barriers to subsequent risk audits highlighted. Although at a very early stage, it may be the case, for example, that the board of Xaxa has underestimated the risks associated with its decision to continue and expand its baby food business in poorer countries and this report would be able to show that.

(ii)   Distinction between internal and external audit risk

Internal risk audit is one undertaken by employees of the company being audited and is usually carried out by the internal audit function. Externally, consultants provide this service to clients. In some cases, this is a non-audit service offered by accounting practices and other consultancies specialise more specifically on risk including the provision of risk audit services.

Advantages of external risk audit

In the case of Xaxa, we believe an internal risk audit would be a less effective option than a full risk audit by an external party. There are several reasons for this:

- An external risk audit will *avoid familiarity* threats by the auditor. The company's internal auditors are likely to be working within the company's culture and perhaps "contaminated" or at least "affected" by it. In the case of Xaxa, this may be less helpful because of the need, as the board has realised, of gaining an outsider's view of the company and its issues. It is not our place to question Xaxa's culture but we have noted with interest, comments made in the media suggesting the company is "self-reliant" when perhaps some external scrutiny would be beneficial.

- An external risk audit will be neutral and *independent in its approach*. Those with experience in the company may feel themselves to have a greater familiarity with its risks and risk control systems but may, in adopting such an attitude, have overlooked or underestimated some risks. A "fresh pair of eyes" will not bring any previous "baggage" and will bring about a more thorough and impartial outcome.

- An external risk audit, assuming it is accompanied by a report to shareholders, will *enhance investor confidence* in the process and in Xaxa's risk management. This may be especially important when a company has been faced with a situation which has caused tension between a board and the shareholders such as at Xaxa. It seems evident that the Oublie Group has a number of issues with regard to the company's risk management and an external risk audit will help to cultivate the important relationship between the board and its institutional investors.

- We believe that current thinking and *best practice can be more effectively transferred* when the audit is undertaken by external parties. External auditors often see practice in many companies in the course of their work and by selecting the most effective practices and sharing that knowledge with subsequent clients, best practice is shared and propagated. Risk audit by internal people is less likely to be aware of latest thinking because of their lack of exposure to other companies and their approaches.

Answer 2 BOB WONG

(a)   **Risk appetite and risk awareness**

Risk appetite

This describes the general posture an entity (in this case, Bob, an individual investor) has towards risk. It describes the investor's position on a continuum between risk aversion and risk seeking. A person with a high risk appetite will be risk seeking and a person with a low risk appetite will be generally risk averse. It is broadly assumed that higher risk is associated with greater gains and losses, whilst greater returns will, over time, be gained with higher risk investments. Lower risk investments are generally assumed, over time, to attract lower returns.

Risk awareness

In the context of Bob's investments, risk awareness describes the ability of an investor to recognise and measure the risk associated with a given investment. Some investments (i.e. the shares in a company, government bonds, company bonds and debentures, etc) have structurally higher risk than others by virtue of what they are and where they lie in the priority of claims in the event of liquidation. For investors seeking to balance a portfolio of investments in line with their personal risk appetite, it is essential to be able to know the general level of risk attached to each one.

Choice of investments

If Bob is generally risk averse, he will seek out investments which have *low levels of uncertainty and predictable levels of return*. The "price" of this certainty is usually a *lower return over time* than a more risky investment, but as part of a portfolio, lower risk investments provide a base upon which it is possible to build with selected higher risk shares. Typical lower-risk investments are company bonds (long-term loans to a company at an agreed rate of interest) or, presumed to be even lower risk, government bonds. These are issued when a country's national debt is financed by individual loans at an agreed annual rate over a fixed number of years.

If Bob is generally risk seeking, it is likely he wants greater returns and is prepared to bear a higher risk in order to achieve them. He will accordingly seek out investments which have *greater levels of uncertainty and more volatile levels of return*. These are likely to be shares in companies in complex or more turbulent environments, possibly less diversified, and with a *possibility of substantial loss as well as capital growth*. Larger companies with diversified interests and a relatively predictable long-term level of return are less likely to be a key part of a risk-seeker's investment. He or she is more likely to opt for smaller companies, those in emerging markets or those in growth sectors which could make a substantial long-term return compared to more established alternatives. Beta factors are one way of measuring and assessing the relative financial risks or volatility faced by an individual company in a market as a whole. Risk seeking investors may invest in companies with a beta greater than one.

(b) **Business risk and financial risk**

Business risks

These are risks which can threaten the survival of the business as a whole and they can arise from many sources. Essentially though, they arise because of the business model which an organisation operates and the strategies it pursues. Some business activities, by their nature, give rise to certain risks which can threaten the business as a whole. Some business risks can affect the "going concern" status and threaten the survival of the business. This is when the continuation of a business in its present form is uncertain because of external threats to the business at a strategic level, or a failure of the business's strategy.

Financial risks

These are the risks which arise from the way a business is financially structured, its management of working capital and its management of short and long-term debt financing. Cash flow can be strongly influenced by how much debt to equity a business has, its need to service that debt and the rate at which it is borrowed. Likewise, the ability of a business to operate on a day-to-day basis depends upon how it manages its working capital and its ability to control payables, receivables, cash and inventories. Any change which makes its cash flow situation worse, such as poor collection of receivables, excessive borrowing, increased borrowing rates, etc, could represent an increased financial risk for the business.

Why risks might vary by sector

The website was correct when it said that risks vary by business sector. A bank, for example, might be especially vulnerable to financial and capital adequacy risk whereas a mining company might be especially vulnerable to health and safety risk. This is because of the different environments, and the business models, strategies and financial structures adopted by companies in different industries.

Sectors exist in *different environments*. This means that the external factors which affect businesses and give rise to risks are different. Some industries, for example, are mainly located within a certain geographical area whilst others are international, thereby giving rise to such risks as exchange rate risk, etc. Some exist in relatively simple and stable environments whilst others are in more turbulent and changeable environments. Thus, in more unstable and complex environments, perhaps with greater levels of regulation, changing consumer patterns and higher technology, companies will be subject to greater risks than those in more stable and simple environments.

Companies in different sectors *adopt different business models*. This means that the ways in which value is added will differ substantially among companies in different sectors. In a service industry, for example, value is added by the provision of intangible products, often with the direct intervention of a person. In a manufacturing company, there will be risks associated with inventory management which a service industry will not be exposed to. Conversely, a company in a service industry such as insurance or banking is more likely to be exposed to certain technical skill shortages and fraud risks.

Different sectors have *different financial structures, strategies and cost bases*. Some companies, by virtue of their main activity, rely heavily on short or long-term loan capital whereas others have lower structural gearing. Others have even more complex financial structures. These financial structures give rise to different costs of capital and differential vulnerabilities to such external factors as monetary pressure. So whereas a traditional manufacturing company might have very little debt, a civil engineering business undertaking individual large projects might take on large amounts of medium-term debt to finance the project.

This means that risks are greater in such a business because of the financial gearing which is lower in the traditional company funded mainly by shareholders' equity or retained surpluses. Banks rely on a range of funding sources and become vulnerable to losses when these become difficult or the price of gaining these funds rises for any reason. Some companies have different cost structures which make them more risky in different economic circumstances. Companies with high operational gearing, such as those having very high fixed costs compared to variable costs, have more volatile returns simply because of the structure of their cost base.

(c) **Mandatory and voluntary disclosures**

Annual reports contain both mandatory and voluntary components. Mandatory disclosures are those which are required, either by statute (e.g. company law), reporting standard or listing rule. The main financial statements, with their related disclosure notes, and the audit report fall into this category. These are the statement of profit or loss, the statement of financial position (balance sheet), the statement of changes in equity and the statement of cash flows. Some parts of the directors' report are also mandatory in some jurisdictions as are notes on the composition of the board and the remuneration of directors. Listing rules in some jurisdictions have increased with regard to disclosure requirements. In many countries, for example, a substantial amount of corporate governance disclosure is required, as is the "comply or explain" statement. The presence of the "comply or explain" statement is often mandatory but the content is used to convey the extent of non-compliance with the relevant corporate governance code.

Voluntary disclosures are those not required by any regulatory constraint but are often made nevertheless. Some of these are made because of tradition and shareholder expectation (such as the chairman's statement) whilst others are thought to be concerned with managing the claims of a company's wider stakeholders. Some companies include disclosure on objectives so that shareholders can understand the board's ideas for the future, possibly including a mission statement or similar.

Likewise, social and environmental information is often included, detailing, for example, the company's policy and objectives with regard to a range of social and environmental measures. Some risk disclosures are also voluntarily supplied, for example, when a company is adopting an integrated reporting approach.

Usefulness of CG disclosure

Corporate governance disclosure in the annual report of a listed company is often required by listing rules although the content of what is required varies by jurisdiction. In most cases, however, corporate governance disclosure includes information on the directors (both executive and non-executive), information on strategy, reports from board committees (including the remuneration committee), risk reporting and information on any unusual or extraordinary events.

The information *about the board* will enable Bob to see the balance of the board of directors which leads the company and also those non-executive directors who help and support the executive board. By studying the experience of the directors, he can eventually take a view on how well the board is likely to lead the company. If the board is in any way non-compliant with relevant laws or listing rules (say on the balance between executive and non-executive directors), this may tell him something about how well other parts of the company are likely to be run.

Risk reporting will enable Bob to gain an understanding of the number of risks which the company feels it faces and the policies the company has in place for managing those risks. Because the specific risks faced by companies vary so much by sector and by company, these disclosures can enable Bob to understand the types of issues which may emerge to threaten the value of his shares in the company. Risk reports are necessarily speculative and incomplete, however, and other risks can materialise which were not predicted by the company. Comparing risk reports year on year and comparing those of companies in the same sector could also prove helpful.

Board committee reports will enable Bob to learn about the role of non-executive directors in the company and how they counterbalance, support and constrain the executive board. In many jurisdictions, the corporate governance report includes a report by the remuneration committee, for example. This enables the non-executives comprising the committee to inform shareholders (or potential shareholders such as Bob) about the policies they adopt in rewarding executives, and to report on historical detail of what the executive board was paid in the financial year just ended. Bob can form a view of whether he believes the policies look consistent with the company's strategy and whether the directors are fairly paid (or overpaid) for their performance.

The *compliance statement*, often referred to as the "comply or explain" statement in a principles-based jurisdiction, will tell Bob the extent to which the company is compliant with the provisions of the relevant code of corporate governance. If it is not compliant, this statement will inform him of the seriousness of any breaches and he can also judge the explanation given, as to why the company is not in full compliance. If there is a serious breach and a weak or unconvincing explanation is given, Bob may well take that into account when considering making an investment in that company's shares.

Tutorial note: *Credit would be given for alternative answers relevant to the usefulness of CG disclosure.*

Answer 3 DEETOWN

(a)   Ethical threats and safeguards

Ethical threat

The term "ethical threat" is used in some professional codes of ethics to describe any factor which may reduce the effectiveness of a professional person and his/her ability to act in the public interest, free from any countervailing concern which might threaten his or her independence.

In the ACCA and IESBA (IFAC) codes of ethics, there are five general ethical threats identified: self-interest, self-review, advocacy, familiarity and intimidation. Each of these can make it difficult for the professional to act without coercion or undue influence. The term is often used in the context of auditing (internal or external). It is important that auditors are free of any ethical threats in conducting an audit so as to ensure that the audit is performed thoroughly and solely in the interests of the shareholders.

Ethical safeguard

An ethical safeguard is a constraint or control placed upon a professional person or an organisation to prevent the occurrence of any of the ethical threats mentioned above. Safeguards are imposed from two sources: those created by the profession, legislation or regulation, and those created from within a given firm's own systems and procedures. The external regulation of audit includes several provisions intended to ensure the independence of an external auditor, whilst some organisations also have their own rules for ensuring that employees or contractors are not compromised in their ability to act independently and without acceding to any vested interests.

Benefits of ethical safeguards

The primary benefit of any ethical safeguard is *to protect an individual or an organisation* from the effects of an ethical threat. The provision of both audit and non-audit services by Hum and Hoo raises several potential ethical threats, particularly to independence. By instituting effective safeguards, these hazards can be avoided. It is important that, as a professional organisation, the *appearance of ethical threats is avoided as well as the actual avoidance itself*. The fact that staff can work on both audit and non-audit work and that the lines between the two are blurred, represents a challenge to the imposition of effective safeguards at Hum and Hoo.

In addition, however, the presence of effective ethical safeguards *underpins public trust and the confidence of shareholders*. The reputation of accountants in society is a crucial component in their professionalism. Ethical threats, unchecked by effective ethical safeguards, undermine the professional reputation and introduce unhelpful factors which make it difficult for accountants to operate normally. Professionals such as auditors, and accountants performing non-audit services, are only helpful to shareholders (in the case of external audit) or service clients (in the case of non-audit services) precisely because their independence cannot be questioned.

A third benefit of ethical safeguards is that they *enable the effective delivery of both audit and non-audit services* without the frustrating factors (ethical threats) which might render some services ineffective. So the fact that an ethical safeguard is in place means that a professional can conduct business knowing that his or her independence will not be questioned. An external auditor, for example, must have the full confidence of shareholders, and safeguards limiting interactions between them and their clients mean that they can be, and be seen to be, independent of them.

(b)   Environmental audit

One of the initiatives which companies have used to convey their environmental policies and performance is the environmental report. These are usually "stand alone" or web-based media containing content on policy, performance against targets on resource consumption (including water, energy, etc) and emissions, including carbon, other chemicals, pollutants and waste.

As with any other audit, the purpose of an environmental audit is to assure that the information given is a true and fair view of reality. This means that if a company makes a disclosure about a given measure, it is essentially accurate.

Demonstrating environmental sustainability

Cherry Hoo correctly identified one of the issues with environmental reporting: it is voluntary in most jurisdictions and not subject to any agreed accounting standard. This means that the ability of a company to "demonstrate its environmental sustainability" *depends upon what, and how much, is measured and disclosed.*

If the company measures all of its environmental impacts, including those inputs which cannot be replaced by recycling, it is likely to be able to produce a more detailed and meaningful environmental account. This would involve stating how much material has been used, how much of it can be replaced or re-used, what the precise environmental outputs are and the extent to which these can be offset or not. This would then be able to be audited and a true and fair view arrived at.

If the company were to elect to disclose less, perhaps in what some commentators have referred to as a "greenwashing" exercise, then it is *likely that the environmental report will only weakly describe the organisation's sustainability.* If the report contained content which was not measurable (perhaps aspirations rather than measureable content), then the audit would be much more difficult to perform (because there is less to assure).

In conclusion, an environmental report will enable a company to "demonstrate its environmental sustainability" if the correct metrics for sustainability are measured and reported on and if the auditors are able to assure, by way of available data and agreed ways of measurement, those metrics. A weaker form of sustainability would be measured by a less detailed form of environmental reporting and audit.

(c)   **Public interest**

The public interest is one of the key themes in professionalism, including in accountancy. To act in the public interest means to act for the benefit of the *collective wellbeing of society* as a whole. This means that accountants should serve the interest of *clients, shareholders, governments and other stakeholders.* In accounting services, accountants need to be aware that when conducting an audit, they need to be impartial and unbiased because they are acting in the interests of shareholders. Society relies upon the premise that accounting reports are true and fair, and useful for decision-making. Anything which might erode that premise is *against the interests of stability in society* and therefore against the public interest.

Why audit committee is a suitable body

Some codes of corporate governance, such as Sarbanes Oxley, specify that some non-audit services can be provided by the external audit firm but only with the express consent of the client's audit committee. Other codes and regulatory instruments also have provisions for the assessment of whether non-audit engagement is valid and acceptable.

The audit committee is well-placed to rule on the purchase of non-audit services for the following reasons:

First, a key part of its purpose and brief is to *take responsibility for the independence of the external audit.* The audit committee has the authority to recommend a change in external auditor if it believes that it is not capable of delivering an unbiased or independent audit. Because it is concerned with auditor independence and has this power to recommend a change in auditor, it is usually able to judge whether non-audit services provided by auditors are affecting auditor independence. The presence of an effective audit committee is also a check and balance against management attempting to capture an external auditor (i.e. they will not seek to capture an auditor because they know they are being monitored by the audit committee).

Second, assuming the company is compliant with its relevant corporate governance code, the audit committee will be made up mainly of *non-executive directors* (NEDs) *with no vested financial interest in the company*. In most jurisdictions, NEDs are prevented from holding shares or share options in companies they are NEDs for. This is to ensure their impartiality and remove any temptation to gain short-term bonuses or to be concerned with short-term issues. Whereas some executives may have a financial incentive to behave in a way which will provide, say, a favourable variance against a budget which underpins their personal bonus, NEDs have no such issues. This facilitates an impartiality which is essential in NEDs being able to identify ethical threats and therefore prevent the activity which causes them.

Third, it is the purpose of the audit committee to *represent the interests of shareholders* against any potential vested interests of executive directors and other company senior management. It is very much in the interests of shareholders to ensure the independence of an external auditor, and an audit committee would be highly dysfunctional were it to permit any behaviour counter to the shareholders' interests. NEDs are an important part of a corporate governance system because they explicitly represent shareholders, sometimes against the interests of executives. In this capacity, they are able to bring scrutiny on shareholders' behalf.

It should be noted that the audit firm themselves is additionally required by the ACCA *Code of Conduct and Ethics* to determine whether providing such services would create a threat to independence. Furthermore, if the client is defined as a "public interest entity" such work is not permitted at all by the Code.

Answer 4 TZO COMPANY

(a)   How Mahmood might act

Conventional ethical behaviour assumption

Kohlberg's three stages of ethical development are the pre-conventional, the conventional and the post-conventional. Each of these has its own likely ethical response.

The conventional ethical response is to believe that *the ethical right is to comply in full* with whatever regulations apply or whatever orders are given in the context they are operating in. It assumes that the highest ethical position is to be in compliance with whatever rules, regulations or requirements are applicable at the time. So the individual's focus is on positioning themselves *so as to maximise his or her ability to comply*. This might involve learning how to adopt compliant behaviour, learning about compliance requirements and familiarisation with the cultural norms which apply.

For Mahmood, it is clear in the case that he has been ordered by his manager to "say nothing" and to "conduct his job as normal". A conventional ethical position would not reflect beyond this. His instructions are clear and *he would see virtue in obedience* to this instruction. The fact that he is a part of an organisational hierarchy and that those in a supervisory position over him have imposed a rule for him to comply with, is sufficient for him.

Post-conventional ethical behaviour assumption

To adopt a post-conventional ethical response is to see a "higher" ethical duty despite whatever laws, regulations, norms or instructions apply at any given time. What Kohlberg referred to as "universal principles" are essentially subjective, meaning that each person can have his or her view of what those are. But in each case, a post-conventional actor will consider the ethical "right" not in line with current regulations (which can change over time) but with his or her higher principles, perhaps those concerning concepts such as justice, fairness, compassion, decency, etc.

For Mahmood, post-conventional behaviour might involve him *questioning the morality of the decision* to include inferior meat in the company's products in the interests of what he sees as the "greater good". He may come to the view, for example, that honesty and truthfulness to customers is a higher or "universal" principle, *even though the board of Tzo Company appears to have decided to introduce the inferior meat into its premium meat product*. In such a situation, he could maintain, but suppress, his beliefs for the sake of keeping his job, or he could act upon his belief. Because he has had no satisfaction from his manager at Tzo, *he might believe it ethically right to inform an external source, such as a newspaper*, as he is considering.

Post-conventional behaviour is often costly to the actor and if Mahmood were to become a whistle-blower in this case, he may well lose his own job and cause others to lose theirs.

(b) **Ethical case**

In recognising that it would be very costly on a personal level for Mahmood to act as a whistle-blower in this case, there is a strong ethical argument that he should do so.

The company is acting in a *concerted manner to deceive customers* by selling food which is not what they believe it to be. As an employee of the company, Mahmood is taking part in a value adding process which results in a product which is not what the customer thinks they are purchasing. It may be that the inferior meat, even if safe to eat for the majority, is unsuitable for some diets or which may offend some consumers' personal or cultural beliefs. In a trades-description sense, this deceit is a breach of customers' trust. It may cause offence to some and possibly even illness in others if they purchased a product unaware of the inferior nature of the contents.

Because the *board of Tzo Company is complicit* in the decision, he is unlikely to get any change of mind from anyone in the company. So the only way to highlight the deceit is to go outside the company. Were he to adopt the normal grievance procedure by observing the chain of command in the company, the involvement of the board of Tzo Company in the use of inferior meat would make it unlikely he would get a sympathetic hearing. In fact by raising the issue internally, he might risk his own safety or the comfort of his position at work. So going to a newspaper may be the only way he can reasonably expect to see the problem addressed.

The division is *falsifying quality control reports* and therefore intentionally misleading whoever it is who receives these – perhaps a food standards agency, a regulator or similar. This control is presumably intended to ensure that the company's main output is of a high quality as stated, and that the quality assurance measures are met for the product. The falsification of the report means that normal quality procedures are being systematically subverted and this is a very serious matter. Again, the fact that the board of directors has sanctioned this makes it unlikely that Mahmood would receive a sympathetic hearing, thus making the case for going directly to the newspaper.

It is in the *public interest* to highlight a situation in which a company is mislabelling food, deceiving customers and shareholders, and requiring its employees to take part in the deceit and remain quiet about it. This is not how business should behave and it could serve to erode society's trust in business in general. Employees have an ethical right to work for a company which is not structurally deceitful and were such a situation to persist, it could undermine management–employee relations and open the company up to legal and reputational damage. Inasmuch as such a situation is probably likely to be disclosed eventually, a quicker rather than protracted conclusion is preferable.

(c)   **Regulatory requirement for auditor report on internal controls**

External reports on the effectiveness of internal controls are intended to convey the robustness of a company's internal controls to an external audience (usually the shareholders). As with other reports, however, the company must make preparations and institute systems to gather the information to report on. This in itself is capable of controlling behaviour and constraining the professional and ethical behaviour of management.

With any report required by regulation, the board must take control of the process and acknowledge its responsibility for the company's system of, in this case, internal controls. This means that it would be unable to knowingly circumvent or undermine the internal controls put in place to control the quality of meat in the factory. The regulatory nature of this requirement would also make it an offence to make a false disclosure, meaning that the directors could be held personally liable for any untruths in the report. So although the use of the inferior meat itself may not be illegal as indicated by the factory manager, making an untrue statement on an internal control report over the use of that meat would be an offence.

Any reporting (including one on internal controls) *creates greater accountability* because stakeholders can hold to account those making those statements. In this case, any stakeholder can then point to what was said in the report and hold the board to account for its performance against any given statement. This includes employees such as Mahmood and consumers concerned with product quality. So if Tzo explained the internal controls behind the production of its "high quality" meat products, it could then be held accountable for any breach in the controls underpinning that quality.

The need to report on internal controls would make it almost impossible *to use the inferior meat without disclosing the fact of its use*, because the penalty for intentionally including misleading or false statements in the report would be high (regardless of whether Tzo is based in a rules or a principles-based jurisdiction). It might then be faced with the choice of continuing to use the meat and admitting it, or discontinuing its use in order to report on internal controls supporting the claimed high quality of its products. Either way, continuing to use inferior meat in a *concealed* way would be very difficult.

A report on the effectiveness of internal controls (such as Sarbanes Oxley s.404) typically requires the inclusion of a *statement on the processes used* by the directors to assess the effectiveness of internal controls. This includes the *disclosure of any material internal control weaknesses* or any significant problems which the company encountered in its internal controls over the period under review. The value of the report as a means of reassuring investors is to use this statement to demonstrate the robustness of the processes. An unconvincing disclosure on this would potentially undermine investor confidence.

Because the report is subject to an auditor's review (or full audit in some jurisdictions), *the auditors can demand evidence of any statement* on the report and follow any claim made back along the relevant audit trail. It is a serious and often easily detectable offence to deceive an auditor or to make a knowingly false statement in an audited or auditor-reviewed report. Such a deceit (of the auditors) would result in an immediate loss of confidence in management on the part of the auditors and, in consequence, also on the part of shareholders and regulators.

Governance, Risk and Ethics

Wednesday 10 December 2014

Time allowed
Reading and planning: 15 minutes
Writing: 3 hours

This paper is divided into two sections:

Section A – This ONE question is compulsory and MUST be attempted

Section B – TWO questions ONLY to be attempted

Do NOT open this paper until instructed by the supervisor.
During reading and planning time only the question paper may
be annotated. You must NOT write in your answer booklet until
instructed by the supervisor.
This question paper must not be removed from the examination hall.

The Association of Chartered Certified Accountants

Section A – This ONE question is compulsory and MUST be attempted

1   Cheapkit is a large clothes retailer in a major developed country. Its business strategy is based around vigorous cost leadership and it prides itself on selling fashionable garments for men, women and children at very low prices compared to its main rivals. For many years, it has achieved this cost leadership through carefully sourcing its garments from developing countries where labour is cheaper and where workplace regulation is less than in its home country.

As a company with a complex international supply chain, the board of Cheapkit regularly reviews its risks. It has long understood that three risks are of particular concern to the Cheapkit shareholders: exchange rate risk, supply risk and international political risk. Each one is carefully monitored and the board receives regular briefings on each, with the board believing that any of them could be a potential source of substantial loss to the shareholders.

For the past decade or so, Cheapkit has bought in a substantial proportion of its supplies from Athland, a relatively poor developing country known for its low labour costs and weak regulatory controls. Last year, 65% of Cheapkit's supplies came from this one country alone. Athland has a reputation for corruption, including government officials, although its workforce is known to be hard-working and reliable. Most employees in Athland's garment industry are employed on 'zero hours' contracts, meaning that they are employed by the hour as they are needed and released with no pay when demand from customers like Cheapkit is lower.

Half of Cheapkit's purchases from Athland are from Cornflower Company, a longstanding supplier to Cheapkit. Owned by the Fusilli brothers, Cornflower outgrew its previous factory and wished to build a new manufacturing facility in Athland for which permission from the local government authority was required. In order to gain the best location for the new factory and to hasten the planning process, the Fusilli brothers paid a substantial bribe to local government officials.

The Fusilli brothers at Cornflower felt under great pressure from Cheapkit to keep their prices low and so they sought to reduce overall expenditure including capital investments. Because the enforcement of building regulations was weak in Athland, the officials responsible for building quality enforcement were bribed to provide a weak level of inspection when construction began, thereby allowing the brothers to avoid the normal Athland building regulations. In order to save costs, inferior building materials were used which would result in a lower total capital outlay as well as a faster completion time. In order to maximise usable floor space, the brothers were also able to have the new building completed without the necessary number of escape doors or staff facilities. In each case, bribes were paid to officials to achieve the outcomes the Fusilli brothers wanted.

Once manufacturing began in the new building, high demand from Cheapkit meant that Cornflower was able to increase employment in the facility. Although, according to Athland building regulations, the floor area could legally accommodate a maximum of 500 employees, over 1,500 were often working in the building in order to fulfil orders from overseas customers including Cheapkit.

After only two years of normal operation, the new Cornflower building collapsed with the loss of over 1,000 lives. Collapsing slowly at first, the number of people killed or injured was made much worse by the shortage of escape exits and the large number of people in the building. As news of the tragedy was broadcast around the world, commentators reported that the weakness in the building was due to the West's 'obsession with cheap clothes'. Cheapkit was criticised as being part of the cause, with many saying that if retailers in the developed world pushed too hard for low prices, this (the collapse of the building) was one consequence of that. In response, Cheapkit's public relations department said that it entered into legal contracts with Cornflower in order to provide its customers with exceptional value for money. Cheapkit said that it was appalled and disgusted that Cornflower had acted corruptly and that the Cheapkit board was completely unaware of the weaknesses and safety breaches in the collapsed building.

One of those able to escape the building was Jess Lui, who was also the leader of a national pressure group 'Protect workers' rights' (PWR) lobbying the Athland government for better working conditions and health and safety practices for workers in the country. Having seen hundreds of people killed and injured in the collapsed building, she believed that although the government could do more, much of the blame lay with Cheapkit and the pressure it continually placed on Cornflower to keep its prices low. Jess questioned whether multinational companies such as Cheapkit should be allowed to exert so much economic pressure on companies based in developing countries. As concern over the state of other workplaces in the developing world became an increasing concern in the media, Miss Lui wrote a letter to the board of Cheapkit, which she also sent to newspapers and other media. Many of the newspapers and television channels reproduced the letter and it became a talking point in many countries because of the issues it raised.

[P.T.O.

In the letter, she said that Cheapkit was an unethical company because it supplied a market in its home country which was obsessed with cheap clothes. As long as its customers bought clothes for a cheap price, she believed that no-one at Cheapkit cared about how they were produced. She said that the constant pressure on prices had created a culture of 'exploitative wages', including at Cornflower.

Miss Lui received a lot of support after her comments on Cheapkit's accountability. She said that large international companies such as Cheapkit needed to recognise they had accountabilities to many beyond their shareholders and they also had a wider fiduciary duty in the public interest. The defective Cornflower factory in Athland, she argued, would not have existed without demand from Cheapkit, and so Cheapkit had to recognise that it should account for its actions and recognise its fiduciary duties to its supply chain as well as its shareholders.

At the same time as events in Athland unfolded, the business journalists reporting on the events and Cheapkit's alleged complicity in the tragedy also became aware of a new innovation in business reporting called integrated reporting, an initiative of the International Integrated Reporting Council (IIRC). Jess Lui read one article which said that integrated reporting might increase an organisation's accountability and require it to account for a wider set of concerns than was traditionally the case. This new understanding led to her including the following comment in her letter to Cheapkit:

'... as the leader of the PWR, it is always in my interests to gain as much information as possible from Cornflower and the other businesses with which it transacts, including, in this case, Cheapkit. Perhaps the integrated reporting initiative offers the advantage of a wider reporting model for businesses, to include accountability for a much more diverse set of concerns than has been the case in the past. The integrated reporting model appears to substantially enhance the existing business model and it would be in the interests of broader accountability if Cheapkit, and other businesses in the garment supply chain, were to adopt this new reporting approach. Anything that requires businesses to report on their wider impacts on society and the environment is a good thing as far as social pressure groups like PWR are concerned.'

The board of Cheapkit discussed the issues raised by the well-publicised discussion of Miss Lui's open letter and the comments from business journalists about integrated reporting. The board was, in principle, a supporter of the integrated reporting initiative and thought it would be useful to explain its position on a range of issues in a press release.

Required:

(a) **Discuss the stakeholder claims of Cornflower's employees and customers, and how these claims may be in conflict.** (7 marks)

(b) **Explain 'corruption' in the context of the case and discuss how corruption at Cornflower contributed to the collapse of the building and the loss of life.** (10 marks)

(c) Cheapkit's board believed that its major risks were exchange rate risk, supply risk and international political risk.

Required:

Explain each of these risks and how each may be of importance to Cheapkit's shareholders. (9 marks)

(d) The board of Cheapkit felt that the reputation of the company had been damaged following publication of Jess Lui's letter. It was decided that it should make a public response to her comments and also respond to points about integrated reporting raised by the business journalists, both of which had received a lot of supportive comment in the media.

Required:

Draft a press statement from the board of Cheapkit to include the following content:

(i)　**An explanation of Cheapkit's role as a 'corporate citizen' given its international supply chain.**

(6 marks)

(ii)　**An explanation of 'accountability' and 'fiduciary duty' as used in the case, and a discussion of how these are relevant to Cheapkit using a shareholder or 'pristine capitalist' perspective.**　(6 marks)

(iii)　**A description of the basic framework of integrated reporting, and the potential benefits to Cheapkit's different stakeholders, of reporting on different capital types.**　(8 marks)

Professional marks will be awarded in part (d) for clarity, tone, logical flow and persuasiveness of your statement.　(4 marks)

(50 marks)

Section B – TWO questions ONLY to be attempted

2 The independent board of governors (an independent oversight body comprised of local residents, parents and other concerned citizens) of the state-funded Chambon school for 11–16 year old children met to consider its most recent set of public examination results. A key responsibility placed upon the school's governors is the delivery, to its local government authority, of a report on exam performance in a full and timely manner. A report on both the exam results and the reasons for any improvement or deterioration over previous years are required from the governors each year. Accordingly, this annual meeting on exam performance was always considered to be very important. Although the school taught the national curriculum (a standard syllabus taught in all schools in the country) as required of it, the exam results at Chambon had deteriorated in recent years and on this particular occasion, they were very poor indeed. In order to address the weaknesses in the school, Chambon's budget had increased in recent years and a number of new teachers had been employed to help improve results. Despite this, exam performance continued to fall. A recent overspend against budget was funded through the closure of part of the school library and the sale of a sports field.

One member of the board of governors was Sally Murol. She believed that the local government authority might attempt to close Chambon school if these exam results were reported with no convincing explanation. One solution to avoid this threat, she said, was to either send the report in late or to select only the best results and submit a partial report so the school's performance looked better than it actually was. There is no central computerised exam results service in the country in which Chambon is located by which the local authority could establish the exam performance at Chambon school.

A general feeling of the governors' meeting was that perhaps the school needed some new leadership and it was time to remove the existing headteacher. Mr Besse had been in the role for many years and his management style was thought to be ineffective. He was widely liked by staff in the school because he believed that each teacher knew best how to manage their teaching, and so he tried not to intervene wherever possible. Mr Besse had sometimes disagreed with the governors when they suggested changes which could be made to improve exam performance, preferring to rely on what he believed were tried and tested ways of managing his teaching staff. He was thought to be very loyal to longstanding colleagues and had a dislike of confrontation.

Required:

(a) Explain, using evidence from the case, the characteristics which identify Chambon school as a public sector organisation and assess how its objectives as a public sector organisation have not been met. (10 marks)

(b) Explain the roles of a board of governors in the governance of Chambon school and discuss, in the context of Sally Murol's suggestion, the importance of transparency in the board of governors dealings with the local government authority. (9 marks)

(c) Discuss the potential advantages to Chambon school of replacing the headteacher in seeking to address its problems. (6 marks)

(25 marks)

3 New Ideas Company (NIC) was launched early this year as a result of a scientific breakthrough at a university. The company was located in a relatively small regional city, some distance from the main centres of population. Because the initial capital needed was large, the scientists behind the company decided to float the company on the stock exchange and the take up of shares was very good. This meant that the initial capital needs were fully funded. The business itself was highly technical, with many shareholders only weakly understanding the science behind the company. Upon reading the share prospectus, some analysts believed that NIC was a relatively risky business and that it could fail within two years unless a very good management team, including suitable non-executive directors (ideally locally based), was in place.

None of the scientists involved in NIC had any experience of business before and had to learn about the roles of a board and how to effectively run a company. Dr Ranjana Foo, the lead scientist who made the scientific discovery, was thought to be the logical person to become chief executive but she herself questioned her suitability for the role. She said she was happiest working alone and in the quiet environment of her laboratory, and was not inclined to invest valuable time learning about running a business as she was not good at relating to a wide range of people.

Colleagues said of Ranjana that, being a good scientist, she was excellent at detail but sometimes struggled to see the bigger picture on a project. Always popular, however, Ranjana liked to think that all of her colleagues liked her and she tended to avoid confrontation and conflict wherever possible.

One potential director of NIC was an experienced local businessman, Dr Idris. Upon being approached about the position, he said that he may have a conflict of interest because he was a major shareholder in one of the potential suppliers of the capital equipment which NIC would be purchasing.

Required:

(a) Assess Ranjana Foo's suitability to become chief executive officer (CEO) of New Ideas Company (NIC). Your answer should include an explanation of the roles and personal qualities of a CEO. (10 marks)

(b) Explain the benefits, specifically to NIC, of the appointment of 'suitable non-executive directors' and discuss the difficulties which the company may encounter in non-executive recruitment. (9 marks)

(c) Explain 'conflict of interest' and briefly discuss how a major shareholding in a potential supplier could be a conflict of interest to Dr Idris were he to become a director of NIC. (6 marks)

(25 marks)

4 After a period of expansion into several overseas markets and some structural decentralisation, Loho Company was considering its internal audit and internal control needs. Although privately owned and therefore not subject to listing rules, Loho's auditors had often suggested that a formal internal audit function would be beneficial.

The launch of several new products and a rapid increase in exports had raised a number of problems at Loho. These included problems in meeting order deadlines, whilst a number of operational constraints had meant that some orders had been delivered to customers late. The increase in overseas business had also, according to Sonja Tan, the financial director, increased the overall risk profile of the business. Credit risk had risen substantially as had a range of risks associated with exporting and overseas investment. In addition to a growth from 150 to 600 employees in its home country, Loho also had recruited a further 200 people overseas in order to facilitate business in those countries.

As part of her continuing professional development (CPD), Sonja Tan, the finance director who was also a professional accountant, had been to a seminar on improving internal controls (IC). She believed that at this point in its growth, Loho could benefit from tighter internal controls. Speaking about this to the board on her return from the seminar, she reminded her colleagues that sound internal controls could only provide 'reasonable assurance' and that any IC system had inherent limitations and could never be totally effective whatever changes were made to improve them. This came as a surprise to some board members who assumed, because internal controls were often very expensive, that they should be guaranteed to be fully effective.

Required:

(a) Construct the case for establishing an internal audit function at Loho Company.   (10 marks)

(b) Explain the reasons why many internal controls can never be guaranteed to be fully effective and discuss why ICs being 'very expensive' are no guarantee of their effectiveness.   (9 marks)

(c) The finance director Sonja Tan learned about improved internal controls as part of her continuing professional development (CPD).

Required:

Explain the advantages of continuing professional development (CPD) for professional accountants such as finance director Sonja Tan.   (6 marks)

(25 marks)

End of Question Paper

1   (a)   Claims of employees and customers
A stakeholder 'claim' is the nature of the relationship between the stakeholder and the organisation. It describes what the stakeholder is seeking from its relationship: what it 'wants'. In some cases, the nature of the claim is clear and meaningfully articulated but in others, it is unclear, amorphous and unvoiced.

The claims of employees and customers are usually clear, with both being articulated in part by market mechanisms and in part by occasional collective representation. This means that unhappy employees leave and unhappy customers stop buying from the business. The employees of Cornflower, located in Athland, are likely to seek fairer terms and conditions, a safer workplace, both physically and psychologically, and more secure employment and better pay from their employers. In some countries, trade unions or labour pressure groups can express the collective will (claim) of employees. The PWR is an example of this.

In contrast, Cornflower's customers, such as Cheapkit, are looking for a continuing supply of cheap garments. Cheapkit's business strategy is based upon the assumption that such supply will be available, and Cheapkit will have invested in capital (land and buildings) basing its strategy on the assumption of continuing supply at low unit prices. Cheapkit therefore has an incentive to maintain the pressure on Cornflower to minimise its costs, including labour costs.

Conflicts in the claims
A potential conflict between the claims of the customers, such as Cheapkit, and employees is in the control of costs at Cornflower. Because Athland is weakly regulated and corruption seems to be tolerated, Cornflower is able to employ local people on 'zero hours' contracts and, in the opinion of some, on 'exploitative wages'. So the price of helping Cheapkit achieve its low cost position in its own market (the customer), is paid for in part by the poor terms and conditions of Cornflower's employees in Athland. Were Cornflower's employees to receive improved terms and conditions, including working in a safe environment, extended job security and higher rates of pay, these increased costs could make it more difficult for Cornflower to retain its low prices to Cheapkit and hence to Cheapkit's customers.

   (b)   Explain corruption
Corruption can be loosely defined as deviation from honest behaviour but it also implies dishonest dealing, self-serving bias, underhandedness, a lack of transparency, abuse of systems and procedures, exercising undue influence and unfairly attempting to influence. It refers to illegal or unethical practices which damage the fabric of society. In the case of Cornflower, the Fusilli brothers seemed to have few ethical problems with attempting to influence a number of activities and procedures in their perceived favour. There was seemingly little attempt to allow processes to take their course or to comply in detail with regulations.

Corruption at Cornflower
The case describes Athland as a country with weak regulatory controls. It is evident from the case that Athland did have the requisite regulation in place over such important matters as building construction, escape routes and building occupancy. The problem was the effectiveness of the state in enforcing that regulation.

The first incidence of corruption in the case was the *employment of inferior building materials*. The motivation behind this was to achieve a lower total capital outlay for the building and also a quicker completion time on the project. In both cases, the intention was to make the capital investment lower, presumably to reduce the debt created by the construction and hence the debt servicing costs. Where building regulations specify a certain quality of material, it is usually because that grade or quality is necessary to ensure the safety and integrity of the building when used and under stress.

Likewise, bribes were offered to *persuade officials to provide a weak level of inspection* (effectively to ignore the regulations) when the building work was being carried out. It is common for building inspectors to be present during construction to ensure that relevant regulations are being adhered to. The Fusilli brothers corrupted these officials to the point where they did not adequately perform their duties. In doing so, the officials failed in their duty to the public interest and were complicit in the weak construction that, in turn, contributed to the building's collapse.

Because of the pressure on internal space in the new building, as well as the additional costs involved, the Fusilli brothers were able to have the building completed *without the requisite number of escape routes*. In the event of an emergency such as a fire or similar, the ability of people to leave the building quickly and safely would be a major determinant of casualty and death statistics. Because each escape route takes up a physical amount of space (with the door itself and the pathway needed to allow passage to the door), the space available for machines and other value-adding activity would be reduced and the building would be more costly to construct. This explains the Fusilli brothers' motive to make this illegal change to the plans. More people may have been able to evacuate the building were such regulations adhered to and a safe number of escape routes provided.

Finally, the *occupancy rules were not enforced* by officials. The number of occupants in a building is a legal constraint intended to ensure that over-occupation does not lead to accidents or other safety hazards. The number of people in the building is also a determinant of the evacuation time and, in turn, the risk to the safety of the occupants in the event of collapse. The fact that three times the regulated number of people worked in the building meant that escape plans were rendered much less effective and this would have significantly contributed to the casualties.

(c) **Exchange rate risk**

Most international transactions involve a currency exchange (unless the countries are in a single currency trading block). Cheapkit needs to pay Cornflower in the currency of Athland whilst selling the garments in its home currency. Because currencies rise and fall against each other as a result of supply and demand for those currencies, an adverse movement of one against the other can mean that the cost of a transaction in one currency becomes more expensive because of that adverse movement. The loss incurred by that adverse movement multiplied by the company's financial exposure is the hazard or impact of exchange rate risk.

The loss to Cheapkit's shareholders can take several forms. The most obvious is the actual loss incurred by an increase in the value of Athland's currency against its own and the consequent increase in costs. This can be a material cost, affecting the buying decision, or it can add to Cheapkit's expenses and therefore reduce its profits on the purchases from Cornflower. In addition though, a large amount of exposure to exchange rate risks can incur risk management costs such as exchange rate 'hedging', as well as the increased uncertainty over the volatility of Cheapkit's profits.

Supply risk

This is the risk that Cheapkit will not be able to obtain the inputs it needs (in this case, garments at the right quality and cost) to sell in its own stores. Increased supply risk is usually associated with complicated or undeveloped supply chains, and dealing with weaker companies in poorly regulated countries. In this case, the collapse of Cornflower's building in Athland means that, at least in the short term, Cornflower will have difficulty in meeting Cheapkit's need for supplies and so this risk has been tragically realised. With approximately half of the 65% of Cheapkit's Athland supplies coming from Cornflower, this incident represents a threat to about a third of Cheapkit's total purchases. Such a large exposure to Cornflower means that Cheapkit is likely to suffer from a shortage of supply as a result of the building collapse.

For shareholders, the value of Cheapkit, and hence the value of the shares, rests upon the successful continuing execution of the business model. Any interruption of supply will mean fewer choices for Cheapkit's customers in its stores with potentially increased prices. In a competitive retail environment, Cheapkit's success, and hence its shareholder value, is dependent on having a range of suppliers to source from, and to play them off against each other in order to achieve the lowest unit costs and the best supply terms and conditions. So the realisation of a supply risk will reduce shareholder value by the offering of less consumer choice and the possibility of increased costs. Both of these will adversely affect Cheapkit's strategic positioning and hence, potentially, its shareholder value. Finally, another supply risk which Cheapkit should have foreseen was the risk that the buildings of a key supplier (Cornflower) *might be vulnerable to such a collapse* as a result of poor government enforcement of building regulations, thus threatening future supplies from this supplier.

International political risk

Political risk refers to a potential failure on the part of the state to fulfil all or part of its functions. It can also relate to any potential influence a government has on the business environment in the country concerned. The state's role is to legislate, to formulate and implement public policy, to enforce justice through regulation and statutes, and to administer the functions of the state (such as education, local services, health, etc). In the case of Athland, the state was believed to be weak in enforcing building and safety regulation, for example, and its failure to adequately do so was one of the causes of the collapse of the building. The ineffectiveness of the Athland state to enforce its own regulations is a realisation of a political risk which not only led to the loss of many lives but also to the loss of a substantial part of Cheapkit's garment sourcing.

International business transactions, including importing from Athland, work effectively when a legal and regulatory environment is in place in all countries dealt with. Contracts of sale and supply need to be enforceable in all countries dealt with, and regulatory controls, such as over the quality of materials, labour and distribution, need to be in effect. All of these ultimately rely upon the stability and effectiveness of the state in which the business takes place. Dealing successfully with Cornflower in Athland, for example, rests upon the assumption that the Athland state is able to enforce its laws and regulations to provide stability in that country. Threats to this include forces of insurrection (uprisings), corrupt officials and other things which render the operation of the state less effective. For shareholders in Cheapkit, the ineffectiveness of the state in Athland means that businesses in that country (such as Cornflower) become unreliable suppliers and this can negatively affect shareholder value.

[**Tutorial note:** *Allow for a range of points made on international political risk. The above is indicative of the most likely approach.*]

(d)

Press statement from the board of Cheapkit.
For immediate publication and/or broadcast.

Cheapkit's response to recent events

This statement is issued by the board of Cheapkit to address several issues of interest to shareholders and which have been raised in the aftermath of the tragic collapse of the Cornflower building in Athland. Cheapkit extends its sincere condolences to the victims and their families.

In response to criticisms made of Cheapkit and other areas of discussion made in the media, Cheapkit would like to make several points to clarify its position on these issues. This is to ensure that stakeholders have full confidence in the company and continue to lend their full support. Cheapkit is a legal, and legally-compliant company, conducting its business in a responsible and diligent manner. It wishes to reassure investors and others that it takes the criticisms made by the PWR leader, Miss Jess Lui, very seriously. We would like to respond to points made in her well-publicised public letter to the board, and also to comment on points raised by several financial journalists about the company's stance on the relatively recent integrated reporting initiative. Any media questions over and above these remarks can, of course, be made to the investor relations department as usual.

(i) **Citizenship**

The company resents and strongly refutes any allegations that it has been a poor or irresponsible corporate citizen. Cheapkit recognises its role as a citizen, both here in its home country but also in Athland and elsewhere in the world in which it transacts. The board accepts two aspects of citizenship. First, any company such as Cheapkit, with its substantial footprint in society, has to acknowledge its *responsibilities*. Just as an individual has the responsibility to *obey the law, fit in with the social and ethical norms of society,* and behave in an appropriate way, so does a business. Cheapkit is a major employer in its home country and, through its supply chains into countries such as Athland, has a large social and economic impact. Its responsibility is to always comply with the laws and social norms which apply in each country it deals with. This extends to being a good employer, maintaining prompt payment of payables accounts, encouraging good working conditions at supplier companies and similar areas of good business practice.

A second and equally important aspect of citizenship, however, is the exercise of *rights*. Cheapkit is a business conducting legal contracts with suppliers, and selling legal products. As such, it has the right *to be protected by the law* in the pursuit of its normal business activities. In addition, *it has the right to receive the support of society* in the pursuit of business in terms of its investors, employees and customers. It has the right, in other words, to have customers free to purchase products without feeling bad about it, and have employees happy to work for the company without fear of criticism from people believing themselves to be in a superior moral position. The Cheapkit board would remind people that it was not us who occasioned the tragic collapse of the Cornflower building in Athland. It was the negligence and corruption of parties outside our control, and therefore it is unfair to implicate Cheapkit in any criticism directed at Cornflower.

(ii) **Accountability and fiduciary duty**

We would like to take this opportunity to address two other important subjects, raised in recent media coverage about Cheapkit: the important issues of accountability and fiduciary duty. Again, we feel that much of what has been said has been misplaced and subjective, and we would like to provide comment to counter some of this commentary.

The board of Cheapkit recognises its accountabilities in several ways. We accept the conventional understanding of accountability as an *ability to call to account* and to accept responsibility for something. Of course, a large business like Cheapkit has many accountabilities including *our primary accountability to shareholders*. This primary accountability is discharged in part using accounting statements and annual shareholder meetings, although integrated reporting (see later in this statement) may enhance this accountability further. This is not to say that we are unwilling to work with suppliers, as necessary, to help to improve their employee conditions. In fact, we fully recognise that such improvements would be to Cheapkit's advantage as well as to the employees of Cornflower.

Miss Lui's letter made reference to her belief that Cheapkit has accountabilities beyond that, including our willingness to be called to account for *events in our supply chain*. This is a matter of ethical opinion. It may be a legitimate view but the board of Cheapkit does not share it. It is unreasonable for us to accept responsibility for events over which we have no direct authority or control. Cheapkit recognises its accountability to its shareholders to deliver sustainable returns and would challenge any view which suggests it should be held to account for the behaviour of others in the supply chain, such as Cornflower.

The board also recognises a fiduciary duty it owes to a range of stakeholders. A fiduciary duty, often understood in terms of *a duty of care and trust* which one party owes to another, can be legal or ethical. Cheapkit has *legal fiduciary duties* to its shareholders and employees in that it must comply with relevant laws and regulations relating to how these are dealt with under its duty of care. The board of Cheapkit is appointed to act in the fiduciary interest of its shareholders and must express this through the pursuit of profitable strategies and the management of strategic risks.

As already stated, the extent to which Cheapkit has a fiduciary duty to other constituencies with whom it has no contractual relationship is a matter of ethical perspective. Miss Lui is of the view that the fact that we purchase from a certain supplier makes Cheapkit complicit in illegal and unethical practice at that company. The construction of the building and the conditions of employment for Cornflower's employees is a not a matter over which Cheapkit has any fiduciary duty as this was entirely within the control of Cornflower's management. Some have said that it was Cheapkit's pressure for cheap prices from Cornflower which created the conditions for the tragic events to occur, but Cornflower freely entered into contracts with Cheapkit at agreed prices and was free to withdraw from those contracts if it did not feel able to deliver. Cheapkit's fiduciary duties extend to, and include those, who collectively own the company, the shareholders, and those with whom the company is legally contracted to extend its duty of care, which is mainly its employees.

(iii) **Integrated reporting**

The Cheapkit board would also like to take this opportunity to respond to some comments made on the usefulness of the relatively recent IIRC initiative and how this might affect the company and its reporting. Like many of the large companies on the world's stock exchanges, Cheapkit is an enthusiastic supporter of integrated reporting (IR).

We see it having a number of potential benefits to the company and its shareholders, but importantly, for many of its other stakeholders also. Designed to be an approach to reporting which accurately conveys an organisation's business model and its sources of value creation over time, the IR model recognises six types of capital, with these being consumed by a business and also created as part of its business processes. It is the way that capitals are consumed, transformed and created which is at the heart of the IR model.

As readers of the business press will be aware, the six capital types are financial capital, manufactured capital, intellectual capital, social and relationship capital, human capital and natural capital. Cheapkit sees three substantial advantages of measuring and reporting performance against these types of capital.

First, the need to report on each type of capital would create and enhance *a system of internal measurement* at Cheapkit which would record and monitor each type for the purposes of reporting. So the need to report on human capital, for example, would mean that Cheapkit and other companies adopting IR must have systems in place to measure, according to the IIRC guidelines, 'competences, capabilities and experience and their motivations... including loyalties [and]... ability to lead, manage and collaborate'. These systems would support the company's internal controls and make the company more accountable in that it would have more metrics upon which to report.

Second, the information disclosed, once audited and published, would create a *fuller and more detailed account* of the sources of added value, and threats to value (i.e. risks), for shareholders and others. Rather than merely recording financial data in an annual report, the IR guidelines would enable Cheapkit to show its shareholders and other readers, how it has accumulated, transferred or disposed of different types of capital over the accounting period. So it would have to report, for example, on the social capital it has consumed, transformed and created and this could include issues of relevance to Miss Lui and others. It might include, for example, the jobs it has created or sustained in its supply chain and the social value of those jobs in their communities, or how it might operate a system of cultural values for its employees. In addition and in the same way as for added value, IR would help Cheapkit to identify, assess and manage its key risks, with this bringing further benefit to shareholders and others.

Third, a fully-developed IR account would show how Cheapkit has created value for *many of the company's stakeholders and not just for the shareholders*. This extends the whole notion of who benefits from a business's activities and it uses the different types of capital to convey this information. So a beneficial increase in social and relational capital, for example, may be of benefit to Cheapkit's communities and suppliers. The requirement to report on this change ensures that those stakeholders who wish to value a particular type of capital from their own perspective can assess the value of the company in that regard and can also assess how the company's value has changed in favour or against their own specific interest in a reporting period. ENDS.

2 (a) Chambon as a public sector organisation

There is a range of ways in which schools are organised. Some are privately owned and pupils are privately supported financially to attend the school. Many such schools do not receive any state funding and are, accordingly, described as being in the private sector. Others, such as Chambon, are public sector organisations. In Chambon's case, it is a public sector organisation because it *receives its funding from central government* ('state-funded'). This means that its budget is funded through state funds (mainly taxation) and it is thus required to deliver value to the country's taxpayers. In addition, the school is under the political control of the local authority. This means that it will be *required to account to the local authority* on whichever targets are set for it. This might include budgetary compliance, teaching quality and pupils' exam performance.

The case mentions that Chambon is *required to teach a national curriculum*, that is, a set of subjects decided at national level and taught at each school in the country. This is to ensure that all of the children being educated in the country (including at Chambon) receive a thorough education containing the subjects specified by national government. In addition, unlike private schools which can organise governance arrangements in more flexible ways, Chambon is required to *observe governance arrangements* set for it by government. These arrangements are likely to include the establishment of an effective board of governors, a means of parent–teacher interaction and the appointment of an effective headteacher. It may also include the removal of a headteacher, by the board of governors, should an incumbent be deemed ineffective in his or her role.

Assessment of Chambon's objectives and whether they have been met

Because it is a public sector organisation, Chambon school will operate in a quite different way to a private sector one. Whereas a private sector organisation's objectives are likely to be concerned with the generation of long-term shareholder value through the ongoing generation of profits, a public sector school's objectives are likely to be quite different. The effectiveness, efficiency and economy ('three Es') model is a useful way of describing whether the objectives of a public sector organisation have been met.

First, to be an *effective* public sector organisation, Chambon exists primarily to educate children and to cultivate an effective learning environment. It does this by employing effective teachers and operating a structure and culture which supports those teachers in their work. Infrastructure such as learning resources, libraries and sports facilities are all important in achieving a conducive learning environment. The closure of a part of the library was a serious threat to this as was the sale of the sports field. Such measures, in turn, may reduce the ability of the school to effectively educate its pupils in future.

The second point of assessment against the three Es model is efficiency. Chambon showed signs of a *lack of efficiency*. Efficiency is defined as the amount of work achieved for a given level of input. Despite budget increases (i.e. higher levels of input), the school's public examinations performance fell. An efficient organisation would have successfully converted the higher levels of resource into outputs, evidenced in the case of Chambon school by better exam results. At Chambon, the increased resources had no apparent effect on exam performance and in fact they deteriorated further, suggesting an inefficient use of those resources.

Third, the school (and the board of governors) *failed to control its budgets* and hence also failed in terms of its economic objectives. The school received higher budgets from the local authority in an attempt to reverse the weak performance and despite this, it still sustained a budget overspend, resulting in the necessity to close part of the library and sell a sports field. This is a wasteful and irresponsible use of public funds for which the board of governors, in part, must share the blame. It is its role to hold the headteacher to account and ensure that the school is managed so as to achieve its objectives effectively and within budget. It is likely that both the head of school and the governors have been negligent in allowing this to happen.

So on each of the three general types of objectives for public sector organisations, Chambon has failed to meet its objectives.

(b) **Board of governors**
The roles which public sector oversight boards are asked to undertake varies between countries and according to the type of organisation. In the case of the board of governors of a school such as Chambon, however, there are typically four general roles.

First, the board of governors at Chambon is required to *comply with imposed local authority rules* on school governance including its own structure and terms of reference, reporting rules and receiving complaints about the school's operations. Upon receiving its annual set of public examination results, it is required to report on those. Other duties may be imposed in addition, such as its duty to hear complaints from service users (e.g. the parents of school pupils) and act on these as necessary.

Second, the board is required to *ensure the school is well-run* and that the headteacher is supported or challenged as necessary. The school exists to provide an important public service and to provide value to the taxpayers who pay for it. In this regard, it is for the governors to ensure that an effective management structure is in place in the school and that the quality of teaching, learning and the pupil experience are adequate and capable of delivering the required level of education.

Linked to this, therefore, it is the role of the governors to make *senior appointments and remove underperforming officers* from their positions. It is the duty of the governors to appoint the headteacher and to ensure that he or she is effectively managing the school to deliver the required level of quality and service to the pupils and their parents. In the case of Chambon, there is evidence that Mr Besse is underperforming and the governors are therefore considering his position.

Finally, the board of governors is usually required to *set and monitor budgets* and to monitor management against key objectives. Because the governors are acting on behalf of the local government authority and the funding agent, they have to ensure that there is sufficient funding in place to deliver the required level of services. Once the funding for a year (i.e. the budget) is agreed, the governors must ensure that there is no overspend. This may be achieved by asking for financial information at various points throughout the year to ensure that the budget is met by the year end.

Transparency and Sally Murol's proposal
Transparency is a default position of openness and full information provision rather than concealment. A transparent organisation is one in which all available information is provided unless there is a strong and defensible reason for hiding a part or all of it. In this case, the school and the board of governors have the duty to report in a 'full and timely manner' its exam performance and the reasons for this.

Transparency is important in a school's report to a local authority in the same way that it is in a private sector business. As a recipient of state funding, it must *account to the funding body* (in this case through a local government authority structure) for the way it has used the funding and the outcomes it has achieved. If the school has been effective and efficient, it can report this, using a range of metrics, and thus show that it has provided value to the taxpayer. So reporting is an instrument of accountability and an important way in which governors must discharge this duty.

Second, it is important that the local government authority receives all necessary information on time because it has a statutory duty to manage education services locally and will *use the reported information for planning*. It may have to redistribute resources from one school to another, for example. In countries where education provision is devolved to local government authorities, there is a legal duty placed upon those authorities to provide an effective provision in that locality and this may involve making changes to local schools. The information provided by schools is often an important input into that process and so full and timely provision of that information is important. Partial, incomplete, late or inaccurate data would mean that the local authority would not have the information necessary to make these important decisions.

(c) **Potential advantages to Chambon of replacing the headteacher**
First, a new headteacher may bring about a *change of culture and staff expectations*. Mr Besse is clearly experienced, but perhaps one reason why he is liked by staff is because he is unwilling to confront underperforming staff. His dislike of confrontation may be one reason why underperformance is tolerated. If an unhelpful culture is allowed to grow and embed itself, it can favour one interest over another. In this case, it may be that the teachers and their conditions have been allowed to be given greater prominence than the quality of the educational experience for the pupils. This could be addressed and reversed with a new headteacher.

Second, a new headteacher *would signal a change* in the school that Mr Besse's regime, with its tolerance of weak educational performance, was over. A new head, with the strong backing the board of governors and the local government authority, would be able to effect the necessary change which Mr Besse so clearly failed to do. By removing Mr Besse, and allowing it be known that it was linked to the deterioration of examination results and financial inefficiency, the governors could convey to the teachers, pupils and parents at the school that his performance was inadequate and a new head was therefore being appointed to improve the school's performance.

Third, a new head would enable the governors, acting on behalf of the local authority, to make the changes necessary to improve exam and budgetary performance. Whilst Mr Besse was resistant to taking such measures, a new head appointed by the governors *would be a 'new broom'* in his or her approach to changing teaching practices and helping to cultivate the educational culture necessary to turn the school around. By introducing more efficiency, new practices and a new style of managing staff, a new head could introduce a new regime and address the weaknesses in teaching and learning, and control costs more effectively, as necessary.

[**Tutorial note:** *Allow other plausible points of discussion here if relevant.*]

3   (a)   **Roles and qualities of chief executive officer (CEO)**
The main roles of the chief executive of a listed company such as New Ideas Company (NIC) are first to *propose and develop strategies* capable of making an acceptable return to shareholders. This involves the CEO having highly developed strategic thinking skills and being able to consider a wide range of potential outcomes and implications when making strategic plans for the business. It is also necessary to ensure that strategies are resourced and so an understanding of investment and the raising of capital is important.

Second, the CEO *implements the decisions of the board*. This means that the various divisions and/or departments in the organisation must work out the strategies agreed, and the CEO must configure and co-ordinate the business to achieve these. This role requires a strong understanding of the business and an ability to relate to colleagues at a high level in a number of specialised areas. Highly developed communication skills are important in this, and the ability to understand the technical and business aspects of the company are both very important.

Third, the CEO must *analyse the performance of all parts of the business* in terms of each one's contribution to strategy and its fit with the rest of the organisational structure. Because successful strategies require all parts of the business, at all levels, to contribute fully, the CEO must have the analytical and processing skills to be able to achieve this. This partly involves analysis of 'hard' numerical data such as variances against budget, etc and also 'softer' qualitative skills such as the ability to assess the human skills and abilities in colleagues and subordinates.

Fourth, the CEO plays the leading role in ensuring that appropriate systems are in place for *internal controls and the management of risk*. The robustness of the organisation's internal systems and their ability to work effectively towards the achievement of strategic goals means that effective internal controls need to be in place, possibly including internal audits. Likewise, a full and detailed knowledge of the risks faced by the business, especially strategic risks, is essential. These roles require the CEO to have multi-conceptual skills and be able to consider a wide range of internal and external issues at the same time. He or she must be able to delegate technical responsibility for these tasks whilst having the knowledge and force of personality to be able to make rapid changes when necessary to respond to new challenges and opportunities as they arise.

Dr Ranjana Foo's suitability
By her own admission, Dr Ranjana Foo is probably ill-suited to the role of CEO of NIC. As the scientist who made the discovery in the first place, she is clearly very able in her own technical field, but this does not necessarily qualify her for the role of CEO. As the scientist who developed the technical product upon which NIC is based, Ranjana clearly has an excellent understanding of the technical aspects of the business. Her limitations are likely to be in analysing the performance of other parts of the business.

As one who prefers to *work alone*, she would be uncomfortable in large meetings such as board meetings where she would be required to interact with people most of the time. Her *preference for a 'quiet environment'* would not be met in the CEO role where she will need to manage other directors and negotiate with others.

In her colleagues' view, *she is good at detailed work but sometimes struggles to see the bigger picture*. This would suggest that her strategic thinking skills are underdeveloped, and this would make it difficult for her to conceive strategic objectives for NIC and put plans in place for their implementation.

Finally, as one who prefers to *avoid confrontation and conflict*, she may be unable to effectively assert her own will and purpose on colleagues who may not fully agree with her on occasions. This is not to say, of course, that conflict is desirable or necessary, but it is sometimes necessary to over-rule one or more colleagues in the interests of the greater strategic good.

(b)   **Benefits of non-executive director (NED) recruitment at New Ideas Company**
As a start-up business, NIC faces a number of challenges. The first is the *lack of business expertise among the scientists*, and particularly with Dr Foo herself. Dr Foo, obviously a committed scientist, is unwilling to invest the time necessary to learn about running a business so will be heavily reliant on the expertise and skills of others in developing the scientific breakthrough into a commercial success.

Because the business is considered risky by analysts, the presence of experienced non-executives is important in *increasing the board's accountability* to the shareholders. With appropriate experience, NEDs can advise on specific issues with start-up businesses, including working capital management and issues capable of affecting cash flow in early trading.

The third benefit of having a suitably-experienced NED presence on the board is to *demonstrate compliance with corporate governance listing rules*. This would have the effect of reassuring shareholders, and the analysts providing information to shareholders, on specific types of businesses. It is important, and especially in the early years of a company's life, to have the confidence of markets. An adequate and fully compliant non-executive presence on the board will help achieve this.

Difficulties in NED recruitment
Despite the increase in non-executive board memberships in many parts of the world, it should not be forgotten that NEDs have relatively little financial incentive for board membership compared to their better-remunerated executive colleagues. In

the case of recruiting non-executives to the board of NIC, the case refers to three specific difficulties which could apply in many regions and not just the one which NIC is located in.

The case mentions that NIC, and the university it grew out of, were located in a *small city away from the main centres of population*. The isolation of some regions makes the chances of locally recruiting an experienced and effective non-executive team very difficult. There is usually very little occupational or geographical mobility ('churn') in such regions with relatively few suitable people being available. There would also be less chance that those available to be non-executives would be sufficiently independent of each other (i.e. they are likely to already know each other quite well through local networks and social organisations).

The *highly technical nature of the company's operations* is another potential difficulty. Given that the company is a highly technical business, it is likely that relatively few people will fully understand the nature of its work and the technical issues behind it. One of the main purposes of a NED is to represent the shareholders' interests on the board and it therefore is necessary for them to have a good understanding of how value is added. In scrutinising the internal controls, risks and the effectiveness of the operations, NEDs need to understand the sources and implications of internal strengths and weaknesses, and also external opportunities and threats. A failure to understand the company's main activities would be likely to deter many potential NED applicants.

The analysts' view, upon reading the company share prospectus, was that, as with many start-up businesses, it was risky. Some predicted that the business could fail within two years. *Uncertainty over a business's future would be a disincentive* for some potential NEDs to commit to joining a board. Some would believe that being associated with a company failure would be bad for their own business reputations and therefore they may be reluctant to join the board as a NED. In the same way, because it is a business which could fail early, the time required to adequately guide and advise NIC may be substantial and more than many would be able or willing to provide. With so much resting upon the successful adaptation of a scientific breakthrough into commercial success, and with a new company start-up developing its own culture and structure, the management commitment required by NEDs is likely to be initially high.

(c) A conflict of interest arises when a person's ability to act with independence and impartiality is hindered by a countervailing interest held in a cause which could be the beneficiary of decisions made. In the case of directors in a business, any countervailing interest which prevents a director acting solely in the interests of the shareholders of the business can be considered a conflict of interest: he or she must act in the interest of shareholders but may also stand to gain or lose personally by decisions made in his or her capacity as director.

In the case of Dr Idris, his shareholding in the equipment supplier *may reduce his impartiality* when it comes to the choice of supplier to NIC. As a director of NIC, he would be duty-bound to always seek out the best value-for-money for all capital purchases in order to return the highest value to the NIC shareholders. In this role, he should have no interest in any of the potential suppliers which may steer him, in principle, towards or away from any particular supplier.

As a major shareholder in the potential supplier, however, he may *stand to gain personally were the supplier to be awarded the supply contract* by NIC. A large contract would generate cash flows and potential profits to the equipment supplier, increase its visibility and make it more likely to receive future supply contracts. This could increase the value of Dr Idris's shareholding in the equipment supplier and hence he may have an incentive to recommend the award of the supply contract to the supplier even although that may not be in the best interests of the shareholders of NIC. There may be an alternative supplier which would represent better value to NIC and its shareholders.

4 (a) Establishing an internal audit function at Loho Company
Some corporate governance reports set out a number of criteria for a company considering setting up an internal audit function. The Turnbull Report, from the UK, for example, lists seven criteria: the scale and complexity of operations; the number of employees; cost-benefit considerations; changes in organisational structure; changes in key risks, problems with internal control systems; and an increase in the number of unexplained or unacceptable events.

In the case of Loho, the case for establishing an internal audit function has grown in recent years because of five of these criteria.

The successful expansion of Loho in recent years has given rise to some problems associated with *growth and greater complexity* of operations. The case mentions new products and new markets overseas. These, being the two major areas of uncertainty on the classic Ansoff matrix, represent a significant increase in the complexity of the company's operations, and the company is manifestly having issues coping with this change. Effective internal audit systems can scrutinise and report on each part of the organisation and ensure that the complexity of each component is understood and controlled.

The growth and increased complexity has also seen an *increase in the number of employees* from 150 to 600 in its home country and the addition of 200 overseas positions. The configuration and co-ordination of this increased number presents Loho with a considerable challenge if they are all to be usefully employed to maximise each person's contribution. This includes oversight of decentralised activities, especially in overseas offices, and potentially managing the cultural and language issues sometimes occasioned by the employment of overseas nationals.

The case mentions that the company has *become more decentralised* as a result of its growth. It is common for growing businesses to increasingly delegate authority to divisions and departments as they grow, or to regional offices if the growth is geographical in nature. The loss of concentration of power at the centre sometimes raises issues with control and co-ordination of the decentralised parts and so an internal audit can help to ensure compliance of those parts with company norms and procedures. These decentralised centres must also be configured so they 'fit' with the rest of the organisation and co-ordinated with the overall strategy, and internal audit can help achieve this.

One of the results of the increase in internationalisation is a *change in some of the risks*. Exporting and conducting business in more than one country increases a number of risks and the case mentions credit risk in particular, which is the risk of failing to be paid on time (or at all) by customers. This can severely affect working capital management and so can, in the worst case, threaten the survival of the business if it is unable to meet current working capital liabilities, such as the payment of suppliers. In some countries or in some sectors where cultural factors may mean that credit risk is a material risk, an internal audit department could enforce credit controls and ensure that mitigation systems are in place to manage those risks. It could also perform regular 'stress test' exercises to ensure that credit controls are effective and fit for purpose.

The final argument for establishing an internal audit function is an *increased number of unacceptable events* at Loho. It would appear from the case that the growth of the company has brought about a number of deficiencies in the operations department which have led to the company failing to adequately meet orders through late deliveries. This level of operational performance will threaten the long-term relationships with customers and could rapidly lead to a loss of trust in Loho among its buyers. An effective internal control function could analyse the causes of these events and help to reduce their impact or find ways in which the company's vulnerability to such events can be reduced.

(b) Why the effectiveness of internal controls (IC) cannot be guaranteed

It is generally understood that, however robust and expensive an internal control is, it can sometimes be ineffective. There are a number of possible reasons for this, with the most common being as follows:

The control can be *over or under-specified*. An under-specified control is one which is not capable of actually controlling the risk or activity intended. Conversely, an over-specified control is one which over-controls and may have the effect of losing the confidence of employees and others influenced by the control. An over-specified control is one which is poor value for money and may constrain activity if the control does not adequately allow normal levels of performance. Controls which do not enjoy the support of those affected are sometimes ignored or bypassed, thereby rendering them less effective than they might be.

Human factors can undermine or circumvent the effectiveness of many internal controls. In this regard, the most common is *human error*, which may or may not be accompanied by *intentional fraud*. It is sometimes believed, by an individual, that personal gain could be achieved were a given control not in place and this can result in that person intentionally circumventing the control.

Likewise, controls can be ineffective if *employees collude* to achieve that circumvention. If a group in a workplace believes a control to act against members' personal interests, they can act together to reduce its effectiveness. This may, of course, result in a sanction if discovered.

The fourth reason why ICs are sometimes ineffective is the *occurrence of non-routine events* when a control is designed for relatively routine behaviour. These might include events from any of the PEST influences, for example, which might render the control ineffective, possibly by 'overwhelming' the control or presenting it with a situation for which it was not designed. Linked to the previous point is the occurrence of unforeseen or unforeseeable events.

Management or employees may exercise *poor judgement or miscalculation*, which means that a control will become ineffective. A brake on a machine tool or a vehicle is only effective, for example, as long as the machine is responsibly and safely used. An excessive speed or the use of a wrong material in a machine tool, for example, would negate the value of the brake, even though the brake is effective in its own right.

Relationship to cost

There are several reasons why cost alone is a poor guide as to the effectiveness of internal controls.

First, it is the *design of the control rather than the cost* which is the primary driver of effectiveness. A wrongly or inappropriately designed control, regardless of cost, will be less than fully effective. It is for this reason that a great deal of technical detail is applied to the design of controls, especially those concerning financial risk. There need not be any direct relationship between design and cost. A highly effective control can, at the same time, be very simple and inexpensive.

Second, *a control can be over-specified*, meaning that the control is more robust, and usually therefore more expensive, than it needs to be. Cost-effectiveness is a key criterion to the adoption of any control, and a control costing disproportionately more than the loss which could be incurred by its failure is seen to be poor value for money.

Third, *almost any control can be corrupted, circumvented or ignored* in line with the limitations outlined in the first section of this answer. With sufficient determination, an employee or service user can act against a control. Similarly, a technical failure (such as loss of power or a computer failure) can render even the most well-designed control less effective.

(c) Continuing professional development (CPD) for Sonja Tan

The case mentions that Sonja Tan attended the CPD session on improving internal controls. This would have been a worthwhile and useful event for a professional accountant and/or company director, and one which fits with the general purposes of CPD.

The first advantage of CPD for Sonja Tan is to *maintain and update the currency of her skills and knowledge*. If she trained as an accountant some time ago, it is likely that changes to accounting procedures and local regulation have taken effect since she qualified. Whilst the knowledge gained during her training would have been sufficient in the early part of her career, her continued effectiveness as a practitioner will be greatly assisted by her CPD. One of the five IFAC (IESBA) fundamental ethical principles is *professional competence and due care*. Mandatory CPD is an effective safeguard against any threats to this principle as far as an individual professional is concerned.

CPD can also *broaden Sonja's skills*. By learning about more general management and management control issues, such as internal controls, she is developing skills alongside her accounting expertise. By learning about, for example, technical computing issues, logistics and other issues relevant to her work situation, Sonja can become a more effective director, especially at a senior level such as FD where a good knowledge of the whole business is assumed.

As a profession, accounting enjoys the support of society and in return, professions such as accounting have to continually ensure that its members are *fit to serve society's needs*. The maintenance of skills and knowledge ensures that the accountant is seen to behave in the public interest and is able to continue to respond to the public need for the profession's skills. Maintaining the support and confidence of society is important for any profession (such as accounting, medicine, banking) and the maintenance of a CPD record is a good way to demonstrate this.

1   **(a)**   2 marks each for examination of the two claims.
      2 marks for discussion of conflict.
      1 mark for evidence of understanding of stakeholder claim (anywhere in answer).

(7 marks)

   (b)   2 marks for explanation of corruption.
      2 marks each for corruption at Cornflower to a maximum of 8 marks. Half mark for identification only.

(10 marks)

   (c)   3 marks for each risk – one for definition and up to two for importance in context.

(9 marks)

   (d) **(i)**   2 marks for explanation of citizenship in terms of rights and responsibilities.
            2 marks for explaining each in terms of the case to a maximum of 4 marks.

(6 marks)

       (ii)   1 mark each for explanations of accountability and fiduciary duty.
            2 marks for each relevant point made on the relevance of each to Cheapkit from the pristine capitalist perspective.

(6 marks)

      (iii) 2 marks for explanation of the basic framework of IR.
            2 marks for each advantage explained to a maximum of 6 marks.

(8 marks)

      Professional marks

(4 marks)

2   **(a)**   1 mark for each explanation of Chambon as a public sector organisation to a maximum of 4 marks. Half mark for identification only.
      2 marks for assessment against objectives to a maximum of 6 marks.

(10 marks)

   (b)   1 mark for each role of governors to a maximum of 4 marks.
      2 marks for each point on transparency to a maximum of 4 marks.
      1 mark for evidence of understanding of transparency (anywhere in the answer).

(9 marks)

   (c)   2 marks for each advantage to a maximum of 6 marks.

(6 marks)

3   **(a)**   Up to 2 marks for each role and quality to a maximum of 8 marks. Half mark for identification only.
      1 mark for each point of unsuitability explained to a maximum of 4 marks. Half mark for identification only.

(Maximum 10 marks)

   (b)   1 mark for each benefit of NEDs at NIC to a maximum of 3 marks.
      Up to 2 marks for each difficulty in recruitment.

(9 marks)

   (c)   Up to 2 marks for explanation of conflict of interest.
      Up to 2 marks for each relevant point made on Dr Idris's conflict of interest to a maximum of 4 marks.

(6 marks)

4   **(a)**   Up to 2 marks for each relevant argument.

(10 marks)

   (b)   1 mark for each reason identified and explained to a maximum of 5 marks. Half mark for identification only.
      2 marks for each relevant discussion point in relation to cost to a maximum of 6 marks.

(Maximum 9 marks)

   (c)   2 marks for each relevant point made to a maximum of 6 marks.

(6 marks)

ABOUT BECKER PROFESSIONAL EDUCATION

Becker Professional Education provides a single destination for candidates and professionals looking to advance their careers and achieve success in:

- Accounting

- International Financial Reporting

- Project Management

- Continuing Professional Education

- Healthcare

For more information on how Becker Professional Education can support you in your career, visit www.becker.com.

Becker Professional Education
is an ACCA approved content provider

BECKER
PROFESSIONAL EDUCATION®

Lightning Source UK Ltd.
Milton Keynes UK
UKOW07f2217290715

256028UK00016B/174/P